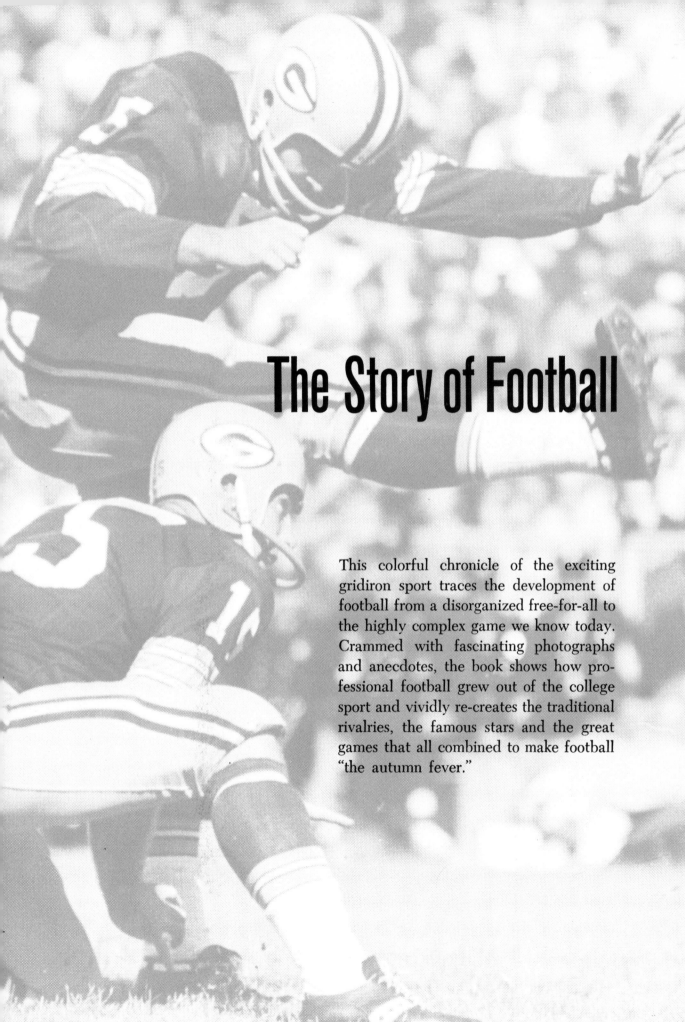

The Story of Football

This colorful chronicle of the exciting gridiron sport traces the development of football from a disorganized free-for-all to the highly complex game we know today. Crammed with fascinating photographs and anecdotes, the book shows how professional football grew out of the college sport and vividly re-creates the traditional rivalries, the famous stars and the great games that all combined to make football "the autumn fever."

RANDOM HOUSE
New York

The Story of Football

by ROBERT LECKIE

Illustrated with photographs

1973 Edition

© Copyright, 1969, 1968, 1965, by Random House, Inc.

Library of Congress Cataloging in Publication Data
will be found on page 199.

Manufactured in the United States of America

To my brothers, John and Bill;

to my brother-in-law, Brud Jury;

to my dear friends Doug Boyd
and Joe Glennon,

to Johnny Sitarsky
and Jimmy Blumenstock,

to Johnny Kelly and Phil Sheridan,

to the brothers Port, Stio,
Hensel, and Caughey—

and to all those other
Rutherford footballers

who were the heroes or the
teammates of my youth.

The Story of Football

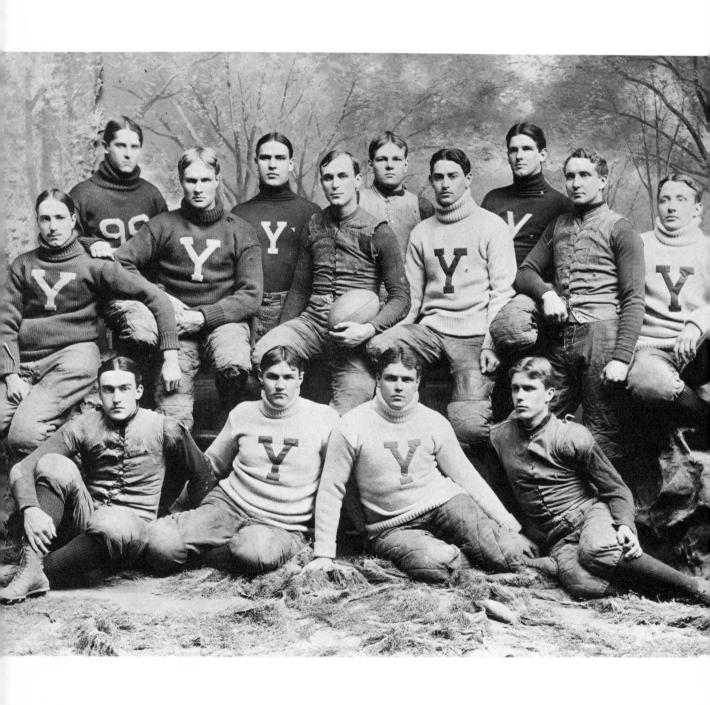

How the Game Began

The origins of football go back almost to the dawn of history. No one knows exactly when the game began, but historians tell us the ancient Greeks played a kind of football game called *harpaston*. It took place on a rectangular field with goal lines at either end. A center line divided two teams of equal but varying size, and the game commenced when the harpaston, or handball, was tossed up between them. Then the members of both teams tried to pass, kick or run the ball over the other team's goal line, even as we do today, more than two thousand years later.

After the Romans conquered the Greeks, they adopted the game of harpaston. It was played in Italy throughout the Middle Ages under the name of *calcio*, and it is likely—though not certain—that the Romans brought the game with them when they invaded Britain. Meanwhile, such widely scattered peoples as the Maoris and Polynesians of the balmy South Pacific, the Faroe Islanders of the raw North Atlantic and the Eskimos of the frozen Arctic were also playing their own versions of a game of football.

Whatever or wherever the origins of the sport, it is in Britain that all its modern versions were begun. They developed from the *melees* or mellays of the Middle Ages.

These were little less than pushing and shoving matches. As many as fifty or a hundred players to a side—perhaps the whole male population of a village—would "get in the game." They tried to kick or push an inflated ball across the "goal" lines. These might be roadside trees or bushes growing a few hundred yards apart, or even the boundaries of the rival towns. The competing "teams" went struggling and surging through the streets, breaking shop windows and infuriating merchants. Often they swarmed over the open fields and the crops of outraged farmers. Fists flew and bones were broken. For every fresh and brawny lad eager to join the sport, there was always a bruised and weary one just as eager to give him his place.

Soon schoolboys joined the fun of these ball games, which were usually played annually on Shrove Tuesday before Lent. As the games grew in violence, however, they began to be forbidden by law. Everywhere there were councils that forbade the rowdy sport, police who tried to stop it, parents who opposed it and clergymen who condemned it.

Nevertheless, "football" flourished, and inevitably it spread overseas to colonial America. There young New England boys delighted in kicking a blown-up pig's bladder through the streets each Thanksgiving Day.

With the growth of the great British schools, the sport lost its mass appeal in England and became the game of schoolboys only. Each school had its own version of the game. Rugby's style was known as "Bigside" after Bigside Field on which it was played. The ball was moved by kicking only; running with the ball was forbidden. As many as a hundred boys might play at one time and, because clearing a path for the kicker was also forbidden, a game of Bigside might become a scoreless tug of war. One day in 1823 a spindly Rugby student named William Webb Ellis watched glumly while a contest struggled toward its goalless close. Dusk was setting in, and at any moment the five o'clock bell might ring, ending the game.

The big oval ball rose into the air. Ellis waited under it. If he caught it, he would have the right to "heel the ball." That is, he could drive his heel into the ground and attempt a free kick for goal. But William Webb Ellis knew that he was too far away from the enemy's goal to make a successful kick. Also, the game had been duller than usual. And so, in a sudden rush of joyous rebellion, Ellis caught the ball and began to *run* with it.

Some of the youths on the other side were too thunderstruck to attempt to stop him. Others were so outraged that they tried to seize him and hurl him to the turf. Unwittingly, they were the first of tacklers—and Ellis was the first of ball carriers.

In one move after another, Ellis gave them the first straight-arm and the first sidestep. He made the first dodge and he was the first man to feel the thrill of bulling straight through an enemy tackler. When at last he pounded, gasping, over the other side's goal line, he had scored the first touchdown in the history of football.

But nobody called it a "touchdown" then. Instead, some of the Rugby boys were calling Ellis foolish for having so openly broken the rules. Others, less rigid, were calling him clever for having thought of such an exciting way to enliven a dull game. The argument was to rage for years, not only among the athletes of Rugby but also among other schoolboys who had either adopted the running game or decided to stick to the "purer" kicking game. Eventually, the sport would split into two separate and distinct games: association football, the kicking game which Americans call "soccer" from the abbreviation "Assoc.," and the ball-carrying Rugby, or "rugger," which was to be the father of our own rugged and thrilling game.

Players dribbling in an 1875 game of association football (soccer).

The Yanks Take to "Football Fightum"

Although football had been born as early as 1823, it was a long time getting established in America.

In the United States, where the colleges rather than the secondary schools had adopted the game, football was actually only a kind of "class rush." Each fall, the sophomores of the big eastern colleges challenged the freshmen. But the game that followed was nothing more than a free-for-all. There was a ball, of course, and it was put in play the moment some bold freshman dared to put his hand on it. But the players were more interested in hitting their opponents' noggins than in following the movement of the ball.

At Harvard, football day was known as Bloody Monday, and the so-called game often ended in a riot. In 1860 both the town police and the college authorities agreed that Bloody Monday had to go. The students replied by going into mourning for a mock figure called "Football Fightum," for whom they conducted funeral rites. But the authorities held firm, and it was a dozen years before football was again played at Harvard.

In that interval America's first intercollegiate football game was played.

Before and during the Civil War a fierce rivalry had been raging between the College of New Jersey at Princeton, New Jersey, and Rutgers at neighboring New Brunswick. The youths of both colleges fought over possession of a Revolutionary War cannon. In 1865, the College of New Jersey, later to be known as Princeton, ended the dispute by sinking the cannon into concrete. Rutgers thought this was most unsporting and sought revenge by challenging the Princetonians to a contest in "base ball," or the New York Game, as it was also called. Princeton accepted and walloped the Scarlets 40 to 2.

Chastened, the Scarlets cast about for another form of revenge. They thought they had found it in association football, or soccer. Again they challenged Princeton. Again the Tigers accepted, delighted to find a new game in which to thump Rutgers. On November 6, 1869, the two colleges met at New Brunswick.

The game began at three o'clock, a few minutes after the arrival of the Princetonians. Twenty-five men on each side laid aside their hats, coats and vests. To distinguish themselves from the Tigers, the Rutgers players wore scarlet caps or sweaters. The teams struggled against each other for a full hour, and Rutgers had its sweet revenge —six goals to four.

Of course, this first of all intercollegiate football games did not much resemble our modern sport, or the form

4

of football to be so rapidly developed in the next decade. But it was not soccer, either, because the rules allowed batting the round black ball with the fist. Moreover, there was that body contact so characteristic of the American game. At one point, J. E. "Big Mike" Michael of Princeton smashed so hard into George Large of Rutgers that he knocked him out of the game. Then Big Mike thundered over Large's prostrate form to crash through the fence on which most of the spectators were sitting. The field on which the game was played was rectangular, as football fields are today.

The next game was played at Princeton, and the Tigers won—eight goals to none. The third and deciding game was never played, possibly because the authorities of both schools had decided that too much football can cause too little study.

Columbia University was the next school to enter the intercollegiate lists. The Lions traveled from New York City to New Brunswick on November 12, 1870, and were defeated by Rutgers 6 to 3. Once again, the contest was a wild scramble. The players kicked and battled each other as much as the ball.

That same year Princeton defeated Rutgers 6–0, and once again the style of play was rough indeed. It provoked a critical outcry so loud that no games at all were played in 1871.

But football was back in 1872, with the Lions of Columbia meeting the Bulldogs of Yale at New Haven. The Yale team was coached and captained by David Schley Schaff, who had learned his football at Rugby. Schaff himself was injured and unable to play in the Columbia game, but even so Yale took the Lions, 3 to 0. After the game, both the Lions and the Bulldogs sat down together for a fine dinner at Lockwoods in New Haven. That same year Stevens Tech of New Jersey became the fifth American college to take up football. Stevens lost to Columbia, but beat both

Rutgers vs. Princeton: November 6, 1869.

New York University and City College of New York the following year.

And so, by 1873, football was definitely on its way. It still looked more like soccer, even though the teams had been scaled down from twenty-five to twenty men each. The only way to score was still to kick or bat the ball over the opposing team's goal, and the game was played in two forty-five-minute halves on fields 140 yards long and 70 yards wide. But the game had that unmistakable rock-'em, sock-'em Yankee flavor that needed only the running ingredient to make it more than ever the All-American game.

And this novelty was to be supplied by Harvard.

Old "Football Fightum" had been resurrected at Harvard in 1872. And the Johnnies, also known collectively as the Crimson, brought him back running. Of course, Harvard allowed a man to run with the ball only if he was being pursued. But even this variation in the rules was enough to keep Harvard from joining the nonrunning teams of Rutgers, Princeton, Columbia and Yale in the first football convention held in 1873. Instead, the Johnnies had to look around for other running teams.

They found one in McGill University at Montreal, Canada. Inasmuch as Rugby had been transplanted to Canada from England, the McGill youths played under rules that allowed a player to pick up the ball and run with it whenever he wished. More, the especially Canadian feature of the game was to count touchdowns, as well as goals, in the scoring. In pure Rugby, a touchdown only provided the chance to kick a free goal from the field. If the kick was missed, the touchdown did not count.

However, the first U.S.–Canadian football game, which took place at Cambridge on May 14, 1874, was played

Columbia and Harvard tangle in an 1878 game.

under Harvard rules. The Crimson won, three goals to nothing. Next day the game was played under McGill rules and ended in a scoreless tie. But it had been so wide-open and exciting that the Harvard men were converted to the Canadian rules. They agreed to follow them again at the third meeting, held in Montreal in October. Harvard won that match—three touchdowns to nothing.

Elated, the Crimson challenged its closest and bitterest rival: Yale. The Bulldogs accepted. But first a meeting was held to discuss the rules. These were called the "Concessionary Rules" because Harvard conceded something to Yale's soccer and Yale yielded a great deal to Harvard's football. Among other things, there were to be fifteen men on each team.

Yale apparently conceded too much, for the Rugby-running Johnnies played the soccer-playing Bulldogs off their feet in that first Yale–Harvard game. Final score: Harvard 4 goals, Yale 0.

On that raw November, 1875, day at New Haven some 2,000 spectators—a record crowd—jammed the stands at Hamilton Park. One of them was a slender and intense young man who was going to go to Yale the following year. Torn between misery at the Yale defeat and admiration for the Harvard style of play, he left the park vowing that when the next Yale team played Harvard, he would be on it. And he would see to it that this defeat was avenged.

The ardent young spectator was Walter Camp, destined to become the father of American football.

7

Walter Camp Changes the Game

Born the son of a New Haven school principal, Walter Camp was a good student. But no one who looked at him would have expected him to be a fine athlete. He was slender—almost skinny—and his only outstanding physical attribute seemed to be his bright and burning eyes.

Walter Camp of Yale. Camp is often called the father of American football.

But Walter Camp was determined to excel in everything, sports particularly. Years later, when he was one of his nation's most outstanding sports figures, he wrote:

If . . . a boy has *the wish to excel* he takes on a contract which involves patience, self-control, persistence, and hard work. No boy or man ever made himself a leader in sports, or in life, without doing a great deal of hard work which at times seemed to be drudgery. No one comes to the top without making certain sacrifices. It is not an easy road, but it is an eminently satisfactory road, because it leads to the desired end.

Camp worked hard and achieved his desired goal: he became one of the country's outstanding sports leaders. After he entered Yale in 1876 he made every varsity team then in existence. He was among the fastest of Yale men, and he was also one of the few who had mastered the new art of throwing a curve ball. Camp became pitcher and captain of the Yale nine, and he was halfback and captain of the eleven. He was a hurdler who was credited with having invented the hurdle step. He was a versatile swimmer and diver who won races in all distances ranging up to five miles. He was a top tennis player and he rowed on his class crew.

Even more important than Camp's achievements on the field or on the water were his contributions to the game of football. For thirty years Walter Camp was to be the outstanding coach or rule-maker in America. During that time he helped Yale to compile what was then a matchless record, and he also served on every football rules committee or attended every football convention from 1878 until his death in 1925. In 1889, he collaborated with the journalist Caspar Whitney in picking the first All-America football team. Eventually he picked the teams himself, and to be named on a Walter Camp All-America was the highest distinction to which any American football player could aspire.

To achieve all of these goals, Walter Camp had indeed done "a great deal of hard work." Untold hours of secret calisthenics, nightly running around the streets of New Haven, and a steadily developing habit of self-denial were the means by which Walter attained his strength of body and of mind. Still, he did not look like much when he came

The Yale championship team of 1876. Walter Camp is standing fourth from left; Captain Gene Baker is holding the ball.

onto the field against Harvard one memorable day in 1876. His six-foot frame weighed only 157 pounds. It was a frame of steel coiled on a will of iron, but only the Yale players knew that.

The Harvard captain, big Nathaniel Curtis, brawny and bearded, laughed aloud at this smooth-chinned slip of a lad. Pointing Camp out to Gene Baker, the Yale captain, Curtis said with a snort:

"You don't mean to let that child play, do you?"

"Look to your business," Baker replied, and a few plays later Curtis understood his meaning. Running with the ball, the Harvard giant bore down upon the Yale "child." Out went Curtis' stiff-arm, which had jolted so many would-be tacklers. Camp could not dive under it; in those days tackling below the waist was forbidden. And so, characteristically, he seized Curtis' arm and swung him around, hurling the Harvard captain to the ground.

"Well, well, well," Curtis grunted, getting to his feet. "That little fellow nearly put me out."

It was a moment of great satisfaction to the seventeen-year-old Camp, and he went on to play a fine game. The real stars that day, however, were Captain Baker and a Yale player named Oliver Thompson, who scored the only goal. He drop-kicked it on the run—against his instep rather than his toe. But the big, oval-shaped Rugby ball was made for just such kicking. It sped straight and true over the crossbar.

The crossbar was only a clothesline drawn taut between two poles, but the goal was genuine enough. Yale avenged its defeat of the previous year—the

defeat which had so upset young Walter Camp. And thus began a Yale winning streak of 47 games which would not be ended until the next-to-last game of the 1885 season, when Princeton topped the Bulldogs by 6 to 5.

During that time, Walter Camp was a star player and coach. More than that, he revolutionized the very game of football.

Eight days after the 1876 Yale–Harvard contest, these two schools, together with Princeton and Columbia, met at the Massasoit House in Springfield, Massachusetts, to form the American Intercollegiate Football Association. The delegates voted to play Rugby football and also to make a goal worth four touchdowns. If a game ended in a tie, a goal kicked after a touchdown would outweigh four touchdowns.

Kicking, of course, was still the prime feature of the Rugby-style football. The big leather oval was kicked high with the wind or low against it. Kickers perfected a "tumbler," a high whirling punt difficult to catch. They also learned to drop-kick on the dead run and to kick the ball when it was rolling or lying motionless. There were also still fifteen men on a side, so Yale, which liked to play with only eleven men, refused to join the new association, although she still attended meetings and played other members.

From 1876 until 1880, then, American college teams played Rugby under an agreed set of rules.

The teams came onto the field wearing stockings, knee pants, jerseys and caps. Usually, though not always, these were in the colors of their alma mater. The

Princeton plays Yale in an 1879 game of Rugby-type football.
Who has the ball?

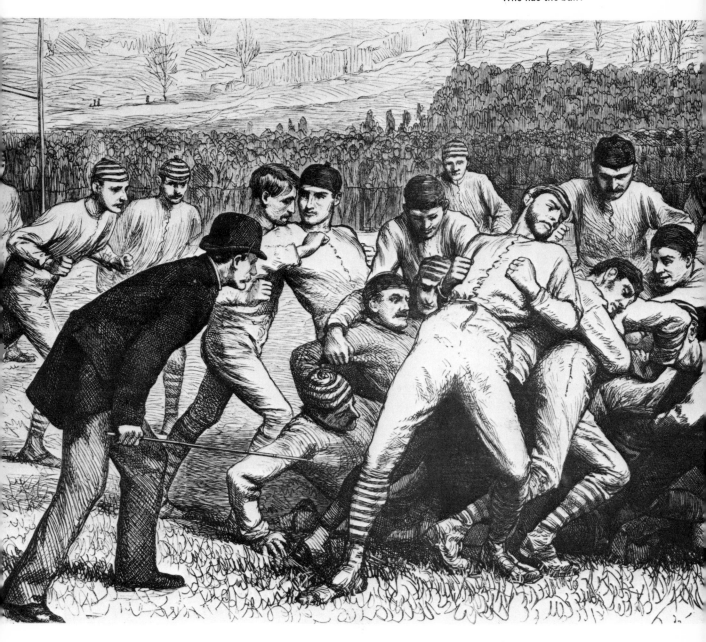

team with the ball—what we would call the kicking team—lined up with the ball at the center of the field. Fifteen yards away was the receiving team, with eight forwards spread out across the field. Behind them were four backs, with three more stationed still deeper.

The kicking team could put the ball in play by a drop-kick, place-kick, punt, dribble, or even a fake. The kicker might run up to the ball and merely tap it with his toe before scooping it up to run. If threatened by an enemy tackler, he passed the ball off to another man, who would run until tackled, whereupon the ball went into "scrummage."

Scrummage or "scrum" was the maneuver which followed the downing of the ball. Once the ball had touched the ground, as it had to in those days to be truly "down," the rival forwards lined up. No one had possession of the ball now. It was placed between the forwards. They battled over it, but they could not touch it with their hands. They could force the other forwards downfield by brute strength, moving the ball along with them. Or they could "heel" it—kick it backward—to one of their waiting backs. But to heel the ball was considered bad form. As a result, spectators and backs alike would watch in yawning boredom while sixteen hefty young men heaved and butted against one another until, perhaps, the ball popped accidentally out of the mass and someone could run or kick again.

Obviously, reasoned Camp and other football pioneers, the game could be speeded up by allowing the ball to be kicked back from the scrummage. And so, in 1880, what was eventually to be the *line of scrimmage* was born. With

it were to come the American football positions as known today, once Walter Camp and Yale had persuaded the Intercollegiate Association to limit the teams to eleven men.

Because one of the offensive forwards in a scrimmage was allowed to pass the ball back with his foot, he became known as the "snapperback." Later, because he played in the center of seven forwards or "rushers," he became known as the "center." Since the defensive rushers were permitted to attack him as he passed the ball with his foot—actually squirting it back by sudden pressure on its end—he needed protection from his own rushers at either side of him. Because, in effect they "guarded" the center, they became known as guards.

It was inevitable, of course, that the rushers at either extreme would be called "end men" and then simply ends. And because the men between the ends and the guards had the best position for making tackles, they eventually earned the name of tackle.

Players known as halfbacks, or backs, were already part of the Rugby game; but the back who received the heeled ball from the center became known as the quarterback. One of the three other backs who customarily played deepest was called the fullback. The quarterback, incidentally, could not run with the ball after he received it from the center. He had to pass it off to one of the other backs.

Thus, in 1880, the basic football formation looked very much like our own T-formation teams, except that the seven linemen up front were spread out wide across a field which was now 110 yards long and 53 yards wide. It remained for Walter Camp to make the innovations which would draw the linemen together in the lineup with which modern players and football fans are familiar.

Naturally, all of these developments did not take place immediately after the 1880 meeting of the Intercollegiate Football Association. But they did occur as a result of it. There was also an unfortunate by-product of the new rule changes. Because there was as yet no system of downs, the team with the ball could hold it indefinitely.

The very next year Princeton and Yale, both of whom had beaten Harvard, met in their famous, or infamous, "block" game. Both teams thought that if they could gain a tie they could win the Big Three title. So Princeton held the ball throughout the first half, and Yale controlled it during the second. The result was a boring stalemate. Neither team scored.

Sportsmen everywhere became enraged. Even the newspapers were critical. It was practically the first time football had been noticed for anything except "brutality." A man signing himself only as "an Englishman" wrote to a newspaper denouncing the "block" tactics. He suggested that one side be allowed to keep the ball for four successive scrimmages.

This letter was reprinted and widely circulated. Walter Camp saw it and agreed. He went even further. To his logical mind it seemed ridiculous that a team which had advanced the ball downfield should be required to give up possession for *any* reason. Four successive scrimmages might not be enough to score a touchdown or to come within kicking distance. But how much better if a team could *earn* the right to keep the ball indefinitely.

Thus in 1882, with Yale again a member of the Intercollegiate Football Association, Camp persuaded the rules committee to adopt *a system of downs*. If a team could gain five yards in three downs it could keep the ball. This idea, together with the introduction of the scrimmage, is the reason why Walter Camp might be called the father of American football. That same year he suggested laying out the field in five-yard chalk lines, thus giving it the appearance of a gridiron. To this day, football is still called the gridiron game, and its players are known as "gridders."

Walter Camp's next revolutionary contribution to football was to be in the matter of scoring. In 1882 games were still decided by goals. There were no points. Four touchdowns made one goal, and a goal kicked after a touchdown took precedence over four touchdowns.

But an argument had arisen over the safety. Up to this time, players had developed the habit of touching the ball down behind their own goal line "for safety." This enabled them to bring the ball out to their own twenty-five for a "free kick." And so, whenever a team had the ball nearer its own goal than its own twenty-five, a player merely touched it down for "a safety." This tactic was used so often during the Yale–Princeton "block" game that it led to the inclusion of the safety as a scoring play. The 1881 convention had decided that, if there was no score by touchdown or goal, the team with four fewer safeties than its opponent would be considered the winner.

There were still no points for the safety and it counted only when the game was tied. Thus, when the Harvard–Princeton game of 1882 ended in a tie, the referee ruled Harvard the winner because Princeton had been forced to make two safeties. Again, there was an uproar; and again, Walter Camp acted.

He introduced point scoring. In 1883 a goal kicked from the field was given a value of 5 points; a goal after touchdown counted 4, a touchdown brought 2 points, and a safety was worth 1. The safety point, of course, was scored *against* the team forced to make it.

As the game continued to develop, it became obvious that a touchdown was harder to score than a goal kicked from the field. So in 1884 the touchdown was increased to a value of 4 points. The field goal stayed at 5, and the goal after touchdown was reduced to 2. The safety was raised to 2.

In 1897 the touchdown was raised to 5 points and the kick following a touchdown dropped to a value of 1 (our modern "extra point"). The field goal fell to 4 points in 1904 and to 3 in 1909. In 1912 the touchdown rose to a scoring value of 6 points.

This scoring system—touchdown, 6; kick after touchdown, 1; field goal, 3; safety, 2—remained unchanged for 46 years. Finally, in 1958, the rules committee allowed a team a choice of kicking for one point after touchdown or running or passing for two points. This was done to reduce the number of ties, and it proved successful.

Thus, in 1883, under the leadership of Walter Camp, American football began to be provided with that wide variety of scoring opportunities which is so peculiar to the game.

One last bottleneck remained to be opened before football could become inimitably American. It concerned the "offside." The word, as used at that time, did not apply to the present violation occurring when a man on either team crosses into enemy territory before the ball is snapped. Instead it was a word the British used to describe a player who got ahead of his own ball carrier or kicker. It is what Americans now call blocking or interference—tactics which were highly illegal in the early Rugby days.

The Americans liked the idea of helping the ball carrier along. They often bumped into an opposing player as though by accident. In 1879, Princeton used two players to escort the ball carrier during a game against Harvard. Walter Camp, who refereed the game, warned Princeton that the tactic was illegal. But the following year, his Yale team was doing the same thing. So were football teams all over the East, where football teams were multiplying, and in the Midwest, where Michigan was pioneering the sport.

14

The Game Gets Rough

Football was always a rough game, but it was to get even rougher after Princeton introduced the "V-trick." The V was first tried from scrimmage when the Tigers met the rising University of Pennsylvania team in 1884. Richard Hodge had his teammates mass in a V formation, with the point forward and the ball carrier inside the V. The play went for a touchdown as the Tigers routed the Quakers 31–0. But then Princeton put the play aside for four years, reviving it at about the same time an exuberant young giant named William Walter Heffelfinger arrived on the Yale campus.

Heffelfinger, who was called "Pudge" and "Heff" by his teammates, was to be a three-time All-America. Compared with today's monsters of 275 pounds and up, Pudge would not seem so big at 205 pounds. But there were monsters in his day, too, and Heffelfinger was still able to hurl them aside during his lightning-like rushes into the enemy backfields. And it was Pudge who was the first to break up Princeton's bone-cracking V formation.

That was in 1888, the year in which Yale rolled up a staggering 694 points to zero for the opposition. The fierce William "Pa" Corbin captained that team; Amos Alonzo Stagg was an end; and the powerful freshman, Heffelfinger, was left guard. Princeton was also unbeaten when the two teams met in the Polo Grounds in New York City. And

Walter "Pudge" Heffelfinger,
Yale's three-time All-America guard.

the Tigers were quick to unveil their revived V.

The Bulldogs tried to slow it down by slugging the lead man on the jaw with the heel of the hand. But he plowed on. Inexorably the Tigers drove toward Yale's goal. Then Heffelfinger got an idea. As the V formed again and the wedge heaved forward, Pudge leaped high in the air with his legs tucked under him. He struck the point of the V like a human cannonball and it shivered and fell apart.

"Hey, you, Heffelfinger!" Hec Cowan roared from the bottom of the ruined V. "Cut that out or you'll kill somebody!"

"I'll quit it if you stop using the wedge," Pudge replied.

But Princeton stuck to her powerful V.

In the end, however, Billy Bull's kicking gave Yale a 10–0 victory in a game rough enough to cause the New Haven *Register* to report: "Both teams got in some quite respectable slugging when they were sure the umpire was not look-ing, and the man who did not have a bloody nose and mouth was considered a little out of fashion."

The New Haven *Union* said: "In less than 15 minutes their jackets were fres-coed with blood. . . . It was a wonder the players to a man did not have to retire and go home with their bones done up in splints."

Soon all the teams in the East were using V or wedge plays. Broken bones became common as the V gained both in momentum and in the element of surprise achieved when the ball was snapped quickly from center with the hands. At the same time, "signals" sent the plays rolling against a predesignated spot.

Again Walter Camp could take credit for both innovations. As early as 1889 Camp's men were signaling what to do on the next play by a "code."

In those days, to know the opponent's signals was considered a great advan-tage. Football "spies" were numerous, and many a coach would hold secret

A lively "scrimmage" between the Harvard and Pennsylvania teams of 1890.

practice or ban all spectators from the the practice field. This was the way in which Harvard was able to surprise Yale when, in 1892, she added the principle of momentum to the mass of Princeton's V-trick.

Lorin F. Deland, a Harvard fan who had never played football, but who excelled as a chess player and a student of military tactics, had seen how much more crushing the V-trick could be if it began on the kickoff rather than at the line of scrimmage. Harvard had to wait until the second half, however, to spring the new play on the cocky Yale eleven. When they did, the Crimson lined up in two five-man squads about twenty-five yards behind Bernie Trafford, the so-called "kicker." At a signal from Trafford they converged in a perfect flying wedge. Trafford tapped the ball, trapped it, and handed off to speedy Charley Brewer, Harvard's 150-pound All-America, inside the wedge.

Harvard's wedge sent the thunderstruck Elis flying in all directions. It would have scored a touchdown if Charley Brewer hadn't tripped over one of his own players on the Yale 25-yard line. Recovering from their surprise, the Yale team held for downs and went on to win 6–0, thus completing another splendid season in which they won all 13 games while scoring 435 points. Between 1883 and 1900, Yale took seven titles and shared one, while Princeton won four and shared one. Harvard and Pennsylvania won three apiece. Yale's frenzied fans had the right to sing:

Let's give a long cheer for Eli's men,
Yale's here to win again;
Harvard's team may fight to the end
But Yale will win.

One reason for Yale's continued success as a high scorer was a silent, wild-eyed slip of an end named Frank Hinkey. Many football stars and coaches considered Hinkey the greatest football player of his time. At his heaviest he weighed only 157 pounds, although his legs were very sturdy. Walter Camp picked him four times for his All-American team. He said that Hinkey "drifted through the interference like a disembodied spirit." Players of that time allowed their hair to grow into long flowing locks, and Hickey did look like a glaring wraith as he raged silently up and down the field. Some sports writers thought he resembled Hamlet, and many of the runners who played against him thought he looked like a maniac.

In four years of play Hinkey never let a play get around his end. He didn't throw the interference aside like Harvard's great Marshall "Ma" Newell, who also made All-America four times during the early nineties. Instead, Hinkey went in low, with arms outstretched. He seemed to plant himself right in the path of the interference. Rival players broke over him like waves over rocks. He would seize the runner by the legs, lift him and slam him to the earth with a shattering tackle.

It was because of Hinkey that Harvard could not score from the Yale 25-yard line after the flying wedge had made its first appearance in 1892. He was easily the toughest football player in the two rough years which followed the introduction of the wedge, below-the-waist tackling and unrestrained slugging. Alonzo Stagg, the All-America end who had played with Heffelfinger, had already made the game harder by devising an "ends-back" formation while he was coach at Springfield College. Stagg moved the ends back of the line and used them as blockers. Another Yale man, George Woodruff, invented the "guards-back" formation at Penn for the same reason—more power in front of the runner. All of these lineups served to place the emphasis on brute strength. And since nothing had been done to outlaw slugging, football was so rough that in 1893, when Purdue met Chicago, the district attorney of Tippecanoe County in Indiana came onto the playing field and threatened to indict all the players for assault and battery.

That was also the year of a particularly rough game between Yale and Army. Frank Hinkey and Army end Butler Ames engaged in what was almost a prize fight. The commandant of West Point, Captain Samuel M. Mills, was so angry that he had his bugler blow recall. To Yale's amazement, the Army team stopped playing and snapped to attention.

"Mr. Ames!" roared Captain Mills. "Mr. Ames! If you hit that man again, sir, I'll put you in the guardhouse!"

"And you, man!" he roared at Hinkey. "You, man! If you hit Mr. Ames again, sir, I'll put you off the Post!"

Then the bugler blatted "as you were" and the game resumed with no fisticuffs.

By 1893 the Yale team had finally accepted the "V-trick" or flying wedge.

But the change had been effected only under threat of bayonets. The next year football very nearly got out of hand; the climax was reached in the bloody Yale–Harvard game played before a roaring crowd of 23,000 persons. It was won by Yale, 12–4, but the best description of the game was made by the Boston *Globe*, which printed a "hospital box score."

YALE: Jerrems, knee injury; Murphy, unconscious from a kick in the head; Butterworth, carried from the field.

HARVARD: Charley Brewer, badly bruised foot; Worthington, broken collar bone; Hallowell, broken nose.

Of course, such minor casualties as black eyes, split lips or bruised and blackened flesh were simply not mentioned. All over the East Coast, newspapers were calling football a brutal or an atrocious game. The New York *Post* said: "No father or mother worthy of the name would permit a son to associate with the set of Yale brutes on Hinkey's football team." Exaggerated tales of the rough American sport even crept into the foreign press.

The exaggerations were comical, of course, but underlying them was an unavoidable truth: the American game of football was becoming far too rough. A year later, amid a growing clamor against the rising number of injuries, the flying wedge was at last outlawed on the kickoff and mass momentum plays were restricted.

Meanwhile, other great names besides those of Harvard and Yale and Princeton were rising in the football world. In 1896 Lafayette won 11 games, tying Princeton and giving mighty Pennsylvania its only defeat in a string of 66

games stretching from 1894 to 1898. Stanford was pioneering in the sport on the West Coast. A young lieutenant named Leonard Wood, destined to be one of America's finest commanders, was taking enough subjects at Georgia Tech to qualify him for the football team. He would be the originator of one of the South's great classics: the Georgia Tech–University of Georgia game. In the Midwest, Purdue was putting together that region's first undefeated seasons. In 1892 the Purdue Boilermakers, coached by Snake Ames of former Princeton fame, rolled over Illinois 12–6; Wisconsin, 32–4; Michigan, 24–0; Indiana 68–0; and Chicago, 38–0.

That same year, Walter Camp at Yale received a significant letter:

Dear Sir:

I want to ask a favor of you. Will you kindly furnish me with some points on the best way to develop a good football team. I am an instructor . . . connected with this University and have been asked to coach the team. I know something of the Rugby game, but would like to find out the best manner to handle the men. I have seen a good many Yale games (as I come from New Haven, you can find out about me from Dr. Seaver) and knowing you are an authority on the game, I would welcome any points you might give me. Hoping that I am not asking too great a favor of you,

Your sincere admirer,
JAMES H. KIVLAN
University of Notre Dame

Football was spreading across the nation, and the Fighting Irish of Notre Dame were already on the move.

Football Fever

Football *had* to become the American game, if not the National Pastime. It had so many qualities typical of the United States. First and foremost was its ruggedness—the thrill of bodily contact, which would attract red-blooded youth. Secondly, it was full of surprises, much to the alternating delight and despair of players and spectators alike. Thirdly, it was played in the most exhilarating of seasons, amid the bright colors of autumn, when there was a bracing tang in the air. Football was like a festival taking place each Saturday afternoon. There were the rival teams and the school bands in their gay uniforms; there were the somersaulting cheerleaders, the team mascots, and the cheering crowds. And, as the sun's warmth gave way to the first chill of dusk and the pungent odor of burning leaves, there was the wildly tooting band and the delirious followers of the victorious team "snake-dancing" home through quiet streets lined with yellowing maples. That was the "autumn fever," as football has sometimes been called. Even today it is hard to think of anything more typically American than a high school football game between neighboring towns.

That was why, as the nineteenth century came to a close, the game spread rapidly across the country—beginning with the Midwest.

Although Notre Dame was eventually to become the most illustrious name in football, the honor of introducing the sport into the Midwest belongs to Michigan. Football began at Michigan as an interclass sport, but in 1879 the Wolverines had a school team which met and routed Racine College in the first game played between Midwestern Colleges. For the following decade or so, Michigan was supreme in its section. It spoiled Notre Dame's football debut in 1887, and dominated those schools which eventually were to make up the Big Ten, or Western Conference.

As early as 1881 Michigan was challenging Eastern supremacy, although the challenge was premature. Coming east, the Wolverines met Harvard, Yale and Princeton within six days and lost to all three. These were the first of the intersectional games that are such a stirring feature of modern football. The feat of playing three football giants in a row at two-day intervals was also something of an achievement.

It was topped, though, by Sewanee's famous trek.

Sewanee, as the University of the South was called, had twenty-one players on her team. They left their Tennessee campus on November 7, 1899. Traveling by day coach, eating when and where they could, without benefit of practice, they met the strong University of Texas team two days later and won, 12–0. The next day they swamped Texas A & M, 10–0, and on the following day trampled Tulane in New Orleans by 23–0. The next day being Sunday, they did not play; but on Monday they routed Louisiana State by 34–0 and on Tuesday they turned back Mississippi, 12–0.

Traveling like nomads, they beat five of the best teams in the South and Southwest within six days, without a single point scored against them —that was truly a team of iron men! No wonder Sewanee closed its season undefeated.

Two of Sewanee's victims, Texas and Texas A & M, along with the University of Arkansas, were the first colleges to play football in what was to become the "slingin'est" league in the land: the topsy-turvy Southwestern Conference. The Longhorns (University of Texas) and the Aggies (Texas A & M) first met in 1894, when Texas won by a thumping score. They have continued to meet every Thanksgiving Day in the area's oldest rivalry.

Thanksgiving, incidentally, soon became the day when the bitterest rivals met in the annual "big game." Richard Harding Davis, who organized and played on Lehigh's first team before embarking on his colorful career as a journalist, described how Thanksgiving and the big game were as inseparable and as American as ham and eggs. Writing of the Yale–Princeton game of 1893, played in New York, he said:

There are two or three facts which tend to show how the development of the Thanksgiving-day game has affected those in high places. One of these is that services in many churches of this city were held one hour earlier than usual last Thanksgiving Day, because the rectors found they could not get full congregations unless the service was over in time to allow the worshippers to make an early start for Manhattan field. And another is that the manager of the Yale team wrote the secretary of the President of the United States to inquire if he could not get prompt information as to just what day the President intended to proclaim as the day of general thanksgiving.

In that same article, Davis described the seriousness with which the players took the game by relating that the victorious Princeton men stood in their dressing room ". . . covered with mud and blood and perspiration," and solemnly sang the doxology. Since the earliest times men have celebrated victory in battle or deliverance from catastrophe with hymns, and these battered young warriors of the gridiron were manifesting the same feeling of exaltation. Moreover, football has always attracted more than its share of athletic clergymen or divinity students. Probably the first of these was the great Amos Alonzo Stagg.

Stagg studied for the ministry while he played under Walter Camp at Yale, but he changed his mind after he came to realize that he was not a good speaker. The sport of football certainly benefited from this decision, for the career of Amos Alonzo Stagg is perhaps the most remarkable in the game's history. From his beginning as a freshman end in 1885 until his retirement as a coach in 1953 at the age of 91, Stagg's career almost exactly parallels the evolution of football. From the days of the first scrimmage—when the game ceased to be Rugby—until our own modern era of the "split T" and "flanker backs" and the "I formation," Stagg not only saw football evolve, he contributed most to its evolution. If Walter Camp is the

Alonzo Stagg (at extreme left) and the Yale championship team of 1888.

"father of football," then Alonzo Stagg is its most prolific inventor.

In addition to his innumerable contributions to football, he also invented the indoor batting cage in baseball and the troughs for overflow in indoor swimming pools. Moreover, he was an associate of Dr. James Naismith's at Springfield when that gentleman invented basketball. He conducted the first tour of Japan by American baseball players and served on the Olympic committee from 1906 through 1932. He coached James Lightbody to an Olympic "triple," coached Clyde Blair to become the first man to run 100 meters in less than ten seconds, made All-America end, struck out twenty players in a baseball game for Yale and rejected the then staggering offer of $4,200 to pitch for the Giants simply because he believed that his life's work was to be with young men.

Stagg began this work at the University of Chicago in 1892, when he became one of the first professional "coaches" in football. When he arrived there, he found that the school had not yet com-

pleted a single college building. So few students answered his call to come out for football that he found it necessary —as was permissible in those days—to play himself.

Gradually, however, Stagg made a Midwestern powerhouse of the Maroon team. And he did it without ever losing his balance, always keeping football in its place. To the tackle who complained that he had wasted four years in college, Stagg replied: "You're dead wrong, boy. You've learned to dress right, speak right, how to act around good people. And if you never passed a college course you still would know a thousand things that not one out of ten other men know."

Stagg still believed that a clear conscience was more important than winning a game of football, and he once requested officials to call back a Chicago touchdown because his team had broken the rules. Stagg's reputation for fair play was so great that he was asked to referee when his own team played Illinois!

Stagg had little patience with self-important people. When a self-styled

22

star showed up for practice in a bright new uniform, he had his quarterback move the scrimmage to a mud puddle and instructed him to give "Mr. Big" the ball. Five dunkings later the glory seeker quit. Although Stagg never used profanity, he was not above calling his players "jackasses," and he formed a Double Jackass Club for especially errant pupils. His arch rival at Illinois, Bob Zuppke, once said that Stagg never swore at his men because he didn't have *men*. "He calls this man, then that man, then another, a jackass. By the end of the workout there are no men playing—just jackasses grazing."

Sometimes, though, the "jackasses" could hee-haw right back at the Grand Old Man. Tony Ketman, a 196-pound divinity student, was a frequent victim of Stagg's practice of teaching lighter blockers to "submarine" their bigger foemen. After a 150-pounder named Oscar Looney had spent the afternoon butting him about, Ketman rose from the field in disgust and said: "Mr. Stagg, I don't mind playing against a man, but I'm darned if I'll play against a goat."

Being small himself—a 150-pound All-America—Stagg was fond of small players. In fact he developed two of the most famous in history. Clarence Herschberger, a 158-pound halfback, was the first All-America from the Midwest. In 1896 he drop-kicked a forty-yard field goal to beat Michigan, 7–6. The next year, the exuberant Herschberger proved to be Chicago's undoing. Just before the Wisconsin game he and a teammate named Walter Kennedy had a contest to see who could put on the most weight at one meal. Kennedy won, 7½ pounds to 7. In further gastronomic combat,

Clarence Herschberger

Herschberger ate thirteen eggs and became so sick he could not play against the Badgers. Wisconsin won, 23–8, and Stagg remarked wryly: "We weren't beaten by eleven Badgers but by thirteen eggs."

In 1899 Stagg and Chicago won their first Big Ten title.

One of the smallest of Maroons, and perhaps the greatest, was Walter Eckersall. The immortal "Eckie" weighed in at 138 pounds, and yet is still considered by many experts as football's All-Time quarterback.

Eckie was a marvel. He could drop-kick with the best of them, and he could get off long, twisting runs that would leave rival teams beating the turf in anguish. He never missed a tackle at safety-man, and his field generalship is regarded as being without any equal. Because he was so light he inspired many another small man to play a game usually associated more with brawn than with brains. One of them, a Norwegian-born youth named Knute Rockne, has described how he saw Eckersall when he was only a high-school player. Eckie led the Western schoolboy champions, Hyde Park High of Chicago, when they walloped Brooklyn Poly Prep of New York, the Eastern titlists, by a score of 105–0. Thirty years later, Rockne recalled:

He played prairie football, mainly wide sweeps around ends; but by instinctive timing he hit the heavier Brooklyn linemen until they were dizzy. With no more than four fundamental plays he worked so quickly and coolly that he made his offense bewildering. Eckersall's sharp, staccato calling of signals; his keen, handsome face, and the smooth precision with which he drove and countered and drove again, handling his players with the rhythm of an orchestra leader—all this gave football a new meaning to me.

Football, incidentally, was taking on a new look at the turn of the century. Rubber nose guards were invented in 1898, and sometimes all eleven players wore them. They were indeed a ferocious sight with the ends of their handlebar mustaches dangling from either side of that long, black, banana-like mask, and their long hair flying in the breeze. Eventually, of course, the mustaches and beards vanished. Alonzo Stagg personally shaved his Chicago players. And Yale set a new hair style when the Elis appeared for a game with their heads close-cropped in the haircut that is standard today. The standard uniform then was a "smock," an affair invented by Ledou Smock of Princeton. It included a laced canvas jacket with padded shoulders, and padded moleskin knee pants. Shin guards were also worn, but helmets were almost unknown. In 1903, Pop Warner introduced a knee guard made of soft wool felt.

The ball itself was also undergoing changes. The "pigskin," a term dating back to the days when an inflated pig bladder served as a ball, was still actually made of cowhide leather. But in 1896 the big oval ball was changed to a "prolate spheroid," which made drop-kicking much easier. With this ball, such kicking stars as Pat O'Dea of the University of Wisconsin began to emerge.

O'Dea was the Wisconsin Badgers' first All-America. Born in Australia, he was known to his teammates as "the Kangaroo." Certainly he could kick like one. Before coming to America, he had already excelled in Australian Football, a game made for kicking. In the States he quickly established himself as "the greatest kicker of all time." Seventy- and eighty-yard punts were the rule with him. In 1897 he drop-kicked a 60-yard field goal against Chicago and another one of 42 yards while on the dead run against Minnesota. The following year, in a howling blizzard, he drop-kicked a 62-yarder against Northwestern.

In 1899, while serving as Badger captain for the second time, O'Dea place-kicked a 60-yarder against Illinois and drop-kicked another against Minnesota. He also punted 100 yards against Yale and ran back a kickoff 100 yards against Beloit. O'Dea was truly a legendary figure, and the legends grew after he vanished from his home in San Francisco in 1917 only to pop up 17 years later in a

24

little California town under the name of Charles Mitchell. O'Dea explained that his football fame had hampered him in his work as a lawyer. "As Pat O'Dea," he said, "I seemed very much just an ex-Wisconsin football player. Probably I was wrong. Mrs. Mitchell, that is, Mrs. O'Dea, always thought I was."

Pat O'Dea also served as a professional "coacher" at Notre Dame for a while. The paid coach was becoming a more common feature of college football. All over America, colleges which had fallen victim to the football fever were laying aside money for a paid, full-time coach. Down south, Auburn had hired John William Heisman, who had coached a series of winning teams at Oberlin, Ohio.

Heisman was the professional of professionals. From 1892 until 1927 he coached at a number of schools, including Oberlin, Buchtel (now Akron), Auburn, Clemson, Georgia Tech, Pennsylvania, Washington and Jefferson, and Rice. From 1927 until his death in 1936 he was athletic director at the Downtown Athletic Club in New York. In his memory, the Downtown Athletic Club renamed their award the Heisman Trophy. It is given each year to the nation's outstanding college player.

Heisman was one of the first football figures to play at two schools. He was a tackle at Brown from 1887 through 1889, and a tackle, center and end at Penn in 1890–91. He had hoped to be a lawyer, but football became his passion. Short, stocky, with a handsome face ruined by a football-flattened nose, Heisman was a perfectionist. He probably ranks only after Camp, Stagg and Warner as an originator and contributer to the game. Most outstanding among his innovations

Pat O'Dea, a University of Wisconsin immortal.

is the forward pass.

Heisman got the idea as he watched North Carolina play Georgia in 1895. Late in a scoreless game, Pop Warner's Georgia Bulldogs were pressing the Tar Heels back. Desperate, the Carolina fullback ran behind his scrimmage line looking for free room to punt. Finally, in a gesture that might have been born of despair, he just heaved the ball downfield. A startled Tar Heel caught it and scampered seventy yards for the winning touchdown.

Pop Warner stormed onto the field to protest. But the officials said they had not seen the play. They allowed this, the first of all touchdown passes, to stand.

Heisman remembered what he had seen.

To him, the pass seemed the answer to the mass momentum plays that were causing so many injuries and were

25

threatening to ruin the game. Heisman saw immediately that the pass would open up football and shift the emphasis away from brute strength. He tried repeatedly to have it legalized, but his efforts were not successful until 1906. In the meantime, he was developing his winning teams down south.

With his flair for the dramatic (he was an amateur actor) Heisman greeted each new football squad with a football and the question: "What is it?" Then, he would give his own answer:

"A prolate spheroid—that is, an elongated sphere—in which the outer leathern casing is drawn tightly over a somewhat small rubber tubing." Then, lowering his voice ominously, he would add: "Better to have died as a small boy than to fumble this football!"

Heisman's teams made few fumbles, and his first Auburn eleven, of 1895, was the first to use the hidden-ball trick. Quarterback Reynolds "Tick" Tichenor stuffed the ball under his jersey to trot to a touchdown against Vanderbilt and win, 9–6.

It has often been said that Pop Warner and his wily Carlisle Indians were the first to use the hidden-ball ruse. But the idea was actually Heisman's. Of course, in those days, practically every maneuver or formation was a "first." And frequently, it was very hard to determine who actually was the originator of a new play. Only in later years, when record books were being drawn up, would the pioneer coaches be asked to recollect when they first saw this or first used that. And then, relying on memory only, they would often be wrong.

One thing is certain, though. The T formation which is so popular today was already in use as early as 1894.

It was used by the University of Pennsylvania, whose football team was coached by another professional, George Woodruff. And its arrival coincided with that of Penn as a football powerhouse. From 1894 through 1898 the red-and-blue won sixty-five of sixty-seven games. The Quakers put together a string of thirty-four before they lost to a great Lafayette team in 1896, and then they won another thirty-one in a row. There were great stars on those Penn teams—men such as Herb McCracken, who would become even more famous as coach at Lafayette, and the four-time All-American guard, T. Truxton Hare. Another Penn immortal, fullback John Minds, has described the formation which Woodruff was using at Penn in those great years.

". . . the regular offensive formation was a seven-man line, with the quarterback directly behind center and the backfield men about four-and-a-half yards back of the scrimmage line: It was the *T formation*."

Also emerging as an Eastern gridiron power in the last decade of the nineteenth century was Princeton. The reason? Probably the most remarkable football family in history: the Poes.

There were six of these Poe brothers, all great-nephews of the American poet, Edgar Allen Poe. They were all small, but every one of them had a fighting heart and iron will. Two made All-America: Edgar Allen, who placed on the first of the All-American teams in 1889, and Arthur, an All-American end in 1899.

Edgar Allen Poe's deeds on the gridiron sometimes rivaled the works of his namesake uncle in the world of letters. This wisp of a man was the scourge of the East. He broke his nose against Penn in one game but was back two weeks later raging against a Yale team led by the giant Heffelfinger. But even Edgar Allen's accomplishments were topped by Arthur, a still smaller man. Against Yale in 1898, this scrawny, white-faced youngster broke up the game by stealing the ball from the arms of a Bulldog back and scampering 98 yards for the winning touchdown. The next year he was back, "smaller than ever," as one Yale stalwart sneered, to snatch victory from defeat in the last-minute play that Princetonians still refer to as "The Kick."

Yale led, 10–6, a score which failed to indicate how thoroughly the Bulldogs had been chewing up the Tigers. With a few minutes left to play, no less than six Princeton regulars had been carried to the sidelines. The crowd was already leaving the field. Then big Bill Roper recovered a Yale fumble. Catching fire, the Tigers drove steadily downfield. With only a few seconds left they had the ball on the Yale 25-yard line. A field goal, worth five points, would win the game. But who would kick it? All of Princeton's kickers were out of the game.

Arthur Poe tapped Captain Bill Edwards on the shoulder and said, "I'll make it." Edwards was astounded. Poe had never kicked a goal in his life, not even in practice. But he had faith in the little man, a faith that proved justified. Poe's toe met the ball with a solid thud. The pigskin sailed straight between the goalposts. The only comfort left to the stunned Yale rooters was the fact that they had seen the last of the worst of the Poe brothers. Arthur Poe was graduated from Princeton University in the spring of 1900.

The six football-playing Poe Brothers of Princeton. Left to right, Arthur, S. Johnson, Neilson (seated in front), Edgar Allen, Gresham, and John.

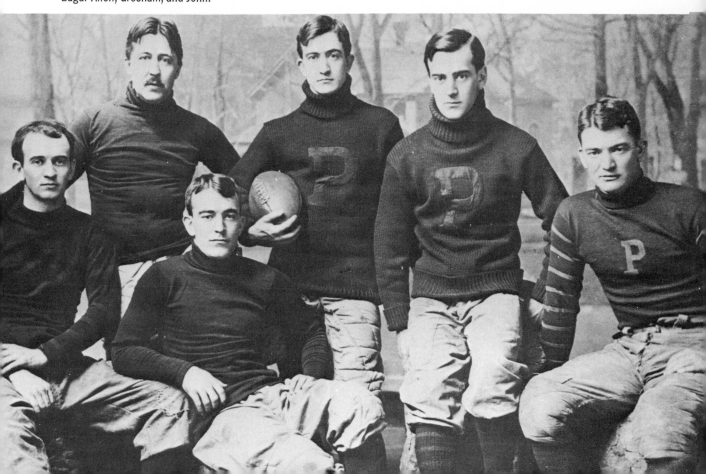

A Point a Minute

In 1901 a railroad train puffed into the station at Ann Arbor, Michigan, and a man in a high starched collar stepped down onto the platform. He was Fielding Harris Yost, an amazing fellow, who had coached five football teams simultaneously in California. The teams were the Stanford University varsity, the Stanford freshmen, San Jose Normal School, California Ukiah and Lowell High in San Francisco. Anyone who had heard of Yost's accomplishments could guess that there were some very interesting football times ahead for the University of Michigan.

There were. Fielding Yost gave Michigan unbeaten teams in 1901, 1902, 1903 and 1904, and again in 1910, 1918, 1922 and 1923. From 1901 through 1905 the Wolverines were the scourge of the gridiron. Football has yet to see their equal. During that period these "Point a Minute" juggernauts rolled up an incredible 2,819 points against exactly 42 for the opposition. They won fifty-five games, lost one and tied one. And they achieved that record in the days of the five-point touchdown, and before the high-scoring forward pass had been made legal.

They owed their success to speed. "Hurry up!" Fielding Yost would shout at his players. "Hurry up! Hurry up! Ye think ye got all day?" It was not long before he was known as "Hurry Up" Yost. And as long as he lived, this rawboned whirlwind who had been born in a West Virginia log cabin would never lose his distinctive mountain accent. The teams which he made famous were always "Meesheegan" to him. "Y'knaow, lad," he would storm at a lazy lineman, "God made ye big! He made ye muscles strong! He gave ye good health! And ye're playing like a wooden Indian in front of a cigar store. If I should put ye in a greenhouse and give ye an ax and a shotgun, ye couldn't get aout!"

Always, Yost appeared on a practice field wearing his starched collars and glittering tie pins, and always he was pleading for more speed, urging his team to pour it on. "Ding 'em in the slats!" he would bellow. "Fight 'em! Touchdown! Oh, no, lad—not that way. *Nay, nay, Pauline!*"

Yost began his very first year by changing the Michigan team completely. He wanted speed up front as well as in the backfield. And in that 1901 team he had it. The lineup contained some of Michigan's all-time greats: Tug Wilson, Al Herrnstein, Dan McGugin, Harrison "Boss" Weeks, Neil Snow, and the incomparable Willie Heston. Heston, a 190-pound wonder who combined power with speed, had played for Yost at San Jose State. Yost called him to Michigan, for in those days colleges were not nearly so strict on eligibility rules as they are today. The great Willie had already been teaching school when Yost's summons arrived, but he loved football so much that he gave up his job.

Willie ran wild during that first year when the Wolverines defeated ten straight opponents. They scored 550 points while holding their enemies scoreless. Because this averaged out to 55 points a game, the team earned their "Point a Minute" nickname.

In one game against Buffalo, Michigan slaughtered the Bisons by 128–0. Toward the end of the debacle a Buffalo substitute staggered over to the Michigan bench.

"Lad," Yost said, "you're on the wrong side.

"Oh, no, I'm not," the youth gasped, and sat down.

The score could never be too high to suit Hurry Up Yost, and he devised a system of signals which gave his teams the chance to run off plays rapidly and catch the enemy defense flat-footed. Boss Weeks, the quarterback, would call out his signal for the next play while his team was getting up from the last one. The Wolverines would jump into position; the ball would be snapped on the first number—and the slower opposition would be overwhelmed while they were still getting into position. If the other team began to figure out that the first number was the starting signal, Boss Weeks changed it to a later number and usually drew his opponents offside.

Michigan's ability to reel off plays stunned the West Coast when the Wolverines went west to meet Yost's old team, Stanford, in the 1902 Rose Bowl game—the first in history. Playing without a substitute, Michigan's eleven ran 142 plays and rolled to an astonishing 1,463 yards on the ground while walloping the Indians 49–0. Today, if a team advances the ball more than 500 yards on the ground, it is considered a rare exhibition of football power.

But while Michigan was riding roughshod over her opponents, Alonzo Stagg at Chicago was also putting together top teams. In 1904, with Walter Eckersall in at quarterback, the Maroons hoped to slow down Hurry Up Yost's point-a-minute terrors. Yost, however, called for secret practices prior to the Chicago game. And he devised a play that called 265-pound Babe Carter out of the line to

In his later years, "Coach" Yost examines an enlarged photograph of his famous 1902 Rose Bowl champions.

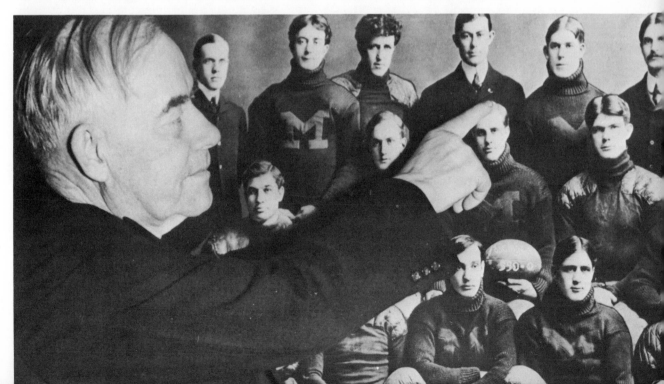

carry the ball. Yost deliberately advertised this play as a touchdown play near the goal, and he saw to it that Stagg heard of it. Then, just before the two teams met, Yost told his men that the play was a ruse. Carter was only a decoy. Thus, the first time Michigan got within Chicago's ten, Carter was called into the backfield. But the quarterback merely faked giving the ball to him, slipping it to Willie Heston instead. While the entire Chicago team ganged up on Carter, Heston waltzed around end for the score.

Stagg, however, had not given up. He was not only tired of losing to Michigan, he was sick of having Hurry Up Yost remind him of it. "We'll give you plenty this year," he told Yost at a track meet in 1905. Stagg was not boasting, for this was the year of the team he called "the greatest that ever wore the C in the days of five-yard football." Besides Eckersall, there was Hugo Bezdek, a fine player who would become famous as a coach at Penn State, and other stalwarts such as tackle Art Badenoch and an All-America end, Mark Catlin. Michigan's powerful line was led by "Germany" Schulz, a legendary center who was one of the iron men of football. He missed only ten minutes in four years of play. But the great Willie Heston, unfortunately, had been lost by graduation.

Just before the game, which Michigan hoped to make its 57th straight victory, Stagg told his team: "Don't let Yost cram this one down my throat."

Out swept the Maroons, but the game soon settled down to a defensive battle between two strong lines. This forced a punting duel between Eckersall and Michigan's Ike Garrels. Neither team

Coach Stagg calls out practice directions to his Chicago team.

had scored by halftime. Between the halves, President Harper of Chicago, who was dying of cancer but who was listening to the game by special telephone hookup, dispatched a message to Stagg. "You must win for me," he said.

Stagg conveyed the message to his players. Inspired, the Maroons returned to the game and hurled back every Wolverine drive. Then Eckersall punted over the Michigan goal. Michigan's Denny Clark caught the ball on the run. But as he stepped out of the end zone Art Badenoch drove him back and Mark Catlin slammed him to the ground for a safety.

Chicago won 2–0. Stagg's team had ended the reign of mighty Michigan and had won the Big Ten title again. Stagg vowed that his team would do even better the next year—if there was a next year.

Football Nearly Perishes

As the twentieth century began, football was still a game of mass momentum. Hurry Up Yost might place his own emphasis on speed; John Heisman might call for adoption of the forward pass; but most of the coaches seemed content to plug along with power plays and pileups.

The flying wedge was not completely gone. Hurdling and the flying tackle were common. Slugging was still a familiar tactic up front, and the most acceptable method of getting the ball carrier through the line was to pull, push or haul him through. Thus the only participant surviving a contest undamaged was apt to be the ball.

Worst of all, young men were being killed and badly maimed while playing football. In 1905 a total of 18 American boys lost their lives in football, and 154 more were seriously injured. Four years later Army's splendid left tackle, Eugene Byrne, was fatally injured during the Army–Harvard game.

In the middle of the 1905 season, President Theodore Roosevelt summoned representatives of Harvard, Yale and Princeton to a White House conference. An outdoor man himself and a lover of sports, Roosevelt was outspoken in his condemnation of brutal play. He said: "Brutality and foul play should receive the same summary punishment given to a man who cheats at cards."

At Columbia the sport was abolished —not to be resumed until 1915. Stanford and California dropped football and picked up Rugby instead. "The game of football," said President Wheeler of California, "must be made over or go."

Nevertheless, the power plays and pileups continued—and deliberately dirty play still claimed its victims. The climax came in Pennsylvania's game against Swarthmore in 1905. The mainstay of Swarthmore's line was Bob Maxwell, a 250-pounder of great speed and agility. The Penn team calculated that, if they could contain Maxwell, they would win the game. Maxwell was hit on almost every play. He staggered from the field a physical wreck. President Roosevelt saw a picture of him in that condition, and he angrily notified the leaders of the sport that if the brutality was not removed from football he would ban the game by presidential edict.

The result was the historic meeting of January 12, 1906, out of which came what is known today as the National Collegiate Athletic Association (N.C.A.A.) Rules Committee, which regulates intercollegiate sports.

Walter Camp of Yale, William Reid of Harvard and Captain Palmer Pierce of Army attended this conference, and they set up a Rules Committee which made the following important changes:

1. Legalization of the forward pass.

2. Creation of a "neutral zone" which separated both lines by the length of the ball.

3. Requiring a minimum of six men on the offensive line of scrimmage.

4. Raising the yardage required for a

first down from five to ten yards in three downs.

5. Marking the field both lengthwise and crosswise with white stripes, thus changing it from a gridiron to a checkerboard.

Although the forward pass was at last allowed, it was hamstrung with many restrictions. Even so, its mere introduction meant that a team must defend against it. This weakened the defensive line and worked to eliminate mass pileups. Power plays were weakened by the requirement that six men be on the line. Five men in a backfield wedge, of course, were not nearly so dangerous as seven or eight.

Perhaps even more important than the forward pass was the establishment of the neutral zone. Previously, play had been hampered by linemen constantly rushing to get the jump on each other, and by the endless wrangling to determine who was or who was not offside. With no space between lines, the forwards had stood face to face trading blows. (John Heisman once wrote of having seen Heffelfinger of Yale and Riggs of Princeton slugging it out thus. "While it wasn't football," he said, "it was even better . . .") With a neutral zone between lines, any offsides and foul blows were easier to detect.

Three years later the game was opened up more when the field goal's value sank from four points to three, but in that one year there were still 33 deaths and 246 major injuries. The clamor of criticism continued, and in 1910 these changes were effected:

1. Outlawing of the flying tackle.

2. Requirement of seven men on the offensive line.

3. Prohibition of crawling.

4. Prohibition of pushing and pulling the ball carrier and of that interlocked interference which was, in effect, the wedge.

5. Permitting forward passes to be thrown at any point providing the passer was five yards behind the line of scrimmage.

6. Dividing the halves into quarters of fifteen minutes each.

7. Dropping the checkerboard field in favor of the old gridiron.

8. Allowing a player withdrawn from the game to return in any succeeding period. (Previously, a player taken out of a game had to stay out. This meant that men who played throughout would be tired toward the end of a contest, and a weary player is most susceptible to injuries.)

Two years later the last of the important changes were made. The field was set at its present size of 100 yards in length and 53-1/3 yards in width. Ten-yard end zones were added for catching passes; the fourth down was provided, and the kickoff was placed at the 40-yard line rather than midfield. The last of the serious restrictions on the forward pass were also removed.

True enough, there would be other changes. Rules on substitutions, for instance, would be altered almost every season. Opponents of the forward pass would, for a time, legislate a penalty of five yards for two incomplete passes in a row, or rule a fourth-down incompleted forward pass in the end zone as a touchback. These changes, however, would not last. But changes are still being made in football because the gridiron game is a constantly changing sport.

Coaches are forever devising new plays and formations, and because some of these sometimes tend to take unfair advantage of the rules, the rules have to be changed again.

Nevertheless, the new regulations formulated in 1906, 1910 and 1912 were the ones that opened up the game, abolished brutality and made football more exciting to both player and spectator. It would remain for logical and inventive coaches to develop the modern game with its thrilling combination of speed, power and deception.

Among the first of these tacticians was Dr. Henry Williams. He invented the Minnesota shift in 1909. Williams' objective was to outflank his opponent; that is, to get on the outside of him so that a play could be run around him. Or sometimes he was simply trying to get four men against three or five against four. To do this, Dr. Williams held his tackles behind the center, with the ends wide. The quarterback was behind the tackles and the other three backs behind him. At the call "Hep!" the four backs shifted into a box position and the tackles jumped into the line. A split-second pause, and the entire Minnesota team was off the mark. There were variations to the Minnesota shift, of course, but the basic idea was that the tackles could jump into either side of the line *together*. Thus, the Gophers would have four men against three on one particular side, which is known as an unbalanced line. Before the defense could adjust, Minnesota would be shooting its play in that direction. With the introduction of Dr. Williams' shift, Minnesota became one of the Midwest's perennial powerhouses.

Out on the West Coast, a disciple of Dr. Williams put together another football powerhouse at the University of Washington. In 1900, Gilmour Dobie had quarterbacked Minnesota to its first Big Ten title. After that he had been an assistant to Dr. Williams. It was his job to look for good football players and Dobie liked them big. "When I'm traveling," he explained, "I ask farm boys how to get to a certain place. If they point with their finger, I move on. But if they point with the plow, I bring 'em to Minnesota!"

Gilmour Dobie's nickname was Gloomy Gil. It was apt. Before a game he would press his face against the dressing-room window and call to his players: "Look, boys, they're as big as bulls and as fast as jackrabbits!"

Gloomy Gil was rarely satisfied with anything less than perfection, and he was always predicting disaster. Yet his early record as a coach is unequalled. He had fourteen unbeaten seasons: North Dakota Agricultural College, 1906–07;

"Gloomy Gil" Dobie

Washington, 1908–16, and Cornell, 1921–23.

Such success never could mellow Gloomy Gil. If someone told him his backs were wonderfully fast, he would shoot back, "That's the trouble—it gets them to the tacklers too soon." After Washington had clobbered California, 72–0, he made his Huskies run a few laps around the field for a workout. And even though he made those Huskies invincible, Gloomy Gil was one of the most unpopular coaches in history. His sour disposition, sharp tongue, and slave-driving tactics earned him few friends —on either side of the line.

Southern football was also coming into its own during the early 1900s. The outstanding schools were Vanderbilt University at Nashville, Tennessee, and Auburn University in Alabama.

Dan McGugin was the Vanderbilt coach. He had been a star guard at Michigan under Hurry Up Yost in 1901 and 1902, and he brought to Vanderbilt Yost's famous formula of "a pass, a punt and a prayer." McGugin's first year was 1904 and the kicking Commodores went undefeated. Southern teams did not score on Vanderbilt until the last game of 1905. Naturally, the Commodores did

not do quite so well against the North, for the East Coast colleges still dominated the football world. But in 1910, Dan McGugin fired his boys up against a fine Yale team with his pre-game speech: "Men, those Yankees out there are the sons of the men who killed your fathers!" Screeching Rebel yells, the Commodores went out to play the favored Bulldogs to a scoreless tie. It was not until some time later that the Vanderbilt men discovered that Dan McGugin's father had been with General Sherman on his march through Georgia.

At Auburn, dandy Mike Donahue, a former Yale quarterback, had taken over a few years after Heisman moved to Georgia Tech. Donahue's 1904 team was undefeated, and from 1913 to 1915 he had a streak of twenty-one wins and two ties. Donahue's teams relied on power plays behind massive lines.

As football passed through these critical and revolutionary years, Harvard emerged as *the* eastern power. The Johnnies, now called the Cantabs, had an undefeated season and were national champions in 1901. They also had little Charley Daly, a 135-pound firebrand of a quarterback. As a freshman Daly once cried out, "Fight fiercely, Harvard!" Although his battle shout has since degen-

Enthusiastic fans at a 1908 Harvard–Yale game.

erated into a joke, Daly's slashing runs and shattering tackles were then no laughing matter.

In 1908 Harvard hired its first professional coach, the tall, handsome and dynamic Percy Duncan Haughton. It was a sad day for Yale when "P.D." took over. He established his position as head man immediately by shouting at his star fullback, who had lounged into practice an hour late: "You, there! Get off the field and don't come back!"

Haughton proceeded to build the first of the "big squad" teams in football history. Where other schools had twenty men on their team, Haughton would have fifty. Before a game he would have three or four teams run through signals, watching with delight the awed reaction of his opponents.

P.D. was a success from the start. In his first season Harvard won nine games and tied another. His method was to split the season into "weeks": Speed Week, Fight Week, Accuracy Week, Hell Week and, then, before the Yale game, Joy Week.

During Joy Week training was relaxed. Haughton made light of Yale's redoubtable Ted Coy. The day before the game, Haughton tied a papier-mâché Yale bulldog to the rear of his car and dragged it through the streets. On game day, the two teams ate together and P.D. made jokes about the opposition, telling his All-America tackle, Hamilton Fish, to make mincemeat of "those blue-bellies over there."

Harvard beat Yale 4–0, and for the first time in years there was a wild celebration in Harvard Yard.

The Yale team, with their superb runner Ted Coy, had their revenge the following year, but thereafter football was Harvard's game. It was especially so in 1912 when a laughing, curly-haired sophomore, Charley Brickley, became eligible to play for the Crimson. Brickley had been practicing drop-kicking almost since the day he was able to lift a football, and he came to Harvard with a great reputation as a schoolboy athlete. Typically, Haughton remained unconvinced, and he poured the pressure on Charley during his first year. But Brickley laughed it off. So did Haughton after Brickley pulled out a near loss to Dartmouth with a third-quarter field goal. Before the Yale–Harvard game of that year, Haughton told Brickley: "There are a hundred footballs out there on the field. I want you to boot every one of them through the goal posts. Use every angle. And don't miss."

Brickley did not miss, and Yale was

Charles Brickley

suffering from a bad case of nerves before the game ever began. With good reason too, because during the game laughing Charley Brickley kicked two field goals and scored a touchdown as the Cantabs downed the Bulldogs, 20–0. Harvard was even more formidable the following year, with the immortal Eddie Mahan at fullback in perhaps the greatest of all Crimson backfields. And what Charley Brickley did to Yale that year remains as one of the outstanding individual feats in football. Four times, from the 35-, 32-, 38- and 24-yard lines, Brickley drop-kicked field goals. Then, to show that his toe was versatile as well as educated, he place-kicked one from the 40. Yale went down by the measure of those goals, 15–5.

It was not until the middle of the 1915 season that Harvard, with a string of 33 victorious games, was to taste defeat. The Johnnies lost to Cornell by 10–0. Even so, Haughton and the Crimson were able to pin a 41–0 shellacking on Yale to add to the 36–0 humiliation of the previous season.

But now the Army's West Point team, coached by Harvard's Charley Daly, began to make its presence known in the gridiron game. And as the youth of Europe went marching off to World War I, a brand-new football movement was in full swing.

Professional football had been established.

Coach Percy Haughton (right) with one of his biggest stars— Charley Brickley.

They Play for Pay

The State of Pennsylvania is the home of professional football, and none other than the great Pudge Heffelfinger of Yale appears to be the first of the professionals.

According to records in the Professional Football Hall of Fame, Pudge received five hundred dollars to play in an 1892 game between two Pittsburgh athletic clubs. Three other players whom Pudge brought with him from Chicago were paid "twice railroad fare" to play. Pudge, of course, won the game for his team. He smashed into the enemy backfield, knocked the runner loose from the ball, scooped it up and thundered over the goal for the winning touchdown. Pudge was also, to judge from the fees paid to players during the next few decades, a very highly paid performer.

The next professional on record, a broad-shouldered graduate of Princeton named Lawson Fiscus, received only twenty dollars and expenses for each game he played for the Greensburg (Pennsylvania) Athletic Association during the 1894 season. Fiscus was nevertheless a splendid sight to see on the gridiron. Both his huge cavalryman's mustache and his enemy tacklers were flying in the wind as he romped downfield with the ball.

The pay was still lower when the first all-professional game was played. This was at Latrobe, Pennsylvania, in 1895. The Latrobe team, sponsored by the local Y.M.C.A., played neighboring Jeannette. Each player received ten dollars. Latrobe won by a score of 12–0.

Fees were to go slightly higher during the next two decades as pro football spread from the Pennsylvania steel and coal regions into similar industrial belts in New York, Ohio and Rhode Island. Actually, these teams were what we would today call semipro. They were fielded by athletic clubs, and the players were young college graduates or high school stars who had gone into the business world. These men played for the thrill of the sport, though they were always glad to pick up a few extra dollars besides. The "gate" was usually what the team coach or manager could collect by passing the hat.

Funds were often raised by means of raffles or socials. David Berry, manager of the Latrobe team and probably the father of pro football, used to hold a minstrel show at the end of each season. Such star players as "Doggy" Trenchard of Princeton and Walter Okeson, the All-America from Lehigh, provided the singing. Berry once raised seventy dollars for Latrobe by holding a football festival in Doherty's Hall. A "watermelon walk" for the youngsters and the "exquisite melody" of the Latrobe Cornet Band were the features. Berry, incidentally, was a newspaper man, like so many sports promoters then and now. He was also a player and a coach. But he retired from active play after his jaw was broken in practice.

Playing for pay was rough, and rivalries were perhaps even more intense than they are now. In one of the early Greensburg–Jeannette games the great Lawson Fiscus was nearly mobbed by irate Jeannette fans who caught him delivering a jaw-breaking kick at a fallen ball carrier. A full-scale riot erupted during the Greensburg–Latrobe game of 1900. Greensburg's Ike Seneca was running for a touchdown when Albert Kennedy of Latrobe brought him down with a vicious tackle. Seneca jumped up and belted Kennedy in the mouth. Coach Russell Knight of Latrobe rushed onto the field to protest, and one of Seneca's teammates knocked *him* down. It was some time before the police could get the crowd in hand. The Greensburg team refused to travel to Latrobe for the return game in Thanksgiving unless it could bring along its own sheriff and twenty deputies.

The rivalry between Greensburg and Latrobe was probably the fiercest of all the professional rivalries. Latrobe's famous marching band would come into town with the team's partisans vowing to demolish Greensburg itself as well as its team. Behind the band came the ladies, all carrying long silken ribbons in the team's colors and little horns to toot for big gains or scores. One year Latrobe won, but Greensburg refused to hand over the ball—the traditional trophy. Latrobe had to fight to get it. Another year Greensburg attempted to kidap Latrobe's new star, Doggy Trenchard, as he arrived at the railroad station. But the Latrobe boys learned of the plot and got Doggy off the train at an earlier stop, hustling him into a carriage and driving him over the back roads to Latrobe.

Thereafter Doggy, so-named for his shaggy locks, played for Latrobe at seventy-five dollars a game. He was carefully shielded from those Greensburg connivers, who were known to be willing to pay him as much as one hundred dollars a game.

This intercity rivalry kept professional football alive in the days of the horse-and-buggy. Civic pride in the city's team was as steadfast as the collegians' loyalty to their alma mater's eleven. Steel and coal-mining companies also helped pro football along. They often subsidized teams in the belief that a football game on Sunday afternoon might offer just the needed release for steelworkers and miners who knew no other day off. These men liked their recreation to be strenuous. The relation between industry and football is best illustrated by the rivalry between Pittsburgh and Philadelphia.

In 1902 Connie Mack fielded a football team called the Philadelphia Athletics, like its baseball counterpart. One of its achievements was to win the first "night game," a contest against Elmira, New York, which was completed in the glare of impromptu lights erected along the sidelines. Connie's great pitcher, Rube Waddell, played briefly in that game, as well as in other victories which led the Athletics to claim the "national championship."

Pittsburgh disagreed and challenged the Athletics. But when Mack arrived in Pittsburgh he found that his three-thousand-dollar guarantee was not forthcoming. Just as he was shepherding his team home again, one of the disappointed fans stopped him.

"What's the matter?" he asked.

"I haven't got my guarantee," Connie snapped.

"How much is it?"

"Three thousand."

"I'll give you a check," the fan said.

As soon as the thunderstruck Connie Mack had established that the "William Corey" who had signed the check was the president of Carnegie Steel, he let the game go forward. The result was a scoreless tie.

In 1902 the first indoor football game was played in Madison Square Garden. The following year a group of teams that included Franklin, Pennsylvania, Philadelphia, Watertown, New York, and Orange, New Jersey, played there. Franklin easily carried off the victory. In an unsuccessful attempt to give pro football a better image, the promotor, Tom O'Rourke, dressed his officials in long-tailed coats and top hats. One of these, the great Frank Hinkey, was rolled about in Madison Square Garden loam when Franklin deliberately ran a play at him. Hinkey rose from the tackle and gave one of the few chuckles of his career.

Rhode Island's entry into pro football was the Providence Steamrollers, a team that would one day be celebrated for the number of professional wrestlers in its lineup. Out in Ohio the Columbus Panhandles, named for the Panhandle Shops of the Pennsylvania Railroad, were playing with the seven Nessers. Six of them were brothers and the seventh, Fred, was the son of Ted, the oldest brother. Father Nesser was the team trainer and Mother Nesser washed the uniforms. One of the brothers, Al, was to play twenty-five years in pro ball before retiring in 1931.

While playing with the Eli's, the great Frank Hinkey was chosen four times for All-America; later he coached at Yale.

Ohio also gave pro football its most violent feud: between the neighboring cities of Massillon and Canton.

Massillon was first to field a team. Eddie Stewart, a writer for the Massillon *Independent*, had bought a flock of football jerseys placed on sale by a local store. He decided he would like a team to wear them and, because the jerseys were striped, he decided he would call the team the Tigers. Next, Stewart sent a challenge to his friend, Bill Day, an attorney in Canton, eight miles away. Day accepted, and the two men scrambled to sign up players who had not already been snapped up by the Pennsylvania teams.

Day appeared to have guaranteed victory for the Canton Bulldogs when he signed Willie Heston for six hundred dollars. But Heston appeared at the camp fifty pounds overweight, and Mr. Stewart of Massillon turned out to be an extremely wily rival. Inasmuch as the Tigers were to be the home team, they were also obliged to provide the ball. They did—a toylike 10-ounce contraption with which they studiously practiced while the unsuspecting Bulldogs were working out with the regulation 16-ounce ball. When they discovered how they were about to be duped, Canton's Bulldogs raised a fearsome howl. But the contract had said nothing about the *size* of the ball, so Stewart's featherweight football was used.

On Canton's first play, the great Willie Heston clutched the tiny pigskin to his breast and went sweeping around right end. He ran straight for a patch of ice which the tricky Tigers had thoughtfully covered with straw. The moment his cleats struck its surface, Willie's feet flew up and his body went down. The entire Massillon team immediately fell upon him with a blood-curdling shout. Heston was thereupon helped to the bench.

With Heston out, and their own ball in, the Tigers went on to win 14–4.

No more games were played until 1906, but the rivalry between the cities flourished, and the unfortunate practice of betting on the game developed. Blondy Wallace became the coach of the Canton Bulldogs. There were to be two Canton–Massillon games during the 1906 season, and the forward pass was ruled legal. In the first of these contests, a Canton end named Eddie Wood caught the first forward pass ever thrown in a pro game. Canton won by a score of 10–5.

But in the next game, the Bulldogs, heavily favored to win, were upset 12–6. Next day, the Massillon *Independent* accused Blondy Wallace of having bribed one of his own players to throw that game so that he could collect on bets made against his own team. Irate citizens of Canton who had lost bets on their team immediately ran the accused player out of town. Then they went looking for Wallace. But Blondy had retired to a safe distance from which he threatened to sue the *Independent* for libel. He dropped his suit, however, after the newspaper confronted him with proof of his dishonesty.

The scandal wrecked pro football in Canton, and slowed down its development throughout the nation. It would not really flourish again until a decade later, when Jim Thorpe—perhaps the greatest all-around athlete in the history of American sports—began to play for pay.

The Touchdown Chief

Jim Thorpe used to say, "I'm an American Airedale." That was because of his mixed ancestry: five-eighths Sac and Fox Indian, one-quarter Irish and one-eighth French.

Jim was born on a ranch in Oklahoma and grew up on an Indian reservation. When he was approximately twelve years old, he was sent to Haskell Institute in Kansas for advanced schooling, but he ran away. In 1904, at the age of fifteen, he enrolled at Carlisle Institute, the government trade school for Indians.

Jim was barely five feet tall and weighed only about 115 pounds when he arrived at the Pennsylvania school as an apprentice tailor. But he was growing. The following year he played guard on the tailors' shop team. Three years later he was over six feet tall and weighed close to 190 pounds. And that was the year—1907—that Pop Warner came back to Carlisle.

Glenn Scobey Warner had coached the Carlisle Indians from 1899 to 1903, between coaching stints at Cornell University, his alma mater. (It was at Cornell that younger law students tagged their twenty-five-year-old associate with the nickname "Pop.") He had also coached at Georgia. This powerfully built man with the shaggy head and craggy face was to be outranked only by Alonzo Stagg as a football innovator. Pop Warner was the inventor of the "double wing" formation and a pioneer in the use of the "single wing" or box. He was forever thinking up new plays and devising new systems. Before he died in 1954, at the age of eighty-three, a poll conducted by the Associated Press rated him as the top coach of all time.

But it is for his colorful Carlisle Indians—players such as Pete Hauser, Frank Mt. Pleasant, Ike Seneca, Sweetcorn, Little Old Man and, above all, Jim Thorpe—that Pop Warner is most remembered. When he first came to the Indian school, Warner did not make a good impression. He used rough language, and the proud Indians quit the team in large numbers rather than take abuse from a white man. Thereupon Pop softened his manner and let his Indians mete out their own discipline by spanking each other after misplays.

The Indians grew to love Pop Warner. He made them victorious, and satisfied their deep desire to beat the white men. Pop also appealed to their fondness for trick plays when he introduced Heisman's hidden-ball play into the East. In a game against Harvard in 1903, the Indians gathered around the ball while Mt. Pleasant slipped it under the back of Johnson's jersey. They then scattered at high speed. The puzzled Harvard Cantabs tackled almost everyone but Johnson, who was the least suspected because he was moving the slowest. He trotted over the goal and fell down, and the ball burst with a bang nearly as loud as the protesting howls of the Harvards. But the score was allowed.

Wily Pop Warner also invented the "deadman" play. A runner, after being

Glenn Scobey Warner

knocked down, remained on his back with the ball in his hands, as if he had been hurt. His teammates would go up to him. The moment the captain asked, "Are you all right, Bill?" the player popped the ball up to him and the Indians took off. With such stratagems and a wide-open style of play, Pop's war-whooping Carlisle Indians soon became one of the most popular teams in the East.

Sometimes they were almost too colorful. Only Pop Warner could handle such wild spirits as Sweetcorn, who shot up a railroad station because he had been left behind on a football trip; or Redwater, who had to be sat on during a train trip because he wanted to jump off "just for kicks." Pop Warner knew how to treat the great Jim Thorpe, too.

Thorpe was inclined to be lazy. If he felt like playing, he was a tiger; if not, he loafed. Pop Warner was at him constantly, trying to goad him into doing his very best.

In a rugged game against Penn in 1907, Thorpe first demonstrated what he was capable of doing. Jim was sitting on the bench, watching the Quakers batter the top Carlisle halfback, Albert Payne. When Payne was finally carried off the field on a stretcher, Warner barked:

"Thorpe! Go in for Payne."

Big Jim ran in. On the first play, he got tangled up with his blockers and suffered a loss. On the next, Jim let the blockers go their own way—while he went his. Sixty-five yards later he was over the goal for a touchdown. The next time he carried the ball he raced 85 yards for a score. Pop Warner was goggle-eyed. Here was a mere newcomer to the sport making monkeys of all those highly trained athletes from Penn. Of course Thorpe was playing purely by instinct. But his instinct was flawless.

Big Jim Thorpe was that football rarity—"a natural." He could do everything as though he had been born to do it. Eighty yards was a common distance for him to punt, and if that big bulky ball happened to be a brand-new one, he could boot it a hundred. When it came to passing, he was among the first to take full advantage of the newfangled play which had been legalized only a year before. And as a runner he was perhaps the greatest, capable of blasting right over enemy tacklers or of faking them out of their shoes. Fully uniformed, he could sprint the length of the field in ten seconds.

42

The versatile Jim Thorpe,
an all-time great.

Thorpe was just as good at tackling as he was at blocking. In fact, he had his own special kind of tackle. He would rarely use his arms and hands, preferring to hurl his iron body crosswise at the runner, whiplashing him to the ground. He blocked that way, too, and rival players frequently complained that Jim was wearing shoulder guards made of steel.

It was this peerless, if untested, player whose debut left Penn crushed, 26–6, while the bearish Pop Warner practically danced with delight. The following spring Jim Thorpe showed his versatility as an athlete. Already a champion boxer, wrestler, swimmer, and a first-rate rifleman, Jim branched out into track. He won the high jump at the Penn Relays.

Eventually he competed in practically every field event. Frequently Pop Warner would show up at a rival school with nobody but big Jim. He would calmly assure Carlisle's astonished rivals that the big Indian was, in fact, the whole team.

In the season of 1908, Walter Camp named Thorpe to his third team All-America. That was quite an honor for little Carlisle. During the next two years, however, the gridiron wizard did not play. He was playing professional baseball for what he called "eating money." Jim had been born poor, and there seemed nothing wrong to him in taking money for playing a sport he loved.

In 1911 he returned to Carlisle. Although he hadn't touched a football for two years, he was better than ever. He was also bigger. That season he became the scourge of the gridiron. It was he, and he alone, who stood between Percy

Haughton's mighty Harvard machine and its second straight national title.

At the outset Harvard quickly drove to a touchdown. The game looked like another routine victory for the Crimson. Then Jim Thorpe got busy. In rapid succession, he drop-kicked field goals from the 22-, the 15- and the 34-yard lines. Upstart Carlisle suddenly led, 9–6! Infuriated, Harvard rolled relentlessly to another score. They then added a field goal. The Crimson was leading 15–9, and it appeared as though the victory was safe.

Undaunted, Jim Thorpe growled to his wearied teammates, "Give me the ball!" Nine times in a row they fed the pigskin to their raging star. Thorpe tore the Harvard line to shreds. The Cantabs *knew* that Thorpe was the man to stop, but they could not do it. On his ninth carry, Big Jim thundered over the goal for the tying score. After that, he drop-

"The scourge of the gridiron" in motion.

kicked a 50-yard field goal. Jim Thorpe and little Carlisle had won an 18–15 upset victory over "invincible" Harvard. The 1911 national title went to Princeton.

The following spring Jim Thorpe was back at track again, training hard for the 1912 Olympics. They were held in Stockholm and it was there that Jim scored perhaps his greatest triumph. He won *both* the decathlon and pentathlon. When he received his awards from King Gustav of Sweden, the monarch said:

"You, sir, are the greatest athlete in the world."

No American football coach whose team played Carlisle during the 1912 season would have doubted the king's word. With all defenses stacked to stop him, Jim Thorpe was unstoppable. He scored no less than 25 touchdowns, totaling, with his kicking, 198 points. His numerous touchdown passes were not, of course, included in that total.

Then came the Army game. The Cadets were as strong as usual. A fine young back named Ike Eisenhower wasn't even able to make the first string. Nevertheless, Carlisle won, 27–6, and the New York *Times* account of the game said that the score failed to show how completely the Indians had prevailed.

"Standing out resplendent in a galaxy of Indian stars," said the newspaper, "was Jim Thorpe, recently crowned the athletic marvel of the age . . . at times the game itself was almost forgotten while the spectators gazed on Thorpe, the individual, to wonder at his prowess. . . . He simply ran wild, while the Cadets tried in vain to stop his progress. It was like trying to clutch a shadow."

In the final game of the 1912 season, played against a strong Brown eleven, Thorpe simply wrecked the Bruins. He got off three long touchdown runs in a 32–0 rout, and it appeared that he had ended his career in an unrivaled blaze of glory.

But then came reports that he had "played for pay" in a Southern baseball league. His amateur status was questioned. Jim quickly admitted that he had made "eating money." A sanctimonious sports world was shocked. The Amateur Athletic Union made Big Jim give back all his Olympic medals. All the men who came in second to him at Stockholm were ruled winners in their events. Jim was declared a professional. It did not matter that the athletes of some of the other nations were openly subsidized. Nor did anyone point out that college ballplayers from all over the country, particularly the Ivy League schools, were regularly playing on summer "semi-pro" teams or hotel baseball "nines" and earned far more money than was paid to Jim.

He was stripped of all his records, and his trophies were sent back to the International Olympic Committee. But no official action could remove one fact from the history of sport: Big Jim Thorpe of America took on all comers from every corner of the world in that year of 1912 and he beat them all.

He turned from football to professional baseball, playing for a time with the New York Giants. But he could not hit a curve. So he returned to his first love: football. In 1915 he revived the fortunes of the Canton Bulldogs and of professional football itself. In the next few years, other former famous collegiate stars were to meet him in the pro teams' extension of the football wars.

It's a Pass!

Although the forward pass became legal in 1906, it was not immediately put into use. Most coaches were suspicious of it. They thought it was too risky. The ball could too easily be lost by interception. Moreover, in those days, a pass became a free ball if it was touched but not caught. And the passer had to run at least five yards back of center before he could throw the ball, thus giving the defense time to guard against him. The "blimp" of a ball then in use was also difficult to throw. Most players curled it against their forearm and hurled it, much like a cricket player delivers a ball. As a result, the ball went high in the air. The receiver had to wait for it, and he needed interference around him to prevent interception.

So the football teams continued to rely on line plunges and power plays. When evenly matched elevens met on the football field the game would often settle down into a kicking duel with both teams playing for the break that would give them the single, winning score.

But there was one exception.

Out of little-known St. Louis University, as early as 1906, a far-sighted coach named Eddie Cochems was experimenting with the forward pass. In the summer of that year he took his team to Lake Beulah, Wisconsin, for the sole purpose of developing the pass. Cochems studied the ball. He could see that it had been designed to fit the instep of the shoe for kicking and the armpit for carrying. There seemed no part of the ball that would allow a purchase for throwing. Then Cochems noticed the seven lacings. Here was just the place!

Cochems told his players—particularly his best back, six-foot-four Brad Robinson— to put their fingers between the two lacings nearest the end of the ball. Its diameter was shortest there. Then he told them to try throwing the ball on its long axis. He recommended that they try throwing it overhand, with a twist of the wrist, much as a catcher pegs a baseball down to second base. They did. With cries of delight they saw the ball going farther and farther downfield. Then, to their astonishment, Brad Robinson threw a spiral. The ball had a beautiful, neatly spinning motion—and it went to its mark as unerringly as a bullet. Robinson came running to Cochems.

"Coach," he burst out in excitement, "I can throw the dang thing forty yards!"

Soon Coach Cochems had developed the first passing combination in history —Brad Robinson to Jack Schneider. In early September, 1906, they teamed up for the first of their "legal" forward passes against Carroll College of Waukesha, Wisconsin. Thereafter the pass was the most powerful weapon in the St. Louis arsenal and Cochems' team went on to win every game, rolling up 402 points and yielding only 11. Moreover, they even stunned Iowa, 39–0, with their newfangled style of throwing the ball. In a game against Kansas on November 3, Robinson let fly a pass to Schneider

46

that carried no less than 48 yards from the line of scrimmage! Even today that would be quite a throw. From 1906 through 1908, Cochems' passing teams gave St. Louis University its finest football seasons.

But Missouri was far away from the East Coast, which was still the headquarters of American football. Many years would go by before the suspect pass became popular. The progressive Pop Warner was quick to realize its potential. But he used it only as a threat to make his double-wing running game function more smoothly. In Jim Thorpe's last game against Army, however, the big Indian had completed six straight passes, the last for a touchdown.

Although the Eastern teams generally scorned the pass, Alonzo Stagg did not look down on it. As early as 1906 his Chicago teams had pass plays in their repertoire. They had no passer, however, who could compare with the giant Robinson of St. Louis.

The University of Illinois was also pass-conscious at an early date. Their football team was throwing the ball on October 11, 1911, the day it met Milliken College. The Marquis of Queensbury was in the stands and this distinguished international sportsman, a descendant of the man who invented the rules of boxing, has left an entertaining account of how the American sport impressed him.

It was my first American football match, and I had been eagerly looking forward for weeks to see one. Unfortunately, from the start it was apparent that Illinois had it all their own way and could play as a cat does with a mouse, but I saw enough of American football to make me an enthusiast and I quite love the game. I had heard it so strongly criticized as a dangerous game that I was agreeably surprised. I think it has many points which Rugby lacks, and a fine freedom is given to the game by the forward pass, which I look upon cursorily as the most brilliant feature of the game. It gives rise to sharp, quick falls when running at the fastest pace. But then, what matter? Every fine sport has its dangers; has not polo, fox hunting, steeplechasing enough dangers that will keep out the timid?

In 1913 an unheralded Notre Dame team came sweeping out of the Midwest to swamp mighty Army, 35–13. The stunning upset did more to make coaches pass-conscious than any other game in history. The New York *Times* reported:

The Westerners flashed the most sensational football that has been seen in the East this year, baffling the Cadets with a style of open play and a perfectly developed forward pass, which carried the victors down the field 30 yards at a clip. The Eastern gridiron has not seen such a master of the forward pass as [Gus] Dorais, the Notre Dame quarterback. A frail youth of 145 pounds, as agile as a cat and as restless as a jumping-jack, Dorais shot forward passes with accuracy into the outstretched arms of his ends, Captain Knute Rockne and Fred Gushurst, as they stood poised for the ball, often as far as 35 yards away.

No other football game in history, with the exception of the first meeting between Rutgers and Princeton 44 years earlier, is as famous as this great game. None was more revolutionary. And yet, out of this game rose many misconceptions which should be corrected.

For one thing, it is believed that the Irish upset of powerful Army lifted them from "obscurity" into the national prominence which they have retained ever since. But the fact is that Notre Dame was among the pioneers of Midwestern football and had succeeded in defeating mighty Michigan, 11 to 3, in 1909. Red Miller, one of the great Irish stars of all time and the first of the famous Millers of Notre Dame, ran wild in that game. In 1902 and 1903 Notre Dame had another smashing fullback in Lou Salmon.

What actually happened at West Point on that momentous day in 1913 was that the proud East had been shocked into acknowledging that college teams from other sections of the country could play football pretty well, too.

The second big misconception is that the forward pass had been a neglected weapon until the legendary passing combination of Dorais-to-Rockne. Other teams, however, had used it before. In fact, Jesse Harper, the Notre Dame coach, had used it himself at Wabash. And just before he came to Notre Dame in 1913, the rules changes of 1912 had stricken the last of the chains from the forward pass. Thus, the time was ripe.

Finally, Harper's team of 1913 was already a fine one. Joe Pliska was a splendid halfback and Ray Eichenlaub was a ferocious bull of a fullback. Few passers have surpassed the skills of wiry little Gus Dorais; and Rockne, of course, was among the cleverest of ends. So Harper had Dorais and Rockne spend the summer of 1913 perfecting their passing game at the Lake Erie beach

resort of Cedar Point. Harper wanted "Rock" to learn how to catch the ball with his hands and on the run, rather than at a halt and against his chest. Rockne himself has described that momentous summer, which was to make both his name and that of Notre Dame famous in the annals of football.

Perfection of the forward pass came to us only through daily, tedious practice. I'd run along the beach, Dorais would throw from all angles. People who didn't know we were two college seniors making painstaking preparations for our final football season probably thought that we were crazy.

But it was Notre Dame's opponents who went crazy that fall. Dorais-to-Rockne was an unstoppable combination. "It was like shooting fish in a barrel," Dorais said in later years. Rockne had worked out a good many patterns that receivers still use nowadays. Although he was very fast, he did not rely on his speed. He cut and dodged, trying to work himself free of the defender before turning it on. Once he fell down as he went out for a pass. Dorais threw short and Rock scrambled to his feet to run back and catch it. "Let's make a play out of that," Rock said, and it was thus that football's greatest opportunist invented the "buttonhook."

In the first three games before the Army contest, pass-happy Notre Dame defeated three opponents by a combined total of 169 points to 7. Notre Dame's entire student body saw the team off as it left South Bend, Indiana, by day coach. "We went out to play the Army like Crusaders," Rockne wrote, "believing that we represented not only our own school but the whole aspiring Middle West."

The East, however, still thought so little of the Midwest that a New York newspaper could report the arrival of the fired-up team from Indiana with the sentence: "Notre Dame College of South Bend, *Illinois,* will play the Army in football today at West Point." According to Rockne, the Army itself felt that way.

The Cadet body and most of the other spectators seemed to regard the engagement as a quiet, friendly workout for the Army. For the first part of the first quarter it looked that way. An Army line, outweighing ours about 15 pounds to the man, pushed us all over the place . . .

The Cadets hit the Irish so hard that they fumbled the first time they got the ball. But then Notre Dame's line held and Army was forced to kick. Dorais' first few passes were fiascos. Army was hurt more by the slashes of Pliska and the battering rushes of Eichenlaub. Then Dorais said, "Let's open up."

His first successful pass, a quick 11-yarder, so surprised Army that the Cadets huddled to discuss it. The Army forwards began charging Dorais. But the agile little Notre Damer was unruffled. He stood far back, calmly shooting his passes to Pliska and Rockne. Then, after a fierce pile-up on a running play, Rockne emerged limping. He limped on the next three plays while Notre Dame moved remorselessly down to the Army 25. The stands were silent, intent upon the Westerners' precise and rapid style of play. Army's coach, Charley Daly, prowled the sidelines like a caged tiger. That was when Dorais called Rockne's number. The wily Rock went limping downfield. The moment he saw that the Army safety was ignoring him, he turned on the speed.

Going over the goal he turned to take the long forward pass that was to change the game of football.

Army coach Charles Daly

Football Coast to Coast

One year after the Irish and the Cadets clashed on the Plains of West Point, Army came roaring back to take the national championship. In doing so, the Cadets broke the stranglehold which the Big Three—Harvard, Princeton and Yale—along with Pennsylvania had held on football in general and the East in particular.

During that 1914 season, the Army team beat every opponent but Springfield by two touchdowns or better, and they avenged themselves on Notre Dame by a score of 20–7. (It was the only game that the Irish lost that year.) Superbly conditioned, Charley Daly's Cadets sometimes just ran their enemies into the ground.

Army unveiled a balanced attack, going from air to ground, from ground to air with devastating effect. One of the ends, Lou Merillat, and quarterback Vernon Prichard were veterans from the previous season. Bob Neyland was at the other end. But the most outstanding players of all were big Jack McEwan at center and—in 1916—Elmer "Ollie" Oliphant at fullback.

With speed to equal his size, McEwan was a roving tornado at center. And Oliphant? Well, at West Point thick-set Ollie is still known as "the Army mule." Though he was only 5 feet 7 inches tall, he weighed 174 pounds, and he hit with such crushing impact that his own linemen were eager to block for him if only to get out of his way. Oliphant's record as an athlete at West Point has never

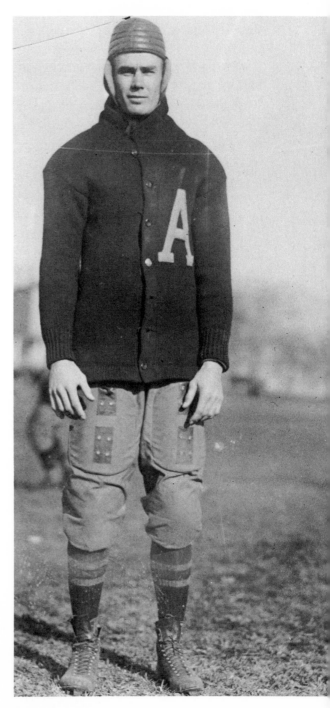

Bob Neyland, Army end.

50

been equaled. He won letters in seven sports: football, basketball, baseball, track, hockey, swimming and boxing. In boxing he was West Point's heavyweight champion. As a football player he was not only a fine ball carrier but he could also punt and drop-kick with the best of them. In addition, he was without a peer as a blocker.

That was the Army mule, a man who played for four years without ever being hurt!

The next new football power to flash across the national scene was another Eastern newcomer: Cornell. The team from "far above Cayuga's waters" had its first all-winning season in 1915 and took the national title. This was the eleven coached by Dr. Albert Sharpe, another former Yale star. The Cornell team was inspired by the fiery playing and leadership of a 165-pound center named William Cameron Cool. Murray

Shelton at end and Charley Barrett at halfback were the team's top stars, and both made All-America. Fritz Shiverick, another back, was an excellent drop-kicker. The Cornell team was depending heavily on him when it met Percy Haughton's "invincibles" from Harvard in the middle of the 1915 season.

Harvard had won thirty-three straight games before the contest with Cornell. And among her players was the peerless Eddie Mahan, one of the main reasons for the Crimson's winning streak. Many sports writers predicted that the game would be a personal duel between Mahan and Charley Barrett of Cornell. In the first quarter, Barrett appeared to have the upper hand. His long punt put Harvard back on its own 20-yard line, after which Mahan fumbled and Shelton recovered for Cornell on the Crimson 25. Then Barrett tore the Harvard line to shreds and scored the game's first touchdown. But after that, he and

Cornell's Charley Barrett gets ready to kick.

Fritz Shiverick,
the Big Red's star drop-kicker.

Captain Eddie Mahan of Harvard.

Mahan collided head-on and Barrett sank to the ground unconscious. He was unable to continue.

Cornell's hopes now rode with scrappy Gib Cool and drop-kicking ace Shiverick. Cool's inspired teammates on the line managed to halt Mahan, while Shiverick kicked a 38-yard field goal to give the Big Red a 10–0 victory. Harvard's long reign over American football had come to an end.

Elated, the Cornellians were very nearly deflated by their rival of rivals, Pennsylvania. A team led by Bert Bell, Lud Wray and Heinie Miller rolled to a 9–0 lead. But Cornell's Charley Barrett scored a touchdown to cut the lead to 9–7, and then in the last quarter broke the game wide open. After sweeping around end to race 40 yards for a second touchdown, he next sprinted 25 yards for a third. Then he kicked a field goal, thereby scoring all of Cornell's points in a 24–9 triumph.

In that same year, 1915, Nebraska went undefeated. The unheralded Cornhuskers upended Notre Dame, 21–19, and established themselves as a national power. For years thereafter, Nebraska would hold a kind of jinx over the Fighting Irish.

The University of Oklahoma was also all-victorious in 1915, mainly because of a fancy passing attack that might fairly be called the Southwest's first aerial circus. The Oklahoma team had taken to the air the previous year when Texas Christian unveiled its first passing combination—Clyde Littlefield to Pete Edmonds. Oklahoma had deliberately adopted this wide-open, reckless playing style in order to offset what looked like an inexperienced squad. And they won

nine games while losing only one and tying one. Frequently they threw as many as thirty or thirty-five passes in a game while ripping through their opponents. The Oklahoma eleven scored more points than any other team in the nation.

In 1915 Pop Warner took over as coach of the University of Pittsburgh eleven. And for three straight years the powerful Panthers never lost a game. They won all eight games in 1915 and again in 1916. The Panthers of 1916 were not only national champions, but one of the greatest elevens of all time. In 1917 they played and won nine games, and in 1918—the year when most colleges had curtailed their football activities in deference to America's entry into World War I—they lost only one game.

Even then, Pitt was noted for its big, rugged line and bone-crushing style of play. With the creative Pope Warner to make up plays and guide them, the Panthers were unbeatable. The backfield included George McLaren, often rated the best Pitt fullback of all time, and the fleet halfback, Jimmy deHart. Up front ranged a line of future coaches. Among them were Red Carlsen, for thirty years Pitt's basketball coach; Tiny Thornhill, who was one day to be Pop Warner's famous successor at Stanford; and a close-mouthed tiger of a man from the Scottish heather—John Bain Sutherland. The grim and relentless "Doctor Jock" would carry on at Pitt where Warner left off.

Elsewhere in the East, Colgate also emerged as a power, and so did Brown University, mainly because of the running and passing of its great Negro All-American, Fritz Pollard. Pollard and the

Brown eleven even beat Yale. Since Yale had been the only team to defeat Colgate during the 1916 season, all the predictions were that the Brown eleven would be the easy victors in their contest with Colgate. But it turned out to be the Colgate Red Raiders who galloped off with a 28–0 victory, proving that football can be a game of astonishing upsets.

In 1916 the Buckeyes of Ohio State for the first time won every regular-season game they played. And Dr. Harry Williams at Minnesota fashioned another powerhouse. The Minnesota Gophers massacred their first four opponents 236 to 14. They later walloped Wisconsin, 54–0, and Chicago, 49–0. The only team between them and a possible challenge to Pitt as national champion was a weak Illinois eleven coached by a "young upstart" from Oak Park High, Bob Zuppke.

Robert Carl Zuppke was to be one of the fabled men of football. Born in Berlin in 1879, he was only two when his family moved to Milwaukee. He worked his way through the University of Wisconsin and played football as a pint-sized substitute quarterback. This little man of the alternating smile and scowl would come to be known by such colorful nicknames as the Wily Dutchman, the Little Napoleon, the Dutch Master and the Old Philosopher. He was probably the game's most quoted philosopher. Among his famous remarks were:

"Some backs run very fast on one spot."

"The movie star may be God's gift to women, but the second guess is God's gift to football fans."

"All quitters are good losers."

"On the first two downs, play for a touchdown. On the third down, play for a first down."

"The tough mug may have a trembling knee."

"A back should keep his feet as long as he can, and his head always."

Zuppke's wit was famous. One of his players once made an unusually hard tackle and blurted out proudly, "Did you see *that* one, Zup?"

The coach dryly replied, "Son, I don't *look* for tackles—I *listen* for them."

The same player kept pestering Zuppke to put him into a game, and Zup always answered: "I'm saving you, son." At last the anguished player burst out, "Saving me for what?"

"The junior prom!" Zup shot back.

When Dr. Williams and his "perfect" 1916 Minnesota team came to Illinois, Zuppke had a ready reply to Williams' question of what the Illinois coach might have up his sleeve.

"Just the hair on my forearm, Doc," Zuppke answered.

In truth, he had a little something else. All week long he had been driving his men. He scrimmaged them *every day* of the week, an unheard-of coaching procedure. "We're all supposed to be killed Saturday," he explained genially, "so we might as well have the satisfaction of killing ourselves instead of letting those Minnesota fellows do it."

On Friday night, the famous sports writer Ring Lardner predicted in the Chicago *Tribune* that Illinois would be defeated by at least 49–0. His reasoning was simply that "the Immortals," as this 1916 Minnesota team was being called, had never been held to fewer than 49 points. They had walloped Iowa 67–0, and rolled up a score of 81–0 against

South Dakota, a team that Notre Dame had barely beaten, 6–0.

Walter Camp was in the stands on Saturday to watch the Illinois team go down in the predicted glorious defeat. Minnesota had built him a little grandstand of his own, close to the field, so that he might watch the Immortals in regal solitude.

Inside the Illinois dressing room, Zuppke told his men: "This Minnesota outfit is superstitious. They never vary on the first three plays. Sparfka, Wyman and Long take the ball in that order. Tackle them in that order."

They did, and stunned the Gophers on their five-yard line. Then the Illinois eleven got the ball and sprang Zuppke's crazy offense. They lined up with huge gaps in their line and the backs in a perfect box. The moment the players were set, the center snapped the ball. Using some of the trick plays which Zuppke had invented—the Corkscrew, the Sidewinder, the Flying Trapeze, the Whoa Back or the Flea Flicker—the

Illinois coach, Robert Zuppke (left), talks to one of his 1929 stars, Russell Crane.

Illinois won the "impossible" victory by a score of 14–9.

In the following year, 1917, a new section of the country claimed the national title. Georgia Tech and John Heisman were considered even better than unbeaten Pitt and Pop Warner. That was the year the Georgia Yellow Jackets also earned the nickname of the Golden Tornado. They rolled up astronomical scores. In three seasons—1915–1916–1917—they scored 1,145 points against their opponents' total of 61. They also set the record for a single game, crushing helpless Cumberland, 222–0.

Sports pages everywhere carried photographs of John Heisman in his turtle-neck sweater and baseball cap, with a little megaphone at his lips. "Hop, lads," he would call through the megaphone, putting his players through his famous shift. "You must learn to hop like a chickadee."

Pop Warner detested shifts. He called them a "fancy movement such as is necessary for the success of a Russian toe dancer." Although Heisman and Warner were unable to get their teams together in the post-season game that football fans were clamoring for, they did schedule a contest for 1918.

It proved to be the game of the year: Heisman's high-flying Yellow Jackets led by such stars as Indian Joe Guyon, a transfer from Carlisle, were pitted against Warner's powerful Panthers. They played at Forbes Field in Pittsburgh. The dressing rooms of the two teams adjoined. Pitt's was silent, while in Tech's John Heisman was delivering an impassioned speech. Pop Warner

Coach Heisman with his traditional cap and megaphone.

motioned his silent players to the wall. They crouched, listening to Heisman haranguing his Yellow Jackets to leave them for dead.

"Okay, boys, you heard that," Warner snapped. "Go out and tear 'em up."

They did, 32–0. That year Pitt was again on top.

The following year, 1919, was the one in which the veterans began returning from World War I. It was also the year in which two teams of war veterans, representing Colgate and Dartmouth, waged a titanic battle on a quagmire of a field soaked by three days of rain. Colgate scored first. With two minutes to go, the Red Raiders had the ball on their own 20. They went into punt formation. Mighty Swede Youngstrom of Dartmouth tore through to block the kick. Then, still on his feet, he scooped up the ball on the five-yard line to dive into the end-zone mud for a touchdown. Dartmouth's fans went wild. Silence fell as Jim Robertson went back for the place kick. Jack Cannell was holding. The soggy ball came back, as heavy as a melon. Cannell plunked it into the mud. Robertson swung his leg. The ball rose slowly and struck the right upright. It fell on the crossbar. It teetered there for a moment, and then dropped over the back side for the point! The epic battle of the veterans had ended in a 7–7 tie.

The Harvard and Notre Dame elevens were also filled with returning war veterans in 1919, and both teams tore through all opponents. But because Harvard's schedule was more rigorous, the Helms Foundation, which has made a careful study of national championship claims, has since awarded the title to the Harvard Crimson. Bob Fisher was the Harvard coach that year, and fleet-footed Eddie Casey was its star.

The 1919 season also saw a "Cinderella team" come out of the South to capture the imagination of the football world. The "Praying Colonels" of little Centre College in Danville, Kentucky, won all of their nine games. They even ripped through mighty West Virginia, which had scored a 26–0 victory over a fairly good Princeton team. In the game against West Virginia, the Praying Colonels had gotten their nickname. Trailing at the half, 6–0, they had knelt bareheaded in prayer. In the second half they came roaring back to score two touchdowns and win, 14–6.

Alvin "Bo" McMillin, Centre's biggest star, was still playing the following year when mighty Harvard took on the upstarts from this tiny college of just 300 students, and drubbed them, 34–14. And Bo was again at quarterback in 1921 when another fine Harvard team met the Praying Colonels. Neither team scored in the first half. In the beginning of the second, Centre moved to Harvard's 32-yard line. McMillin took the ball and circled right end. He cut to his left, saw an opening and dashed for the left sidelines. Then he turned on the speed. Two Harvard tacklers, intent on heading him off, dived at him. Bo stopped short; the tacklers hurtled through the empty air—and the Centre star swept the remaining distance to the goal line. The final score was 6–0.

It was Harvard's first defeat since losing to Yale in 1916. It was regarded then, and is still regarded, as one of the great football upsets of the century. When the Praying Colonels returned to Danville, they were piled aboard a fire truck and driven along the main street through delirious crowds. The Associated Press reported: "The townspeople and the students went berserk with hilarity. They literally painted the town with huge scrawled whitewash figures, 'C–6, H–0.' . . ." But then, having won new glory for the South, the Praying Colonels were themselves upended in the last game of the season when Texas A. & M. won glory for the Southwest by defeating Centre, 22–14.

Obviously no one section of the country could claim a monopoly on football. East, South, Southwest and Midwest— all the colleges were playing it well. And then from the West Coast came reports of the "Wonder Teams" of the University of California.

Coached by Andy Smith of Pennsylvania, the Wonder Teams never knew defeat. From 1920 through 1924 they won forty-four games and were tied four times. The 1920 team was probably the best, led by quarterback Charley Erb and one of the all-time great All-American ends—Harold "Brick" Muller.

Like Jim Thorpe, Muller was an all-around athlete. Standing six feet two and weighing 215 pounds, he was a high-jumper and a sprinter. Not only could he churn ahead for long gains on end-around plays and race downfield for passes, he could also drop back to take the ball in his big, powerful hands and hurl it farther and faster than any man then living. But because California's eight opponents in 1920 did not include a Midwestern or Eastern victim, the football experts thought that the Golden

Bears had played an inferior schedule. The test came in the Rose Bowl on New Year's Day when the Golden Bears were pitted against the champion Buckeyes of Ohio State. The California eleven, led by Muller, proved that it was indeed a wonder team by winning 28–0 and thereby clinching the national title.

The year before, Ohio State had been propelled into national prominence, mainly because of the brilliant play of its triple-threat star, Chick Harley. Although he weighed only 157 pounds, Harley was to Ohio State what Heston had been to Michigan. His deeds have been best described by another famous Ohioan, James Thurber, writing in a New York newspaper.

[Harley] was the greatest football player we Ohioans have ever seen. If you never saw Harley run with a football we Ohioans could not describe it for you . . . It was a kind of a cross between music and cannon fire, and it brought your heart up under your ears. He could pass and punt and place-kick and block and tackle, but it was his running that got you. Usually in the last few minutes or seconds of a game he would get away like a flame and score the winning touchdown. He won the conference championship . . . he beat Michigan to avenge a quarter-century of defeats. Camp put him on his All-America. Columbus went raving crazy. The only game he lost was his last against Illinois in his senior year. I can see him now, the tears in his eyes and everybody crying, and the team crying and everybody in the stands crying.

Football, even then, was a deeply emotional sport.

California's "Brick" Muller

Jim Thorpe Runs Again

While college football was rocketing into national prominence, professional football had been foundering. Scandals, rowdy spectators and badly disciplined players had given it an unsavory reputation. Jim Thorpe was the man who would rescue pro football—almost single-handedly—and make it a thriving business again.

Tired of baseball barnstorming, dissatisfied with his secondary role on the New York Giants, the big Indian returned to his first love in 1915. He signed to play with the Canton Bulldogs.

Gus Dorais and Knute Rockne, both recently graduated from Notre Dame, had already begun playing part-time for the pros, and they had introduced the forward pass to the professional teams. Jim Thorpe, in turn, taught the Bulldogs to run out of the exciting double-wing offense he had learned from Pop Warner at Carlisle. Other professional teams copied the attack. This, together with the forward pass, made the "paid" games more thrilling than ever and revived professional rivalries. Jim Thorpe became the top star of the pro teams. He drew the crowds, and he knew it, too.

Once, in a game against a pro team led by Knute Rockne, Jim was surprised to find Rockne flattening him on two end runs.

"Rock," Jim cautioned, "these people want to see Big Jim run." But Rockne's third tackle was even more ferocious.

Shaking his head in mock solemnity, Jim went into the backfield again and waited for the ball. "I'm coming over, Rock," he said, and headed straight for the former Notre Damer. Rockne closed for the tackle. There was a shattering sound as they collided; then Jim Thorpe stepped over the Rock's prostrate form to go cantering downfield. Coming back he saw Rockne being helped to his feet.

"That's right, Rock," he said, patting him on the shoulder. "You just let Big Jim run!"

And run he did during those six years when pro football was getting its first legs.

"He had a way of running I never saw before," said Pete Calac, Thorpe's teammate at Carlisle and Canton. "Jim would shift his hip toward the guy about to tackle him, then swing away and then, when the player moved in to hit him, he'd swing his hip back, hard, against the tackler's head and leave him lying there."

Jim also proved himself a demon on defense. The owner of the Canton Bulldogs, Jack Cusack, had had special shoulder pads made for Jim out of shoe leather. "They hit like iron," said George Halas, who played against Thorpe as a pro. "It felt as if he had hit you with a four-by-four. If he hit you from behind, he'd throw that big body across your back and nearly break you in two."

The real professional football activity had moved from Pennsylvania to Ohio, and the Massillon–Canton feud had been revived and grown hotter. One

Jim Thorpe of the Canton Bulldogs
leaps to tackle a ball carrier.

Indian Joe Guyon, Jim Thorpe and Pete Calac,
three Carlisle stars who played for the Canton Bulldogs.

year Massillon hired forty-five football stars for a game against Canton and used only a third of them. The idea had been to keep the players out of Canton's reach. Gradually, though, the game moved even farther west, into Illinois and Indiana. Midwestern stars were heavily in demand. They generally signed to play by the game and would play for the highest bidder. In one season the inexhaustible Knute Rockne played for six different teams on six successive weekends.

Sometimes college stars—many of whom were short of funds—could not resist the temptation to make a few dollars by playing under assumed names. It was not unusual for two college teams to play each other on a Saturday. Then, under different names and representing rival cities, they would frequently play each other all over again on the following Sunday.

This practice made the college authorities angry at the professional teams. Joseph Carr, manager of the Columbus Panhandles, realized that college animosity could kill the pro game. Moreover, pro fans were complaining about the way the teams changed every week. Carr decided that it was important to form a league that would force teams to keep a certain number of players under contract and to honor the contracts of other teams. They must also agree to keep their hands off players still in college.

On the night of September 17, 1920, the pioneers of professional football met at Ralph Hays's automobile agency in Canton. They formed the American Football Association. Jim Thorpe was elected president, and a membership fee of $100 a team was set. There were eleven members: Canton, Cleveland Dayton, Akron and Massillon (all of Ohio); Rochester, New York; Hammond and Muncie, Indiana; and Chicago, along with Rock Island and Decatur, in Illinois. The Decatur team was known as the Staley A. C. Coached, managed and led on the field by George Halas, it would soon be known as the Chicago Bears.

Three teams claimed the championship at the end of the first year. As a result, Massillon gave up the game in disgust, and the league was reorganized. Jim Thorpe, who had only been a figurehead president, was replaced by Joe Carr. In 1921, the first official championship was won by the Chicago Bears. Green Bay, Wisconsin, had a team in the league that season. The Packers came in fourth.

So 1921 marked the beginning of the National Football League, although that name was not adopted until 1922. Pro football was beginning to find its way to real popularity.

The Rock and the Gipper

The decade of the 1920s has been called The Golden Age of American Sport. Baseball had its Babe Ruth and golf its Bobby Jones. There were Big Bill Tilden and Helen Mills in tennis, Man o' War and Earl Sande in horse racing, Jack Dempsey and Gene Tunney in boxing, Johnny Weissmuller and Gertrude Ederle in swimming. And in football there was Knute Kenneth Rockne.

Unlike the other famous athletes of the day, "the Rock's" fame resided more in his astonishing career and personality than in his ability to perform. True, he had caught those immortal passes on the Plains at West Point, and he had also played pro football while doubling as an assistant coach and chemistry instructor at Notre Dame. But it was his life story and his way with people that captivated the American public—even more, perhaps, than the colorful and winning football teams he coached at Notre Dame.

Knute Rockne was the immigrant boy from Norway who had been dismissed from high school because he was always cutting classes to practice football. He had grown up in poverty, only to be cast out early into the school of hard knocks. But he had the good sense to realize that he had made a serious mistake. He proceeded to educate himself while working at one of the most difficult jobs in the Chicago post office. He was the only one willing, or able, to memorize the arrival and departure times of hundreds of trains. After four years of this, he had

accumulated $1,000 in savings. So at the age of twenty-two, equipped with a cheap suitcase, he went down to Notre Dame.

Ten years later he had become an example of the American success story. His teams were playing annually in front of half a million spectators. They were meeting, and generally defeating, the best teams from every section of the land. Rockne himself was one of the most sought-after speakers in America. His fame rivaled that of presidents Harding, Coolidge and Hoover. Newspapers quoted his witticisms almost as often as they quoted comedian Will Rogers. In a sport in which coaches are frequently more important than the players, Knute Rockne was regarded—and is still regarded—as the greatest of them all.

Oddly enough, as the Rock was always the first to admit, he contributed almost nothing new to football. Camp, Stagg, Warner, Heisman and others were the game's great innovators. The "Notre Dame shift," which was to be copied by teams throughout the land, was not Rockne's. He himself once said, "The game which I have taught, with some important changes, was brought to Notre Dame by Jesse Harper, whom I succeeded in 1918. Harper was one of Alonzo Stagg's best quarterbacks at Chicago. Stagg brought his game from Yale. Ergo, just as we all trace back to Adam, so does Notre Dame football go back to Stagg and Yale."

Knute Rockne watches anxiously from the sidelines.

The Rock uses a little psychology on his players.

But the *style* of Irish football was unquestionably both Rock's and Notre Dame's. Again and again the teams from the little Indiana school came from behind to beat bigger and wealthier teams. For Notre Dame was then a "poor boy's school," where almost all of the student body worked to pay their way. With its never-say-die spirit, its dramatic and daring football, its habit of consistently drubbing bigger schools, Notre Dame was naturally a college for the American public to take to its heart.

Bob Zuppke once said, "Football made the nation college-conscious," and there was undoubtedly much truth in the statement. In the same way, Knute Rockne may have done more than anyone else to make the nation football-conscious.

Babe Ruth did not invent the home run, but he made a more spectacular use of it than any other player of his time. Like Ruth, the flat-nosed, bald-headed genius from Norway seized upon football and gave it a color it had never had before.

Rockne did this at the time when big teams and big stadiums and big intersectional rivalries were blossoming all over the country. He "sold" football to America. Harry Mehre, one of his finest players and later a successful coach at Georgia, once explained it this way: "Rock sold football to the man on the trolley, the elevated, the subway . . . the baker, the butcher, the pipe-fitter who never went to college. He made it an American mania. He took it out of the thousand-dollar class and made it a million-dollar business."

Much of Rockne's success stemmed from his insight as a psychologist. Once, between halves in a game with Georgia Tech, Notre Dame's star fullback, Rex Enright, lurched into the dressing room in disgust. He hadn't been able to gain at all.

"Manager!" Rockne cried. "Get some low-cut shoes for Enright. How can you expect a man to run in those high-button clodhoppers he's got on!"

Convinced that his shoes had been the difficulty, Enright ran wild in the second half.

Because of his keen insight into human nature, Rock rarely delivered a halftime speech. Instead, he would light a spark under a slumping team with a single phrase. "Let's go, *girls*," he simpered once to a losing squad. Another time he let the team stew in lonely silence. Just before they were to return to the field, he opened the door, poked his head inside, and lisped: *"Excuse* me! I thought this was the Notre Dame dressing room."

He could also make a quiet appeal to their fondness for him. In 1930 Rockne was stricken with phlebitis. Before the important game with Southern California, he sat in a silent dressing room in full view of his players while the trainer bandaged his puffed and ravaged legs. The Irish went roaring out to route the Trojans, 27–0.

Rockne's hold on his players was complete because he was fond of them as human beings. He was interested in their families, the careers they planned for themselves, their problems in class or in their relations with other students. For many years the Rock was not only the coach but team trainer as well. He had a wide knowledge of anatomy, fortified by an unusual aptitude for chemis-

In 1930 Notre Dame routed the University of Southern California, 27–0.

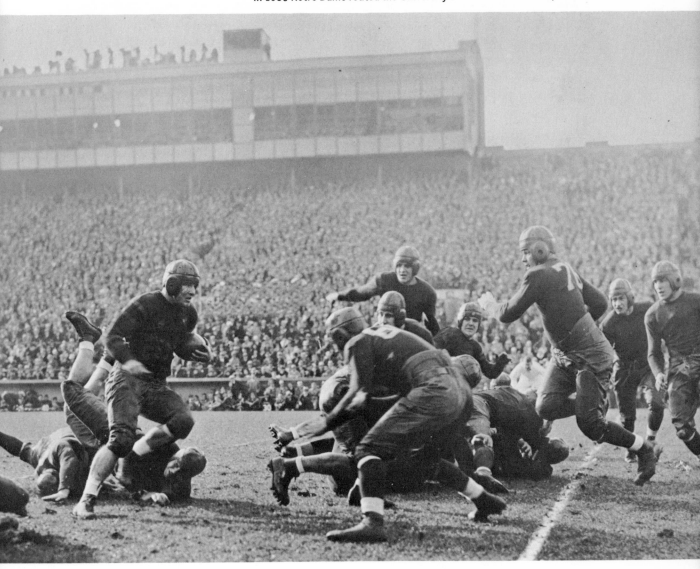

try which made him instrumental in a Notre Dame priest's invention of synthetic rubber.

Rockne would swab his players down with oil of wintergreen and daub them with iodine. "Get nine hours' sleep," he would say. "Don't worry if the pain keeps up tonight. Just try again tomorrow night. If you can't sleep then, there's still no need to worry. Because you'll certainly sleep the third night."

There was, of course, a bit of a sly dig in those words of advice, for Rockne could be cuttingly sarcastic. During his years of success—he had five unbeaten and untied teams and three national champions during twelve years at Notre Dame—his biggest fear was overconfidence.

"Show them your scrapbooks," he said to a team that was on the verge of defeat. "They don't know how good you are."

Sluggish players would be stung by such remarks as, "There are some dumb people and some dumber people. You come next." And he would tell linemen: "The only qualifications for a lineman are to be big and dumb." But then, wheeling on the snickering stars, the backs, he would snap: "But to be a back, you only have to be dumb."

Some players resented such needling. One quit in a rage, shouting: "I'll never play for you again!"

Rockne snapped back with a crushing retort: "You never have!"

His sharp tongue could also be turned against himself. One year, with a fine team, he decided to scout mighty Army in its game against Navy. To do this he left an assistant to direct the Irish against an ordinary Carnegie Tech team.

Tech toppled the Irish, 19–0. When Rockne heard himself being called a "dumb Swede," he replied: "The only thing dumber than a dumb Swede is a smart Norwegian."

His ability to sting young men in their pride was never so evident as in Rockne's first meeting with George Gipp. On an autumn day in 1917 the Rock was strolling along the Notre Dame campus. He heard somebody kick a ball and looked up to see a 60-yard punt spiraling overhead. Next he saw the punter—George Gipp, a lean, 175-pound six-footer. Gipp was wearing street shoes!

"Why aren't you out for the freshman squad?" Rockne asked.

"Football isn't my game," replied Gipp, who had come to Notre Dame on a baseball and basketball scholarship.

"Afraid?" Rockne taunted.

"Me afraid!" Gipp scoffed.

"Oh, you're tough?"

"As tough as I need to be."

"Think it over." Rockne needled him. "I'll be handing out equipment over at the Field House in an hour or so. I've got just the pair of cleats for you."

"A special pair?" Gipp inquired.

"Yeah. They belonged to Ray Eichenlaub."

"Who was he?"

"A *real* Notre Dame man," Rockne snorted, and walked on.

But he had measured his man correctly. George Gipp was at practice that afternoon, and Jesse Harper and Rockne soon found that they had that rarity—a "natural" athlete—on their squad. Gipp would often loaf during training, but once the whistle blew he was a marvel of balance, speed and grace. And he was also a daredevil.

68

The legendary George Gipp,
who claimed that football wasn't his game.

During his first game as a freshman, the Irish freshman team was tied, 7–7, with Kalamazoo. Late in the fourth quarter Notre Dame was unable to make a first down on its own 38. Gipp went back to punt. The ball was centered, and the Irish ends sprinting downfield heard the thud of a foot meeting the ball. To their astonishment the enemy safetyman suddenly turned around to face his own goal posts. A roar went up from the crowd, and the safety shook his head. "The son of a gun kicked a field goal!" he sputtered.

Not content to settle for a tie, Gipp had drop-kicked the ball 68 yards.

Gipp's first varsity season, 1917, was cut short by a broken leg. And the following year—Rockne's first season as head coach—Gipp dropped out of school. But he was back in 1919 and he proved to be just the man to run and pass from Rockne's split-second "One-two-three, shift!" His speed and elusiveness in a broken field became legendary. He ran his blockers like a general directing troops: *"Take him to the outside. . . . Let this one go. . . . Go after the safety man. . . ."*

Many a time Gipp's quick thinking saved a game. Against Army in 1919 the Irish were trailing 9–0 and knocking on the Cadet goal. Just as the teams were lining up, Gipp saw the referee lifting the horn to his lips to signal the end of the half. "Gimme the ball, quick!" he called. The center snapped it to him, and George drove over the line for a touchdown. From there Notre Dame went on to win, 12–9, giving Rockne an undefeated season in his second year at the helm.

The following year the Rock and the

Gipper were better than ever, going undefeated a second time, even though the national title was awarded to the Wonder Team from California. Gipp's gridiron feats became legendary. Only Jim Thorpe had received equal acclaim. Although most observers thought that Thorpe was the better runner, they rated George the better passer and kicker.

Gipp proved them right when he played against Army. Before the game, he and Red Reeder, of the Cadets, engaged in a field-goal kicking competition. At the 40-yard line, Reeder dropped out. But George nonchalantly carried four balls to midfield. He drop-kicked two of them between one set of goal posts, then turned and did the same with the other pair. The crowd roared its approval. Then, during the game itself, Gipp displayed his passing and running ability. Throwing for two touchdowns, carrying for 124 yards from scrimmage and returning punts for long gains, he rolled for a total of 332 yards in one of the best performances of his career. Notre Dame won, 27–17.

The following week, in a game against Indiana, Gipp suffered a dislocated shoulder and broken collarbone. He was taken out, and his injuries were bandaged. He pleaded to get back into the game, but Rockne refused. The Indiana eleven shot into a 10–0 lead which they held going into the last quarter. Then the Irish caught fire, advancing to the one-foot line. Indiana stiffened, and Rockne finally sent in the Gipper.

On the first play he tore into the end zone for a touchdown, and then he kicked the additional point. Although every move was an agony, he continued to play. Throwing the ball sidearm, Gipp passed and ran the ball down to Indiana's 15-yard line. Then he went back for a drop-kick. The Hoosiers rushed him and he lofted the ball over their heads into the hands of Eddie Anderson on the 1-yard line. The Indiana team now concentrated on Gipp. But while he faked possession of the ball beautifully, Joe Brandy hurtled across the goal with the winning touchdown.

A week later George Gipp had a nasty cough. He was so ill that he could not play against Northwestern. Nevertheless the crowd kept chanting, "We want Gipp! We want Gipp!" Rockne put him in reluctantly and quickly pulled him out after he threw two incomplete passes and was smeared while returning a punt.

George Gipp never played again. He had come down with a bad attack of tonsilitis, which soon developed into pneumonia and a strep throat. There were no wonder drugs available in those days; Gipp was plainly dying. Knute Rockne came to his bedside and watched sorrowfully while life grew fainter and fainter within that splendid frame. Here was a boy of twenty-three with everything to live for. That very day the White Sox had bid for his services on the diamond. Walter Camp had named him All-America fullback. But there was no hope at all. Notre Dame had lost one of her greatest gridiron heroes.

The Invincible Big Red

The East, meanwhile, was producing a succession of outstanding small-college teams.

In 1921 the Leopards of Lafayette had what was probably their best team of all time. Coached by Jock Sutherland, the Lafayette eleven and their exploits projected the dour doctor into national prominence. Sutherland depended on sheer power. No one ever got more out of straight off-tackle smashes and power reverses than he did, and the Leopards of 1921 and 1922 performed brilliantly for him.

Another coach, Earle "Greasy" Neale, at a small Pennsylvania college named Washington and Jefferson, got equally satisfactory results from his team. During his first fling at collegiate football Neale put together an eleven that many experts considered good enough to be rated as national champions. His Presidents, undefeated in 1921, were invited to the Rose Bowl to play California. They held California to a scoreless tie, dominating the play offensively and giving Brick Muller one of his rare bad days.

Russ Stein, captain of the Presidents, was an outstanding tackle on defense and a powerful fullback on offense. But the team's top man was Wilbur "Fats"

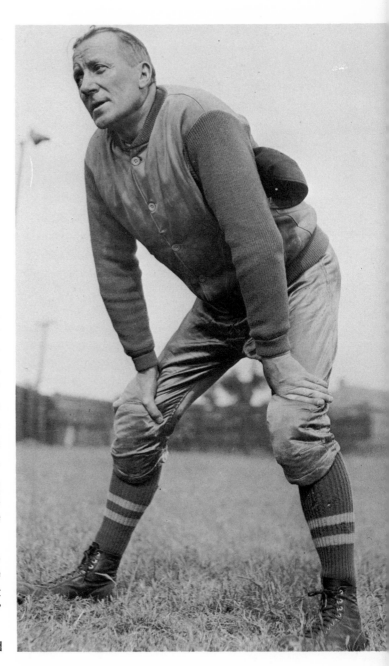

Jock Sutherland

Henry, a giant tackle so fast that he was often called upon to run tackle-around plays.

Fats Henry's habitual smile was a sharp contrast to the legendary pessimism of Cornell's new football coach, "Gloomy" Gil Dobie. Dobie, after nine years of turning out champion teams at the University of Washington, had moved east to coach at the Naval Academy. As might be expected, he had developed fine teams there. For three years he kept Navy close to the top of the Eastern standings. In 1919 the Dobie-coached Middies even upended a strong Army team, 6–0, but after the close of the season Dobie quit the Naval Academy. When asked why, he replied, "I'm just leaving—period." Later he complained that there were "too many admirals trying to run football when they should be at sea."

But the Navy's loss proved to be Cornell's gain. He made The Big Red a national power. As always, he was the complete drillmaster, working tirelessly with his teams, driving them until they could function almost as one man. He taught his ball carriers to hit at the exact moment when their mates were exerting their maximum pressure against the enemy line. "Run for three yards," he would say. "Anything after that is gravy." They followed his instructions, and the gravy turned into touchdowns.

Power and precision, power and precision—those were the qualities that kept the Big Red on top during those three seasons of 1921, 1922, 1923—the first two of which brought national titles. Throughout those years the names of Eddie Kaw and George Pfann were national bywords. Kaw, an All-America halfback for two seasons, was perhaps the cleverest runner in Big Red history. He was not fast. Rather, he twisted his way through a broken field with a peculiar stop-and-go motion that left tacklers clutching handfuls of air. Kaw would elude as many as a half-dozen men on his runs for the end zone. George Pfann, the All-America quarterback, was a power runner. He bowled tacklers over or broke free of their grasp on the sheer strength of his thigh muscles. Pfann was also a first-rate signal caller. He made the Big Red machines function so flawlessly that many fans believed he could have called the plays out loud and the enemy would still have been unable to stop the Cornell eleven.

But even with such backs operating behind a hard-hitting, mountainous line, Gil Dobie still found it difficult to give his players credit. Kaw and Pfann were just good men to him—never great. Gloomy Gil could not use a superlative except to belittle. Someone might be the worst, but never the best. That was probably because his only standard was perfection itself. That was also why his teams kept on winning until he retired in 1938. His lifetime record during 33 years of coaching was 14 unbeaten teams totaling 180 victories, 45 losses and 15 ties.

If anyone should have been gloomy, it was Gilmour Dobie's opponents.

The Gallopin' Ghost

A streak of fire, a breath of flame;
Eluding all who reach and clutch;
A gray ghost thrown into the game
That rival hands may rarely touch . . .

Thus wrote Grantland Rice, the dean of American sports writers, in a tribute to Red Grange, the superstar of American football.

Red Grange *was* the greatest. No football player ever captured the imagination of the American public as completely as he did. Modest and unassuming, not particularly powerful, with a height of five feet ten inches and a weight of 170 pounds, he became one of the sports idols of his country. His fame was so great that mothers had only to say, "Red Grange eats spinach" or "Red Grange always obeyed his parents" to get balky children to eat or do something they did not like.

And he flitted through rival elevens like a ghost. He ran like the wind and the mere sight of him tucking the ball into his armpit and starting toward his end could bring mighty throngs to their feet with a single great roar of expectation. He seldom disappointed them. In three years on the Illinois varsity he ran for 31 touchdowns in 20 games and gained 3,637 yards from scrimmage or in running back punts and kickoffs. And this was a record compiled against teams with defenses deliberately stacked to stop Red Grange!

Sometimes rival players who were determined to "get Grange" would delib-

Red Grange, the superstar of American football.

erately slam into him even though he didn't have the ball. They would pile onto him or kick him when he was down. Often Red was a mass of bruises when he finished a game. But he never whimpered, and his teammates respected him. That alone was a great achievement, because it would be hard to blame Red's teammates for being jealous of his unparalleled celebrity. They knew, however, that the redhead actually did shun

73

the limelight—and that he was as game a football player as ever ran onto a field. His coach, Bob Zuppke, never had to drive Red.

In the October, 1936, issue of *Esquire* magazine he later wrote an excellent description of his greatest player.

Grange was a genius of motion. I saw that and made a team-picture with him at the focal point. He ran with no waste motion . . . I once made a trip to the Kaibab Forest on the edge of the north rim of the Grand Canyon and as a deer ran out onto the grass plains, I said: "There goes Red Grange!" The freedom of movement was so similar to Red's.

Red had that indefinable something that the hunted wild animal has—uncanny timing and the big brown eyes of a royal buck. I sketched a team around him like the complementary background of a painting. Those were not great teams that Grange ran for. But they fitted around him, helped to set him off.

Red had come to Illinois from an incredible record as an all-around high school athlete in his native Wheaton. He had planned to concentrate on basketball and track, but he also turned out for football. He quickly dropped off the squad, however, overawed by the sight of so many big, powerful players. But he came back at the insistence of his fraternity brothers.

Then the great "Zup" saw him. During a freshman-varsity game Red caught a punt and whirled through the entire varsity for a touchdown. Zup noted Red's high knee action and his extraordinary pickup. He saw, too, that the talented freshman had one bad

habit: he ran wide, toward the sidelines, instead of cutting back. So Zup told the freshman coach to correct that fault. Red learned to start out easily around his end, cutting back sharply and then reversing his field again farther down the gridiron. His passage downfield described a long figure S. Zup saw him improving and envisioned great things for Red's first varsity year, 1923.

Zuppke's vision didn't fail him. Illinois won the national title and Red Grange became a household word.

"Old 77" exploded on the sports world like a bomb in a game between Illinois and Nebraska. Walter Eckersall was the referee, and he saw the sophomore with the big 77 on his back score 3 touchdowns and gain 208 yards during 39 minutes of play. Red's last touchdown came in the fourth quarter. He caught a Nebraska punt on his own 35-yard line and sped straight down the sidelines with the astonished Eckersall trailing him almost every step of the way. The headlines read: GRANGE SPRINTS TO FAME.

Red also saved the day against Iowa. In the last quarter the Hawkeyes led, 6–3. But Red caught pass after pass from his splendid teammate, Earl Britton, before sprinting around end for the winning score. That year the Fighting Illinois eleven shared the Big Ten conference title with Michigan, which also won all of its games. That year, also, Red Grange was everybody's All-American—everybody's, that is, except for the Michigan student daily, which put him on the *second* team. Michigan paid for that when the two teams met the following year and the Wolverines also paid for their coach's pre-game prediction.

"Old 77" exploded on the sports world like a bomb.

"Mister Grange will be carefully watched," said Hurry Up Yost. "Every time he takes the ball there will be eleven hard, clean Meecheegan tacklers headed for him at the same time. I know he is a great runner. But great runners have the hardest time gaining ground when met by special preparation."

The Wolverines kicked off. Red Grange caught the ball on his five. He sped up the center of the field and cut hard right to avoid one group of "hard, clean Meecheegan tacklers." He slanted hard left to the other sideline to avoid another batch. Then he raced the remaining distance to the goal. The first time he touched the ball he had run 95 yards for a touchdown!

The next time, Red swept around left end. He picked up his blockers, using them as only he knew how. He flashed his change of pace, his unbelievably quick pickup, his flawless leg-cross— and raced 67 yards for a second score.

After an exchange of kicks, Illinois had the ball again. Red swung toward his right end, while an escort of blockers drove the "hard, clean" tacklers to his right. Then he cut inside them and moved 56 yards for his third touchdown. The fourth time Red took the ball the same play sent him speeding downfield for 45 yards and his fourth touchdown. Twelve minutes of the first period had gone by. Red Grange had held the ball four times and had run 95, 67, 56 and 45 yards for touchdowns!

Bob Zuppke sent in a substitute to ask Red Grange the inevitable question: "How do you feel?" Red's answer was "Tired!" Zuppke took him out to the roar of an absolutely thunderous ovation. Some 67,000 fans had jammed the new Illinois Memorial Stadium for this dedication game.

The crowd roared again when Red came back into the game in the final period. On his first play he ran 19 yards to score.

Five runs, five touchdowns, and 282 yards.

It was football's greatest individual performance, carried out against a team that had made "special preparation." The feelings of the Michigan coach, Hurry Up Yost, were not helped when his wife remarked: "Don't you think it would have helped if you'd sent in someone to tackle that red-headed boy?" After the game the *Michigan Daily* observed sourly: "All Red Grange can do is run!"

"And all Galli-Curci can do is sing!" Bob Zuppke retorted in a quip that is now part of football history.

Actually, Red Grange could also block, tackle, pass, punt and kick placements.

But for Zuppke to have used him as a blocker would have been like using a great soprano as an accompanist. In that "team-picture" which Zuppke had painted, the other ten men were to do the blocking.

Best of all the blockers was halfback Wally McIlwain, with fullback Britton close behind. But everybody was blocking when Illinois went east to play powerful Pennsylvania in 1925.

Red could kick, too.

The Quakers were also "specially prepared." They thought that Red Grange could run only to his right, and they were stacked to stop him there. But wily Bob Zuppke had devised plays which sent Red sprinting to the left, the Penn short side, after the shift. On the day of the game, however, it did not look as if anyone could sprint in the sea of mud that enveloped Franklin Field. And yet, next morning, The Chicago *Tribune* ran an eight-column banner on Page 1 proclaiming: ILLINOIS 24, PENN 2; GRANGE! The Chicago *Herald-Examiner* said:

Philadelphia, Oct. 31—They've seen Red Grange in the East, folks . . .

They saw him take the ball on the first play from scrimmage . . . and reel off fifty-six yards to a touchdown before most of the crowd knew whether his number was 77 or 30. After that they *knew*.

They saw him take the kickoff . . . and run it back fifty-nine yards to Penn's twenty-five-yard line. Then they spent the rest of the afternoon watching him compile an aggregate of three hundred and sixty-three yards in the thirty-six times that he carried the ball, which is a little bit better than a first down for every trip.

Walter Eckersall thought Red's game against Penn was even greater than the one against Michigan the year before. He said that, in scoring three of the four Illinois touchdowns, Red had "practically single-handedly" defeated undefeated Penn. He added:

Near the end of the second quarter, after he had wrecked Pennsylvania's hopes for national laurels, Coach Zuppke decided to give his Man o' War a breathing spell. He beckoned. Grange straightened up from the weird, mud-bespattered pyramid of gnomes. He removed his yellow head guard, revealing for the first time his red thatch of hair, and started for the sidelines.

. . . a vast throbbing silence fell upon the far-flung tiers of watchers. With one spontaneous, beautifully sportsmanlike motion, 63,000 human beings rose to their feet in tribute to the lad walking slowly through the . . . mire. And while the women . . . gazed in wonder at the slight figure far below, every man afoot removed his hat.

It was the only time the ghost had galloped in the East and he had galloped well. But it was not the first time that gridiron gallopers had come riding out of the West.

The year before, there had been the Four Horsemen of Notre Dame.

The Four Horsemen of Notre Dame

Outlined against the blue-gray October sky, the Four Horsemen rode again. In dramatic lore they were known as famine, pestilence, destruction, and death. These are only aliases. Their real names are Stuhldreher, Miller, Crowley and Layden.

Again it was Grantland Rice writing. This time he was reporting on the Army–Notre Dame game of 1924, the first to be played in New York.

The following day an alert publicity man at Notre Dame had "The Four Horsemen" photographed as they sat in full football uniforms astride a quartet of steeds. The picture was reprinted all over the country. Almost overnight the great Notre Dame team of 1924 became immortal. This is the year in which Knute Rockne won his first national championship. It is also the season from which his own and Notre Dame's fame dates.

The Four Horsemen of Notre Dame (left to right):
Don Miller, Elmer Layden, Jim Crowley, Harry Stuhldreher.

Another great sports writer, Allison Danzig, has written: "From then on the names of the university and the coach became synonymous for champion football. And interest in all football skyrocketed in a stampede toward the box office that packed the stadiums and led to a pyramiding of interest and gate receipts and a mad scramble for star players. Red Grange was galloping into the headlines of the nation's press at the same time, and it was in this same month of October, 1924, that he broke out in his rash of four touchdowns in twelve minutes against Michigan. Between the Galloping Ghost and the Four Horsemen the nation went slightly football mad."

There is little doubt that this was the greatest "pony" backfield in history. Don Miller and Jimmy Crowley, the halfbacks, weighed 162 and 164; Elmer Layden at fullback weighed 162, and Harry Stuhldreher, the quarter, was just 154. Yet they tore rival lines into shreds. They ran with a rhythm, speed and grace that left an indelible imprint on the minds of those who saw them. And they ran behind a line that was to earn its own great measure of fame as "The Seven Mules." The mules were Ed Hunsinger and Chuck Collins at end, Rip Miller and Joe Bach at tackle, John Weibel and Nobel Kizer at guard, and the incomparable Adam Walsh at center. Walsh was a tiger; he once played an entire game with two broken hands. He was witty, too.

In one game the Horsemen were playing behind a second-string line and could get nowhere. Rockne sent in the Mules, led by Walsh. "What's the matter, boys?" Walsh asked, handling the ball for the snap from scrimmage.

"Maybe you need a little help." They got it, of course. With the Mules plowing the field ahead of them, the Horsemen cantered to a 40–0 victory.

But the real wit was Crowley. "Sleepy Jim," the man who Rockne thought "looked as though he were built to be a tester in an alarm-clock factory," was a master of repartee. He received his nickname the day Rockne inquired if he got enough sleep at night. "Yes," Jim countered, "but not enough out here in the afternoon." After an Eastern game in which one official nearly penalized the Irish into defeat, the same official said to Crowley: "You were lucky to win today."

"Yes, Cyclops," Jim shot back. "After watching you officiate you don't even begin to know how lucky we were!"

Crowley, who could pass and run, made his first attempt at punting in a game against Princeton in 1923. A burly Tiger broke through to block the kick and score the safety that gave Princeton her only score in a 25–2 defeat. After the game a friend needled Jim: "I see you're a triple-threat man this year."

"Yes," Crowley snapped. "Trip, stumble or fumble."

Although Crowley had the reputation as the greatest wit, all the Horsemen were light-hearted young men. They delighted in teasing their opponents, especially famous stars. One of these was brawny Ed Garbisch, Army's All-America center. When the Irish met the Cadets in their memorable 1924 game, they deliberately ran plays against him. As he picked himself up, one of the Horsemen would ask, "Is that the great Mr. Garbisch?"

"Yes," another one replied, nodding

his head solemnly. "That's the great Mr. Garbisch."

On another smash, Crowley turned to Miller in feigned amazement. "You don't mean to say that that's the great Mr. Garbisch?"

"If the number is correct," Miller replied, "that is none other than the great Mr. Garbisch in person."

Such needling did not fail to get under the Army star's skin and spoil his game. Notre Dame won, 13–7. Garbisch was nonetheless an all-time Army great, and he went on to kick four field goals and beat Navy, 12–0, that very same year.

At times, needling was a good medicine for the Four Horsemen, too. *Their* hat-size was frequently in danger of growing larger. Once one of them stormed up to the Notre Dame manager and demanded new stockings and belt. "Okay," said the manager, "but turn in your old ones."

"What for?" the Horseman exploded.

One of the Mules, Rip Miller, who was to be famous as a coach at Navy, was within earshot. He turned to the manager in mock rebuke. "What do you mean talking that way? Don't you know who he is? He's one of the Four Horsemen!"

"Nooo!" the manager exclaimed.

"Yessirree!" Miller insisted, and the chastened Horseman slunk away, only to come back next day to return the new equipment. He'd keep the old things, he said.

Of the many stories—and more numerous legends—concerning this great backfield, none is more curious than Knute Rockne's own account of his first glimpse of them. He produced this estimate: "Not so hot."

Later he wrote in *Colliers* magazine:

These men and the others of the freshman squad in 1921 were soundly beaten by such teams as Lake Forest Academy and the Michigan State Freshmen. Stuhldreher of the lot had the most promise. He sounded like a leader on the field. He was a good and fearless blocker and as he gained in football knowledge he showed signs of smartness in emergencies. Layden had speed—he could run a hundred-yard dash in under ten seconds at a track meet. But speed and some kicking ability seemed to be all his football wares. Jimmy Crowley was only less humorous in play than in appearance. He looked dull and always resembled a lad about to get out of or into bed. He showed very little as a freshman—certainly none of the nimble wit that made him as celebrated for repartee as for broken-field running. Don Miller traveled that first year on the reputation and recommendation of his brother, "Red" Miller, the great Notre Dame halfback who made such havoc when his team beat Michigan in 1909.

And yet, by the middle of the following season, these four young men were the first-string backfield. They had met and meshed. In mind and body and outlook each seemed to be a perfect foil for the other, and they emerged as perhaps the best coördinated and most colorful backfield in history.

The official debut of the Four Horsemen was actually against Carnegie Tech. [Rockne wrote.] I moved Layden from left halfback, where he had been alternating with Crowley, a fullback. These boys surprised the fans at Pittsburgh with their perfect timing as they functioned for the first time as a unit backfield. Layden amazed me by his terrific speed at fullback. He adopted a straight line drive that made him one of the most unusual fullbacks in football. He pierced a line through sheer speed—cutting it like a knife.

Thereafter the Four Horsemen rode through rival lines on gridirons from Princeton to Palo Alto. And at Palo Alto they rode into immortality. There they met a mighty Stanford team coached by the great Pop Warner. There they played in the Rose Bowl for the only time in Notre Dame's history, and there they met a blond tornado of a fullback named Ernie Nevers.

Only Red Grange and the Horsemen themselves overshadowed this splendid athlete. Rockne called him a "fury in football boots." And he played against the Irish with both of his ankles taped. Even so, he bent and burst the Notre Dame line. Again and again he led Stanford downfield on long drives only to find his own forwards tiring against that stiffening Irish line. Twice these long drives were thwarted by unwise quarterback calls, and Notre Dame was quick to convert enemy mistakes into touchdowns.

Had the game been considered solely as a battle of fullbacks—of power against speed, as represented by big Ernie Nevers against little Elmer Layden— then it might have been said that the victory went to the fleet of foot. Layden scored three touchdowns. His first came as he knifed over from the Stanford three. He made his second, by plucking one of Nevers' long passes out of the air and racing 70 yards to a touchdown. The

Ernie Nevers (left) and Pop Warner of Stanford.

third was scored on another interception which he brought back for 35 yards and a score. In the end, Notre Dame triumphed, 27–10.

The Stanford University Indians had the statistical edge on the Irish. But that, again, was only proof that, while power can grind out the yardage, speed and daring can make the sudden stab that puts points on the scoreboard.

Pop Warner pointed out that Stanford had 17 first downs to Notre Dame's 10, and jokingly suggested that first downs ought to count as points. Sleepy Jim Crowley shot back:

"Yes, and next year the major leagues are going to give runs for each man left on base!"

So the Four Horsemen and the Seven Mules rode back to South Bend as all-victorious national champions. Already there was a rising clamor to pit this team against Red Grange and Illinois. But the "dream game" was never played, and the Galloping Ghost and the Four Horsemen went clattering into football history, side by side, as equals.

The Ghost Goes Barnstorming

As the 1925 football season neared its end, a controversy began to rage both in the streets of Chicago and on the campus of the University of Illinois. Would Red Grange turn pro? *Should* Red Grange turn pro?

College authorities still resented professional "raids" on their teams, and educators advised young men not to take up the pro game as a career. Thus, when it became known that a promoter named C. C. Pyle was trying to persuade the great redhead to cash in on his fame, a storm of protest erupted. Red himself gave the tipoff to his plans. "Most of those guys will forget me next year," he snorted in reply to the legions pleading with him to "stay pure" and remain in college. "Will they lend me a dollar next year?"

Red had been a poor boy. He had never owned a complete suit until midway through college. If he could make money doing what he did best, he saw nothing wrong with it. After all, he said, he could capitalize in less honorable ways—by becoming a fake writer or a fake actor. So after his last college game, against Ohio State, he and Pyle approached George Halas of the Chicago Bears and made an agreement.

The contract, in effect, reduced the Bears to the role of playing second fiddle to Red Grange. It called for a huge share of the gate receipts for Pyle and Grange. But the hiring of Red Grange

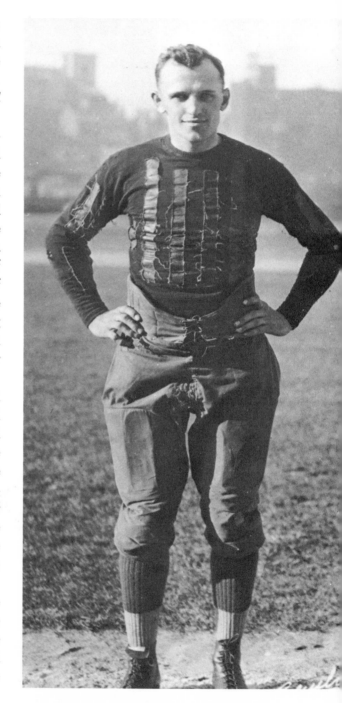

was to be the making of professional football.

Enormous crowds everywhere flocked into the stadiums to see the fabled Ghost galloping for pay. His first game was against the Chicago Cardinals on Thanksgiving Day, and drew a sellout crowd of 38,000 fans. The contest was a financial success but a football flop. Paddy Driscoll, the Cardinals' kicker, craftily angled all of his punts away from Grange. The redhead had no chance to make a spectacular runback. Of the three kicks he caught, his longest return was twenty yards. Running in the mush and snow, Red gained only 36 yards from scrimmage. But he and Pyle split $25,000 as their share of the gate receipts.

Three days later, Grange galloped for 150 yards as the Bears beat the Columbus Tigers, 14–13, before a throng of 28,000 spectators. And then he began the barnstorming tour that was to net him and Pyle more than $50,000 apiece and to make pro football.

In the next twelve days the Bears played no less than eight games. In Red's third game he returned to his old form, racing for four touchdowns as the Bears beat Eddie Kaw's team of All-Stars in St. Louis. Moving east, he drew a throng of 35,000 in Philadelphia to see the Bears beat the Frankford Yellow Jackets. The next day a mammoth throng of 68,000 people crowded into the Polo Grounds in New York to cheer as Red scored a touchdown to beat the Giants 14–7.

The tour moved on to Washington, Boston, Pittsburgh and Detroit, where a bruised and weary Red Grange had to miss the game because of a shoulder injury suffered in Pittsburgh. He could hardly move his arm for the final game against the Giants in Chicago, but nevertheless he played: to keep his word to Halas. Without Red on the field, as the Bears had learned in Detroit, the crowds dwindled away to almost nothing. But the whole Bear team was tired and battered, and the Giants won, 9–0.

A later tour through the South and Far West earned both Pyle and Grange another $50,000 apiece. Thus, a record income of $100,000 in three months made Red Grange the most highly paid player in pro football history. He would not equal it again, and, in truth, he would rarely rise to the heights he had scaled as a college player. There were several reasons for this. The players on his own team often felt disinclined to block for a man who was being paid so much more than they were, and rival players—also poorly paid—took great delight in spilling him on the seat of his pants.

Nevertheless, Red's sensational barnstorming tour was responsible for the general increase in players' salaries. The magic of his name monopolized sports pages for pro football. A sport that had often been held in disdain began to be treated with respect. And as gate receipts rose, so did the pay of the players.

Professional football can be thankful that the Ghost decided to go galloping for pay.

George Halas, coach of the Chicago Bears.

As a barnstorming Chicago Bear, Red Grange carries the ball against the All-Star Collegians in an end-of-season, January, 1926, game.

Old Favorites and New Champions

In 1921 Bob Zuppke had introduced the last of the basic football innovations: the huddle. Teams no longer lined up immediately after the ball was downed, waiting for it to be snapped on a pre-arranged signal. Instead, they gathered in a huddle around the play-caller, who gave the signal as well as the next play. At the time, Zuppke came in for severe criticism for his huddle. But it soon grew popular, especially after Illinois took the national title in 1923.

By that time football was being played very much as it is played today. And because the sport was such a big attraction, the games had to be played rain or shine. Huge crowds of people, many of whom had traveled hundreds of miles for a game, could not be turned away with "rain checks" as in baseball. On November 24, 1923, fifty-five thousand people sat through a three-hour downpour at Harvard's Soldier Field to see Yale beat Harvard for the first time since 1916. The score was 13–0.

That game became famous, not only because the Bulldogs scored their first touchdown in 16 years against the Cantabs, but also because a Yale halfback named Raymond "Ducky" Pond really lived up to his name. He picked up a Harvard fumble on his own 33-yard-line to go splashing and skidding 67 yards for the winning touchdown.

Southern Methodist University at Dallas, Texas, also won fame in 1923. Coach Ray Morrison trained his "Immor-tal Ten" in the use of the forward pass, creating an "aerial circus" that brought S.M.U. an all-winning season and its first Southwestern Conference title. The Immortal Ten, after playing together as freshmen in 1921, had sworn to end the victory famine which had befallen the Mustangs. They did, and they are still a legend at S.M.U.

The year 1923 marked the beginning of difficulty in selecting a national champion. Yale, Cornell, Michigan, Illinois, California, S.M.U. and others all claimed the distinction. As previously mentioned, the Helms Foundation eventually decided that the Illinois team—led by Red Grange—deserved the top rating. Although Notre Dame was everybody's champion the following season, the difficulty of finding a unanimous choice reappeared in 1925. More and more of America's finest colleges were playing top-flight football.

Dartmouth had perhaps its greatest season in 1925. And her players had perhaps the highest scholastic rating per man of any other college eleven before or since. Andrew "Swede" Oberlander was the star. The Swede was a fine runner and a great passer. His movements were highly rhythmic and it is said he used to set, look and throw to the chant:

Ten thousand Swedes
Came out of the weeds
At the Battle of Copenhagen

Cornell thought there were at least that many Swedes on the field the day Oberlander led Dartmouth to a 62–13 rout of the Big Red, thus ending Gloomy Gil Dobie's reign. It was a close first quarter, 14–13. Thereafter the Swede passed for 6 touchdowns and scampered 55 yards for another. But the Midwest, which had supplanted the East as football's dominant power, was not impressed. "You people in the East don't know what a good football team is," one of the Chicago coaches told a reporter just before the Chicago–Dartmouth game. "You'll see one tomorrow. Dartmouth is just another ball club for Chicago." The spectators had something to see all right, on the day of the game. The Swede went out to throw four touchdown passes, and the Dartmouth Indians routed the Chicago Maroon, 33–7.

The University of Michigan had a team that rivaled Dartmouth's that season. In fact Hurry Up Yost always said that his 1925 eleven was the best team he ever coached, not excluding any of the Point-a-Minute steamrollers. It was a smart team, too, and its spectacular success owed much to the passing and catching of its two Bennies.

Benny Friedman was one of the greatest of all passers, both as a collegiate star and as a pro. Bennie Oosterbaan was one of the greatest receivers; he made All-America end three times. Yet, this "greatest" of Yost teams lost to Northwestern, 3–2. The game was played at the mammoth Soldier Field in Chicago, and the field was a black slop of mud. It rained, hailed and sleeted by turns. With a 55-mile gale blowing, no one, not even the great Benny Fried-

man, could pass. So the Northwestern Wildcats steadily punted themselves into field-goal position. After they scored their three points, Michigan got a safety —and that was all the scoring.

In 1925 a short trim back named Eddy Tryon led Colgate to its first unbeaten season. Tryon did everything well and played at his best when the going was worst. He was the nation's top scorer.

The Huskies of Washington were also clamoring for number one recognition in a year that boasted many top teams, but the eventual champion was a newcomer among football giants: the Crimson Tide of Alabama.

The debut of the University of Alabama among the elite was managed by Wallace Wade, who was later to win perhaps even greater fame at Duke University. Wade was a cool, canny and tight-lipped perfectionist. He rarely showed emotion. If his team won a great victory, he would merely grunt, "You boys did all right today." If they were upset, he would also say, "You boys did all right today." In 1925 his team was a high scorer and had only a single touchdown scored against it. Quarterback Pooley Hubert and speedy Johnny Mack Brown were the outstanding players. And the Crimson Tide settled the dispute about who was best by beating Washington, 20–19, in the Rose Bowl.

That was one of the most thrilling games ever played. Alabama came from behind with three touchdowns in the third period. Two of them were scored on long passes from Hubert to Johnny Mack Brown. From this triumph Brown went on to become a popular movie star.

The Crimson Tide was rolling again

in 1926 with a team that surprised everyone, including Coach Wade. There were no stars, just eleven team players who played a game as cold and calculating as the mind of their coach. Again Alabama finished at the top of the heap. But Stanford, with one of Pop Warner's best teams, tied Alabama, 7–7, in the Rose Bowl. They were awarded the Rissman Trophy, an annual award then symbolic of national supremacy.

Also starring that year were the fabled "Iron Men" of Brown University. The Bruins were unbeaten, although Colgate tied them in the last game of the season. The Iron Men earned their nickname when they defeated Yale and Dartmouth on successive Saturdays without a single substitution.

Many fans thought that Navy was tops in 1926. This was the Middies' first year with Bill Ingram at the helm, and his team beat everyone they played until the final game with Army. That contest —played before 110,000 screaming fans in Soldier Field, Chicago—ended in a 21–21 tie. It was probably the most thrilling game of the most famous rivalry in football.

Another newcomer among major teams in the Golden Twenties was Boston College. The Eagles were coached by Major Frank Cavanagh, one of the most beloved and colorful figures in football lore. The "Iron Major" was a renowned professor of law, a superb trial lawyer, an eloquent orator and a delightful entertainer, as well as an outstanding coach. During his first two years with Boston College, he astounded the gridiron world by putting out a team that beat Yale two years in a row. He guided the Eagles to an unbeaten season in 1920, and again in 1926. Then he shifted to Fordham, where he made the Rams a national football power. They had their first unbeaten season in 1929.

Yale, incidentally, sprang back in full strength after its two setbacks at the hands of Boston College. The Bulldogs were playing for Thomas Albert Dwight Jones. "Tad" Jones, perhaps even more than Walter Camp, was the living, breathing spirit of Yale. Just before the annual contest with Harvard, which is still spoken of as "The Game" in Yale–Harvard circles, he would tell his squad: "Gentlemen, you are about to play football for Yale against Harvard. Never again in your lives will you do anything so important."

Coach Tad Jones, often called the "spirit of Yale."

In 1927 the University of Illinois was back. Bob Zuppke was still coach, and he had a fleet-footed fellow named Grange in the backfield. This one was Garland Grange, brother of the incomparable Red. Garland was even faster than Red, according to Zuppke, who said: "Red was exceptionally fast, but he wasn't quite as speedy on the straightaway as his brother, Garland. Gardie didn't have Red's elusiveness—no player has ever had it—nor did he have Red's pickup. He had more dash and fire, though." The championship 1927 Illinois team was made up of lightweights. There were only two linemen who weighed more than 190 pounds, and Gardie Grange, at 171 pounds, was the heaviest man in the backfield.

Some less familiar names trailed close behind Illinois in 1927. Among them were Texas A & M, the University of Tennessee and New York University.

Joel Hunt was, and is, the name that the Texas Aggies most remember. A star for three straight seasons, this 168-pound back scored 128 points in 1927, the year in which the Aggies won every game except a tied match with Texas Christian. Hunt was good at everything, but he ran with the ball best of all. He was trickier than he was speedy, and down at College Station they will say: "He wa'nt so fast, but you couldn't catch him in a telephone booth!"

Ken Strong of New York University was really fast. He was well-named too. Weighing 201 pounds, he was one of those big men who could churn out the hundred in ten flat. Strong was the outstanding player when the colorful Chick Meehan coached the N.Y.U. Violets through their most successful seasons:

1926, 1927 and 1928. In 1928 Ken Strong gave the Violets one of their greatest victories, a 27–13 victory over one of Carnegie Tech's finest teams. Judge Wally Steffens, coach at Carnegie Tech, said of Strong:

"I've seen Heston and I've seen Eckersall. But here is the greatest football player I ever saw. It is the first time I have seen one football player run over my team. We beat Notre Dame, 27–7, last Saturday. We were undefeated. But Strong runs and passes and kicks us into the ground."

Ken Strong was also a great star with the pros. He might have been a baseball immortal as well, had not a wrist injury cut short his career with the Detroit Tigers.

The Violets of N.Y.U., fine as they were, met their nemesis in a new Southern power, the University of Tennessee. Under General Bob Neyland, Tennessee was to compile one of football's outstanding records. From 1926 through 1934 the orange-shirted Tennessee Volunteers won 76 games, lost 6 and were tied 5 times. In 1938, 1939 and 1940 the Vols won all thirty of their regular season games. For as long as Neyland was in charge they went to a bowl game almost every year. And Neyland, in the opinion of none other than Knute Rockne, was "football's greatest coach."

He was a perfectionist who ran his teams with military precision. His motto, which still hangs in the Tennessee dressing room, was: *One Good Interferer Is Worth Three Ball Carriers!* He covered his blackboards with other slogans, such as: "The Team That Makes the Fewest Mistakes Wins," "Play for and Make the Breaks," "When One Comes Your Way,

The colorful Chick Meehan, above, of N.Y.U.
and his nemesis, Coach Bob Neyland of Tennessee.

Score!" The spirit which he infused into his Volunteers is typified perhaps by the lineman who blocked a kick for a touchdown at the cost of one of his front teeth. Asked if he regretted the loss of his tooth, he merely grinned and said, "I'd swap a tooth for a touchdown any day!"

Neyland's defensive record was absolutely matchless. In 25 years, during 188 regular season games, the Volunteers gave up exactly 5 points per game! They did not, oddly enough, do as well in post-season contests. Frequently they lost to underrated teams.

The Volunteers had stars galore. Among them was the great Bobby Dodd, a wily quarterback who would one day be a famous coach. Others were the professional ace, Beattie Feathers; the peerless triple threat, Gene McEver; and, perhaps best of all, huge Herman Hickman.

Neyland always said that Herman Hickman was the greatest guard ever to tread the gridiron. Rival teams derided this short, 225-pound youngster (he was only 19 in his senior year) as the Fat Boy. N.Y.U. once had the ball on the Tennessee 3-yard line and decided in the huddle: "We'll go through the Fat Boy. He can't even move." After three plays the Violets were back on the 14. Hickman's methods were simple. He broke through, picked up the blocker and hurled him at the runner. Later, when he was a coach himself and weighed a vast 310 pounds, Hickman had to stop scrimmaging with his men for fear of injuring them. Big and tough as he was, Hickman was also known as "The Bard of the Great Smokies," and could recite poetry by the hour.

90

Coach Howard Jones of Southern Cal—Rockne's arch-rival and close friend.

Although the Volunteers of Tennessee were undefeated in both 1928 and 1929, there were other teams which achieved perfect seasons. Boston College was one; so were the rising powers of Southern California and the University of Detroit. Detroit, as might be expected with Gus Dorais holding the coaching reins, had a top-flite passing team. The Titans rolled to victory behind the passing and running of Lloyd Brazil, All-America and all-time Titan great. But Detroit was not destined to remain a perennial power, as were the Trojans of Southern California.

Southern Cal became great under Howard Jones. Howard was the younger, quieter and less famous Jones boy, the other being the colorful Tad of Yale. Howard had also coached at Yale, as well as at Syracuse, Ohio State, Iowa and Duke, before finding his happy home on the sunny campus of the University of Southern California. No man was more dedicated to football. He would spend hours lining up chips with his players' names on them, moving them around to explore all their possibilities. He often became so engrossed in planning strategy for his Southern California team that he drove through red lights, missed appointments or forgot his way home.

Jones was another man who depended on drill and precision rather than pre-game theatrics. He was stern but polite, and his strongest oaths were words such as "Ye gads!" or "Pshaw!" To a player who had lost a game by failing to cover a pass, he merely said, "That was your pass, you know." But the player felt the rebuke so strongly that he cried for an hour.

It was Jones who collaborated with Knute Rockne to arrange the great intersectional Southern Cal–Notre Dame game, one of the most colorful of all rivalries and one which, played at the end of the season, has often decided the national championship.

The Trojans under Jones won two of those national championships—in 1931 and 1932—as well as five Rose Bowl games and eight Pacific Coast Conference titles. In fact, the Trojans felt they were number one in 1928. Led by their great tailback, Morley Drury, the Trojans were unbeaten and won the Rissman Trophy. But the Helms Foundation thought that the top honor belonged to Georgia Tech.

Like Southern California, Georgia Tech was unbeaten in 1928. The team was a splendid football machine and perhaps the finest ever put together by the beloved Tech coach, Bill Alexander. The Yellow Jackets probably outranked the Trojans on the strength of their famous victory over California in the Rose Bowl. One of the most bizarre incidents in football lore occurred that day.

A Georgia Tech player fumbled on his own 40-yard line, and California's center, Roy Riegels, scooped up the ball. With a horde of Yellow Jackets pursuing him, Riegels reversed his field. He broke into the clear and began racing for the goal line 60 yards away.

But it was his own goal.

Seventy thousand spectators watched in amazement as Riegels went sprinting toward disaster with teammate Benny Lom in frantic pursuit. Lom yelled at Riegels to turn around and head back in the right direction. But Riegels thought Lom was urging him on to greater speed. At last Lom overhauled Riegels on the 3-yard line and spun him around. But by then it was too late. The pursuing Yellow Jackets overwhelmed Riegels on his own 1-yard line. Shaken, California went into kick formation. Riegels centered the ball to Lom, and a Tech tackle broke through to block the kick and score a safety.

That was the margin of victory as both teams went on to score touchdowns. The game ended, 8–7, in favor of Georgia Tech. Afterward, the disconsolate Roy Riegels explained: "After I picked up the fumble, somebody shoved me and I bounced right off into a tackler. In pivoting to get away from him I completely lost my bearings."

Bob Zuppke of Illinois had a witty explanation. "No wonder a center ran the wrong way. Centers spend all their time looking at the world backward and upside down."

But Roy Riegels did not let this famous "wrong-way run" get him down. He went on to star as captain of a strong California team in 1929.

Captain Roy Riegels of U.S.C. races 70 yards to his own goal in the Rose Bowl disaster of January, 1929.

Triumph and Tragedy

The year 1929 marked the beginning of the Great Depression in America. But the collapse of the stock market had no effect on Notre Dame's football, for 1929 marked her return to the top of the football heap.

There were other fine teams that year. Jock Sutherland at Pittsburgh produced one of his typical steamroller elevens. Purdue was undefeated and won its first Big Ten crown, and Texas Christian also gained its first conference championship. A rising coach named Bernie Bierman made the team at Tulane University in New Orleans an irresistible force in the South, while Tennessee continued unbeaten for the third straight year.

But it was the Irish who overshadowed everyone else. They beat the powerful Southern California team that toppled victorious Pitt, 47–14, in the Rose Bowl; and to many experts they looked superior to the Four Horsemen team of 1924. Jack Elder, Frank Carideo, Larry Mullins and Marty Brill were, indeed, a fine football foursome. But there were others who starred in that 1929 backfield, among them Bucky O'Connor, Joe Savoldi and the back who ran like a horse—Marchie Schwartz. Carideo and Schwartz were to become two-time All-Americas. Another was Jack Cannon, often considered one of the All-Time All-America guards. A young fellow named Frank Leahy also played on this eleven.

Jack Elder was the fastest man on the squad, and it was he who saved Notre Dame's record in the final game against Army. Led by Chris "Red" Cagle, the Cadets were driving toward the Irish goal. But Elder plucked a Cagle pass out of the air and went flying down the sidelines a distance of 97 yards for the game's only touchdown.

Although Elder was not back the following season, the Irish were even better. The 1930 eleven was Rockne's masterpiece. He pushed his preference of speed over power to such a degree that one of his guards, Bert Metzger, weighed only 153 pounds. But Metzger was so fast he could topple rival linemen who were almost twice as big. He became famous as Notre Dame's "watch-charm guard."

Carideo, Schwartz, Savoldi, Mullins and Brill were all better in the 1930 season, and they tore through nine top-flight opponents. What they did to Penn made even the memory of the Red Grange slaughter fade by comparison. The final score was 60–20, and would have been far worse if Rockne had not sent in hordes of substitutes. The New York *Times* reported that the Irish attack exploded with "seven kinds of forked lightning," adding: "It left [80,000] dazed onlookers wondering whether any team that ever stepped on a football field could have equalled this one in the cyclonic speed and brute power of its runners, the annihilating force of its interference and the almost matchless perfection of its play in every detail." The Penn rout was also a personal triumph for Marty Brill. Unable to make the Penn team, this young Philadelphian had transferred to Notre Dame. There he had become the "blocker" of the Irish backfield. But against Penn the wily Rockne let him run with the ball, and he reeled off three electrifying touchdown runs.

Even so, the fans on the West Coast predicted that the Irish would be put in their place when they met Howard Jones's powerful Trojans. Pop Warner had already called this Southern California team one of the three best he had ever seen.

When it came time for the game, Joe Savoldi was declared ineligible and Moon Mullins was out with an injury. The experts declared that Southern Cal would take Notre Dame by as many as four or five touchdowns. The actual final score? Notre Dame 27; Southern Cal, 0.

The acclaim that came Knute Rockne's way was close to hysterical, and he began to benefit from it. He signed a contract to become sales manager for a big auto manufacturer, and he agreed to participate in several movie productions. In March of 1931 he was in Kansas City on business. From there he was planning to fly to Los Angeles for the opening of a chain of sporting-goods stores. Then a ticket mixup caused him to lose his seat on the airplane. As he turned to leave the terminal, a man recognized him and offered his seat. Rockne took it with thanks.

"Soft landings, Rock," someone had said in farewell a few days before.

Rockne had laughed. "You mean happy landings," he had answered.

But there was neither. Almost as soon as the little airplane took off into the intense and bitter cold, ice began forming on its wings. The pilot fought desperately but over Bazaar, Kansas, the engines coughed and died and the plane crashed into a cornfield.

Everyone was killed. The great Knute Rockne had perished at the pinnacle of success. The nation was stunned.

Ten thousand sorrowing Americans jammed the Chicago railroad station to see his body arrive. President Hoover sent his condolences. So did the King of Norway. Members of Rockne's last great team carried the casket into the church for funeral services that were broadcast all over the world. And from the Cleveland *Press* came the statement that was the dead man's epitaph.

"In the past generation it was Buffalo Bill. This generation it is Knute Rockne."

Line-Bustin' with the Bronk

Pro football had established itself during the Golden Twenties. Just as Red Grange had given the game headline value, the National Football League president, Joe Carr, gave it stability.

Much of the publicity provided by Grange had proved harmful to the pro sport. Educators were angry that the great redhead had been "lured away" from his studies. So Carr called an NFL meeting in Detroit in 1926 and had the league members adopt a rule pledging that the pro football teams would not attempt to sign a college player until after his collegiate eligibility expired. Violations were to be penalized with a $1,000 fine or loss of franchise, or both.

Gradually, also, the NFL was settling down into a ten-team league divided into a Western and an Eastern division. The Chicago Cardinals, the Chicago Bears and the Green Bay Packers were still teams. In 1925 Timothy J. Mara had bought a league franchise for $2,500 and created the New York Giants. In 1932 the flamboyant laundry tycoon, George Preston Marshall, along with three other men, took over a franchise in Boston. This was later moved to Washington, D. C. In 1933 Art Rooney put a team in Pittsburgh. It was in 1933 also that Bert Bell and Lud Wray, the old Penn stars, created the Philadelphia Eagles from the remains of the Frankford Yellow Jackets. Next year Dan Topping took over a franchise in Brooklyn; Detroit replaced Portsmouth and the old Cincinnati franchise operated in St. Louis for a single season.

Until 1937 there were nine teams in the NFL: Cardinals, Bears, Packers, Giants, Pittsburgh Steelers (then Pirates), Eagles, Brooklyn Dodgers and Detroit Lions. Cleveland rejoined the league in 1937 with the Rams, so there were five teams in each division.

Under Carr's guidance players no longer jumped from team to team. Each team's followers got to know their players, and rivalries began to develop between cities. Philadelphia thirsted to defeat Pittsburgh; Washington wanted to scalp New York; the Bears and the Cardinals carried on an inter-city feud in Chicago, while Chicago, Detroit and Green Bay hated one another by turns.

From the outset the Green Bay Packers were the storybook team of pro football. They had begun when Curly Lambeau met a sports writer named George Calhoun on the street and they said to each other, in effect: "Let's start a football team." Lambeau, who had played one year under Rockne at Notre Dame, was to be on the team, as well as to coach and recruit players. Calhoun would handle business and promotion. From the Indian (later Acme) Packing Company came the uniforms, the practice field and the name. And from the residents of the little city nestled on the shores of Lake Michigan came a spirited loyalty unsurpassed within or without the pro ranks.

Curly Lambeau (center), the guiding force behind the Packers, confers with Don Hutson (left) and Irv Comp.

Lambeau was a shrewd showman from the outset. At a time when most teams were playing off-tackle football, he gave his fans the most exciting style of play then imaginable. In 1929, Lambeau hired the colorful Johnny Blood to play for him. Blood, whose real name was McNally, was a fast, slashing runner who could bring the fans onto their feet the moment he headed for a hole in the defense. His unrealized potential as a pass receiver became evident the following year when Arnie Herber of Green Bay joined the team. Herber was an unknown rookie, whose short stubby fingers, seemed unsuitable for grasping a football. But even though Arnie held the ball with his *thumb*, rather than his fingers on the lacing, he could heave the ball for tremendous distances. And he threw pass after pass to the speedy Blood as the Packers rolled to three straight league titles from 1929 through 1931.

In 1933 the pros made the pass legal from *anywhere* behind the line of scrimmage rather than from five yards back. This was a change that just suited Herber, even though George Halas and George Preston Marshall had promoted it as a way of favoring their teams.

In 1936 a tall slender end from Alabama, named Don Hutson, joined the Packers. On Hutson's first play as a pro, while Blood decoyed the Chicago Bears' defense to one side of the field, Don streaked down the other side to take an Arnie Herber pass for a touchdown. Don Hutson was to catch a total of 101 touchdown passes before retiring as a pro immortal. And many of them were thrown by Cecil Isbell after the Purdue

The 1933 backfield of the Green Bay Packers.
Left to right: Arnold Herber, John Blood,
Roger Grove and Clark Hinkle.

Beattie Feathers gains 8 yards
against the Redskins
in a 1938 game.

star replaced Herber as the Packer passer.

Stars equally exciting were appearing on other teams. The Washington Redskins had Sammy Baugh, Cliff Battles, Andy Farkas and Turk Edwards. On the Giant roster were Mel Hein, Ed Danowski, Tuffy Leemans and Ward Cuff. Ernie Nevers, whom Pop Warner called the greatest player he had ever coached—much to the dismay of Jim Thorpe—starred for the Chicago Cardinals, along with Gus Tinsley and Ki Aldrich. Dutch Clark and Lloyd Caldwell were favorites with Detroit fans; Parker Hall and Johnny Drake starred for Cleveland; Whizzer White sprinted down the field for Pittsburgh, and Joe Carter and Emmett Mortell sparked the Philadelphia Eagles. And while the Brooklyn fans boasted of Herman Hick-

man, Ralph Kercheval and Ace Parker, the followers of the Chicago Bears sang the praises of Beattie Feathers, Bill Hewitt, Joe Stydahar and Bronko Nagurski—the Bronk.

Some experts rate Jim Thorpe as the greatest of the early pros; others single out Ernie Nevers. But most will put their money on the peerless, line-busting Bronk. He had never played football in his life until he came to the University of Minnesota, but in 1927 he was a star end. In 1928 he was selected as an All-

America tackle, and in 1929 he was an All-America fullback. His great versatility, which sprang from his incredible strength, seems to give Bronk the edge when it comes to selecting the greatest early pro.

"You can't get away from Nagurski for the all-around combination," Coach Jeff Cravath of Rice once said. "Eleven Nagurskis would wreck any other one-man team, although eleven Thorpes and eleven Nevers wouldn't be any shove-around . . . But seven Bronks on the line would be too good to run against."

The Bronk

And four Bronks in the backfield would probably have been too much to stop. Although his size has always been exaggerated, he was still a marvel of power, with his height of six feet three inches and his weight of 200 pounds. Moreover, it is likely that the modern athlete's diet and methods of conditioning would add another thirty pounds or more to that steel frame.

It was often said that Bronko Nagurski didn't need any interference because he ran his own. He struck with his head up and his body straight out like a cannon. His knees pumped high against his cheeks and he struck with the force of a runaway plow. Few players, before or since, have dealt out punishment as he did. He seemed to exult in collision. To attempt to stop him head-on was almost suicide. The only way to bring down the Bronk was to adopt his own method of tackling when he was playing tackle on defense. You had to hurl your body crosswise at his legs and whip him to the earth.

With the Bronk hurtling through their opponents' lines, the Chicago Bears eventually wrested pro supremacy away from the Green Bay Packers. The Bears had completed 23 games in a row without a defeat before they entered the 1934 championship game against the Giants in New York. The meeting was billed as a clash between football's two iron men: Bronko Nagurski and Ken Strong. But it was played on a frozen field more suitable for ballerinas. Cleated football shoes simply could not grip the turf, and the running game of both teams got almost nowhere. Still, the Bronk scored one touchdown, and the Bears were leading, 10–3, at the half.

Two Giant tacklers are having a hard time slowing up Bronko Nagurski in the thrilling 1934 championship game between the Bears and the Giants.

While the first two quarters were being played, however, New York's wily coach, Steve Owen, was scouring the city for basketball sneakers. During the intermission he and his players put them on. The Giants returned to the field like a team of skaters matched against eleven sliders. The cleated Bears—the Monsters of the Midway, as they were called— skidded around helplessly. But the Giants' Ken Strong ran for two touchdowns, one of them a 42-yard dance on ice through the ranks of the bumbling Bears. The final score was 30–13, and the Giants had their first National League title.

More than that, the pros had shown themselves to be even more clever than the collegians. The football world buzzed with the story of how the crafty Giants had "sneakered" the title game away from the Bears and Bronko Nagurski. But there was some comfort for the Bronk. During that same year, 1934, the football team at Minnesota, his alma mater, began a victory march under Coach Bernie Bierman that is unrivaled in college football records.

Go, Go, Gophers!

"I never made an emotional speech in my life," Bernie Bierman once said, and it was true. The closest that Bierman—unquestionably one of the finest of coaches—ever came to emotion was during the Tulane–Georgia game of 1929.

Georgia led at the half, 15–14, and Bierman decided to let an assistant deliver a pep talk. At the climax of his speech, the assistant hurled his hat to the floor, jumped on it and roared: "*Georgia?* I can lick the whole darn State of Georgia myself!"

At that point, Bernie Bierman set his own foot on the hat and whispered, "So can I."

That was Bierman: cold, cryptic, confident—and very, very successful. It was he who brought Tulane's Green Wave into national prominence, leading them to the Rose Bowl, where the Greenies were defeated, 21–12, by one of the greatest Southern California teams. And it was he who made the Golden Gophers of Minnesota national champions for three straight years—1934, 1935, 1936—a feat still unrivaled in football annals.

Bierman's first year as coach at his

Coach Bernie Bierman of Minnesota.

own alma mater—he had starred for Minnesota under Dr. Henry Williams—was 1932. He spent it building a powerhouse while the eyes of the football fans were focused on the rival powers of Southern Cal and Michigan. The California Trojans were whirling to their second straight national title. Their star was little Cotton Warburton, one of the most thrilling broken-field runners to carry a ball. Michigan also won all its games in 1932, and Harry Kipke, a Wolverine immortal, had replaced Hurry Up Yost as coach.

The following year the Wolverines were again supreme, even though many experts thought that powerful Princeton ought to have had at least a share in the title. Princeton was being coached by Herbert Orrin "Fritz" Crisler, and under him the Tigers of the Nassau dominated the East from 1933 through 1935.

But even if 1933 was a big year for the Wolverines, the Gophers held the kingpin team to a scoreless tie, thereby serving notice that the Michigan reign was doomed.

The following year Minnesota arrived with an explosion of power. After the Gophers had crushed Michigan, 34–0, Harry Kipke said: "The reserves alone would beat almost any team in the country." When the Minnesota team beat Indiana, 30–0, Coach Bo McMillan moaned: "It is a team without a weakness."

They had already defeated a great Pittsburgh team earlier in their incredible 1934 season. The Panthers had shot out to a 7–0 halftime lead. "Two touchdowns will win," Bierman told his Gophers between halves. They went out

and ground out two of them on the straight power plays that were typical of Bierman's coaching, and won the big one, 13–7. The 34–0 rout of Wisconsin at the end of the season was merely an anti-climax. One of the greatest teams of college football—led by 230-pound fullback Stanislaus Kostka and All-Americas Pug Lund at halfback and Butch Larson at end—had played its last game.

But the Gophers, the giant team with the tiny mascot, rolled on. A handsome young fellow cast in the same hard mold as Bernie Bierman played guard for Minnesota in 1935. His name was Bud Wilkinson. He made All-America while his team won every game.

The Southwest was also producing winners that year. Texas Christian University was rampaging behind the immortal Sammy Baugh, and Southern Methodist was providing Coach Matty Bell with a Cinderella team in his first season as head man. Ten seniors and one junior had suddenly jelled into an unbeatable combination. When the Horned Frogs of Texas Christian met the Southern Methodist Mustangs for the conference title, the Mustangs triumphed on a last-quarter, fourth-down pass from punt formation. That victory took Southern Methodist to the Rose Bowl, where they lost to the Stanford team, 7–0.

Southern Methodist had already been awarded the Rockne Memorial Trophy, a new emblem of national supremacy. (The trophy had been donated by the Four Horsemen after Notre Dame retired the old Rissman Trophy by winning it three times.) But the loss to Stanford undermined the Mustangs' claim to the national title, and it looked as if unbeaten Minnesota was the true champion.

The following year, 1936, the Associated Press decided to eliminate the difficulty of picking a collegiate champion by conducting a poll of sports writers. Minnesota, with Bud Wilkinson at quarterback, won the first AP championship with no trouble at all. Three years in a row, Bernie Bierman's power-playing giants had mowed down the opposition. No wonder the Minnesota fans were proud to roar:

"Go, Go, Gophers!"

Charles "Bud" Wilkinson

Four Cliff-Hangers and One Berwanger

The "cliff-hanger" or thrilling game that leaves fans either wild with joy or crushed by disappointment is almost as common to football as the crazy bounce of the ball itself. Time and time again—in high school, college, service or with the pros—a blocked kick, desperation pass or long run has changed the complexion of a game. A team that has been scenting victory suddenly tastes defeat. This is the true cliff-hanger, and although football has certainly abounded in such games through the years, there are four that experts generally consider to be the most outstanding of all.

These are the Princeton–Chicago game of 1922, the Yale–Army game of 1929, the Southern California–Notre Dame game of 1931 and the Notre Dame–Ohio State game of 1935. All had that great quality of keeping the fans groaning and whooping by turns. And in each of those games, a team came from behind to win and to make the so-called "impossible" an incredible reality.

In 1922 Princeton had an eleven which its coach, Bill Roper, called "The Tiger Team of Destiny." Week after week this team snatched victory from defeat. Because it wouldn't be beaten, it couldn't be beaten. Three of its games were won by field goals or by extra points. Although these Tigers had been picked to lose in almost every game, and had won, no one expected them to turn back a strong Chicago team.

The expected Maroon triumph seemed assured when the fourth period began, for Chicago held an 18–7 lead and had Princeton back on her own 2-yard line. The Tigers went into a huddle and decided to throw a pass! They had decided on the play on the spur of the moment, and Chicago was astonished to see Jack Cleaves drop back into his own end zone and rifle the ball to Johnny Gorman. Gorman almost got away, but he was finally pulled down from behind on his own 40. That play turned the tide. Even though Princeton had to punt, Chicago got the ball in its own territory rather than inside Princeton's. The Chicago stands became silent. Then, on the very first play, a substitute center made a bad pass. The ball bounced off a halfback's shoulder and popped into the arms of Princeton's Howdy Gray. He raced away with it for a touchdown, and Ken Smith's perfect kick made the score 18–14.

Now the huge Chicago throng was pleading for a touchdown. But Princeton held and got the ball again. A series of passes swept them downfield, where an interference penalty put them on Chicago's 15. "Hold, Chicago! *Hold!*" the crowd screamed. But the Tigers drove to a first down. Chicago stiffened. However, the Tiger Team of Destiny was not to be denied. Four plays later Princeton was over the Chicago goal again and the score stood 21–18 in favor of Princeton.

Now it was the Chicago team that came roaring back. Passing and bucking they struck down to Princeton's 1-yard line. The crowd was in a frenzy. "Hurry!" they shrieked at the Maroon quarter. "Hurry!" Their frantic cries only confused the Maroon play-caller. He had two full minutes to play. Had he taken his time and struck calmly at the Tiger line with a mixture of plays, Chicago should have been able to shove it over. Instead, he sent John Thomas battering at the center, where the Chicago star

met a stone wall. Princeton held, and Chicago went down to defeat in what Alonzo Stagg called "a mad, wild last twelve minutes into which enough heart palpitation for forty games was packed."

Seven more years were to pass before a cliff-hanger of equal "suspense" was to take place. This time the scene was the mammoth Yale Bowl. A throng of 80,000 had turned out to see an awesome Army team, led by the brilliant Chris Cagle, take on a Yale eleven rated as a 2–1 underdog. The Cadets got to work quickly. Cagle intercepted a pass and dashed 45 yards for a touchdown. As the second period began Cadet John Murrell broke away for a 35-yard touchdown jaunt. The score: Army 13, Yale 0.

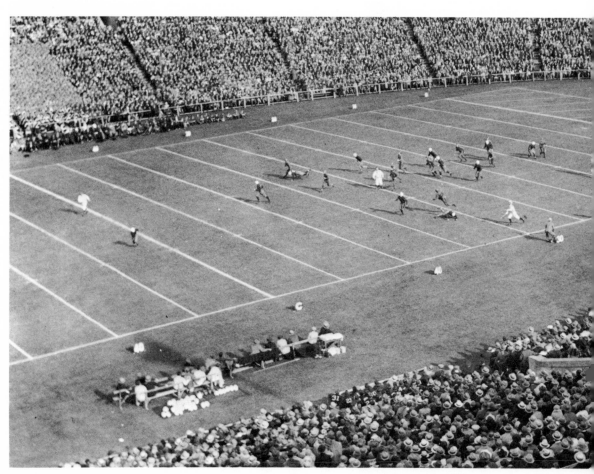

A hush came over the crowded Bowl.

"Little Boy Blue" was warming up. Yale's head coach, Mal Stevens, had signaled to his sophomore quarterback, Albie Booth. Was he going to send this five-feet-six, 144-pound midget in among those gold-jerseyed goliaths from West Point? He was, and a roar went up from the crowd as little Albie trotted out onto the green gridiron.

Suddenly Yale came alive. Once again, as he would do throughout his sophomore year, Little Boy Blue had given his teammates a wonderful lift. They crowded around him. He seemed dwarfed by that encircling ring of white helmets. Then the Yale team turned and struck at Army in a fury.

Ten men of nearly equal size hurled themselves upon the Army stalwarts while one little man carried the ball. Almost single-handed he moved it downfield for 32 yards and the first Yale touchdown. Bedlam broke loose in the Bowl.

It changed to pandemonium in the third period as Albie Booth got loose again and again. He dodged among the helpless Army giants like an elf of steel and carried the ball 35 yards for the second score. After he drop-kicked his second extra point, a shout of thunder rose from the Bowl. Yale was ahead, 14–13.

Army tried to fight back. But the Yale line had been transformed into a wall

The Yale Bowl was jammed for the 1929 "cliff-hanger" between Army and Yale.

Yale's "Little Boy Blue," Albie Booth.

of seven raging tacklers. Army had to punt. The ball rose high in the air. Waiting for it back on his own 35-yard line was Little Boy Blue.

Albie Booth caught the punt and moved toward his right. A swarm of Cadet tacklers hemmed him in. He danced among them. He should have been hurled to the turf, but he kept on his feet and suddenly broke into the clear. While the Yale blockers erased the last gold jersey between him and the goal line, he raced 65 yards for his third touchdown. After he kicked the point, the score stood at 21–13. And that was how the game ended. The smallest man on the field had blasted Coach Biff Jones's hopes for an easy Army victory. Booth had scored three times against the same Army line that would yield only one touchdown—Jack Elder's interception run—to one of the mightiest Notre Dame teams ever fielded. The achievement made Albie Booth a Yale immortal.

In 1931 the Notre Dame team was determined to get its third straight national title. They wanted to win it "for Rock." Even though Hunk Anderson now coached the Irish, his players were the men whom Rockne had trained before his tragic death. They remembered him, and so did Notre Dame. A spanking new red-brick stadium had been erected and named Rockne Memorial Stadium. There were 52,000 fans inside it the day the Trojans of Southern California came to play what many considered to be one of the greatest of Irish teams.

Notre Dame had not been beaten since the last game in 1928, when, pro-

phetically, they had bowed to Southern Cal. The Irish line was considered impregnable. The splendid Marchie Schwartz was still in the backfield, ably assisted by powerful Steve Banas. Schwartz very nearly ran wild for the first three periods. He reeled off gain after gain and scored one touchdown. Banas scored another, to put Notre Dame ahead, 14–0.

Could the Trojans match the two touchdowns already scored by the mighty Irish and go on to win with only seventeen minutes left to play? Not very likely.

But Southern Cal had stars of her own. Big Aaron Rosenberg was the mainstay of a hard-driving line. Ray

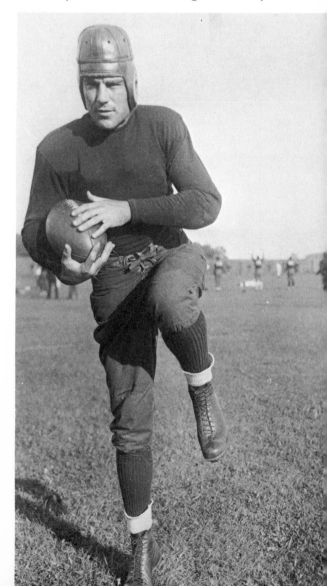

106   Marchie Schwartz of Notre Dame.

Sparling was a speedy pass receiver, and in the backfield were Gus Shaver and Ernie Pinckert. They teamed up. A missed pass to Pinckert was ruled as interference, and Southern Cal had the ball on Notre Dame's 40-yard line. Shaver took a lateral and shot around end to the 24. Then Shaver and Quarterback Orville Mohler drove to the 14.

As the fourth quarter began, Shaver gained only a yard—but then Ray Sparling took the ball on a surprise end-around and wheeled all the way down to the 1-yard line. Shaver hit center twice, and took it over. Nevertheless, after Joe Kurth broke through to block the extra point, the Notre Dame lead of 14–6 looked safe.

But Southern Cal was now on fire. Another interference ruling put the ball on the Irish 24. Mohler and Shaver drove down to the 10, and a roar went up from the stadium as Shaver took a lateral again to race around end for his second touchdown. After the extra point was kicked, the huge throng could scarcely believe that only one point now separated the two teams.

Once again the aroused Trojan line held the powerful Irish attack. The crowd held its breath as Schwartz went back to punt. Then a great shout arose as Marchie got his foot on the ball and dropped it back on Southern Cal's 20. There were only four minutes left to play, and 80 yards stood between Southern Cal and the Irish goal posts. But Gus Shaver was undaunted. He dropped back and hurled a mighty spiral into the air. Sparling, speeding under it, made an "impossible" catch on the Notre Dame 40.

Now the crowd spoke with the voice of thunder, and the Southern Cal eleven could barely hear Shaver's signals. Another interference ruling put the ball on the 17-yard line. But now the Irish rose up in fury to stop Southern Cal's advance. Again, a penalty put the ball down to the ten. Southern California was thrown back. Then, with a minute left to play, Trojan guard Johnny Baker came out of the line to try a field goal. This was Baker's third game against the Irish, and he had yet to taste victory. Silence fell on Rockne Stadium. The ball came back, it went down. Baker swung his leg—and the white sleeves of referee Frank Birch shot up in the air to signal victory! Southern Cal had won, 16–14, and the two-year reign of the Trojans had begun.

107

Four years later, this great comeback was equalled by the Irish themselves.

In 1935 Ohio State was challenging Minnesota, not only for conference honors but for national ranking as well. The Buckeyes were coached by Francis Schmidt, a man who delighted in running up big scores. His Scarlet Scourge tore through opponent after opponent. Toward the end of the season Ohio State met Notre Dame, now coached by Elmer Layden of Four Horsemen fame. It was the first meeting between the two schools, and even though the Irish had a fine team they were not considered the equal of the Buckeyes.

Coach Elmer Layden, one of the original Four Horsemen.

There were 81,000 spectators in the stadium at Columbus as the Scarlet Scourge began to take Notre Dame apart. At the end of the first half, the score was 13–0 in Ohio State's favor. The Buckeyes had held the Irish to two first downs, while racking up nine themselves. They came out for the last half prepared to apply the crusher. But the Irish were bracing, even though a line of reserves now held the forward wall. Between this line and the splendid punting of Bill Shakespeare, Notre Dame held Ohio State scoreless in the third period. But the Irish had also failed to score. Ohio State's two-touchdown lead made the outcome seem a foregone conclusion as the Buckeyes punted out on the last play of the third quarter.

Notre Dame's Andy Pilney caught the punt and returned it 28 twisting yards down to the Buckeye 12. Suddenly the golden Irish helmets rose higher. The mighty crowd leaned forward. Was it possible? Andy Pilney's answer was a quick pass to Frankie Gaul on the 1-yard line. From there Steve Miller crashed over for Notre Dame's first touchdown. A groan shot up from Notre Dame's partisans as Ken Stilley's conversion kick hit the uprights and fell back. The score remained 13–6.

Two minutes later Notre Dame had the ball again and Andy Pilney was once more on the rampage. Running and passing flawlessly, he brought the ball down to the 1-yard line. Again Steve Miller tried to carry it over, but he fumbled! Ohio State recovered and Notre Dame's cause seemed doomed.

The Buckeye's young star, "Jumpin' Joe" Williams, seemed to have driven the last nail into the Irish coffin as he got away for 23 yards and put the ball at midfield. But the Fighting Irish had been well named. That battered line of reserves held again. Ohio State kicked out of bounds on Notre Dame's 22. There were only a few minutes left to play. Could Notre Dame possibly tie the score?

Once more it was Andy Pilney who gave the answer. He threw and caught passes to lead the Irish all the way down to the Buckeye 15. There was scarcely more than a minute left to play. Pilney dropped back. Spotting Mike Layden free in the end zone, he threw. Layden caught the ball, and bedlam broke loose in Columbus.

Then a great quiet came creeping over that vast throng. Quarterback Wally Fromhart went back to try the placement this time. As the ball came toward him a horde of scarlet jerseys converged on Fromhart. His foot dug into the turf, and the ball bounced harmlessly off that wall of Buckeyes.

Ohio State was still in front, 13–12. A gallant effort seemed to have come to an unsuccessful end.

Except that Ohio State fumbled the next time they got the ball and Notre Dame recovered!

Less than a minute to play, and once more the magnificent Pilney was fading back to pass. But Ohio State had every receiver covered. So Pilney ran. Three times he seemed to have been stopped or trapped, and three times he reversed his field. His madly churning legs carried him 32 yards down to the Buckeye 19-yard line. And that was the end of the game for Andy Pilney. He lay on the

sidelines, writhing in agony. He was placed on a stretcher, carried to an ambulance and rushed to the hospital.

All, it seemed, had been for naught. There was only time for a few more plays. Bill Shakespeare missed a pass. Dropping back again, he threw. The ball traveled 35 yards diagonally, and Wayne Millner suddenly appeared out of nowhere to catch it in the end zone.

Notre Dame was ahead, 18–13! No one cared when Marty Peters missed the kick. Ohio State had time for one play, but it was smothered by Notre Dame. The cliff-hanger of cliff-hangers had come to an end, and the riotous joy of the Irish was unalloyed when it became known that the gallant Andy Pilney had only pulled a ligament in his leg.

Three weeks later the great Jay Berwanger appeared in his last game for Chicago. The Maroon was not winning in those days. In the mid-thirties some educators were saying that there was too much emphasis on football in American colleges. Chicago was one of the institutions which had begun to deemphasize the sport. And it was the bad luck of Jay Berwanger to play for the Maroon at this time.

Individually, however, Berwanger's fame rivaled the collective celebrity of the great Minnesota teams of the period. And in the Chicago–Illinois classic of 1935, Jay Berwanger brought off his own cliff-hanger.

Late in the third period, Illinois was ahead 6–0. They punted. Jay Berwanger caught the ball at the 50 and went charging downfield, his knees churning high. The first tackler to hit him was stretched

Jay Berwanger, the unanimous A.P. All-Star choice who refused to turn pro.

out unconscious. Four more dove at him and fell back to the ground. Berwanger hurtled on. At last, on the 1-yard line, he was pulled down from behind. With typical modesty, he gave the ball on the next two plays to a teammate. But the Illinois eleven held. Then Jay Berwanger took the ball and went vaulting over the massed Illinois bodies for a touchdown.

Now came the vital try for point. Berwanger stood cooly with dangling arms. He kicked and the ball sped straight and true for the winning point! No wonder Berwanger's delirious teammates carried him from the field on their shoulders. No wonder that Berwanger became the first player in history to receive the Heisman Trophy, now awarded annually to collegiate football's most outstanding player. And no wonder another honor, probably greater, was to come his way.

In 1936 the National Football League held its first "draft" of college players. This was the system that was to make the pro sport. Losing teams were to get first chance at the college stars. In that way no one team could dominate the sport, no matter how wealthy or successful it might become. Jay Berwanger was the very first collegian to be chosen. He was picked by the Philadelphia Eagles, but despite the honor he refused to turn pro.

Slingin' Sam, the Passin' Man

In 1936 the pros held their second draft, and one by one the eligible college stars were chosen. The next-to-last choice went to the Boston Redskins, who had won the Eastern crown. George Preston Marshall, the Redskins' owner, was holding his breath. Would anyone select his choice before he had *his* chance?

No one did. When his turn came, Marshall jumped to his feet and yelled, "Sammy Baugh!"

As a youngster Sammy Baugh had been able to do anything with a ball— whether it was a basketball, baseball or football. But most of all he loved to throw a football.

He hung an old tire out in the back yard in Sweetwater, Texas, and began tossing footballs through it. Hour after hour he threw, until he could hit the middle almost without fail. Then he began to swing the tire before he threw, and soon he mastered hitting a moving target. Finally he began to run to his left or to his right, jumping and dodging imaginary tacklers, and then whipping the ball through the moving target.

Although he had mastered the pass, Sammy went out for end on his high school team. But after the coach had seen him rifle back a poorly thrown ball two or three times he put him in the backfield.

Oddly enough, Sammy became more famous as a baseball player in high school. His rifle arm enabled him to

"Slingin'" Sammy Baugh

make the long throw from third base, and he went to Texas Christian on a baseball scholarship. But in college he starred at football instead of baseball, and became perhaps the most outstanding triple-threat player in the country in 1936.

Why seven pro teams that could have chosen him let his name go by remains a mystery. At the time, of course, it was thought that the Southwest Conference was simply "pass-happy." In pro football a player couldn't pass like Baugh, the experts said. Those big pro linemen would teach him a little respect. But George Preston Marshall had seen Baugh play and he believed in him.

Marshall had never been a man to take another fellow's word for anything. It was he who had insisted that the title game of 1936 be played in New York, even though his team was based in Boston. Boston, he argued, simply would not support pro football. Harvard was the magic name in Beantown.

Already Marshall was planning to move his team to Washington. He was sure that, if he could get the sensational "Slingin'" Sammy Baugh, he would draw crowds there and make money.

After he got Baugh in the draft, Marshall let his coach, Red Flaherty, watch Sammy in a workout.

"That's the greatest passer football has ever seen," Flaherty said. "We'll take it all in thirty-seven."

They did. With Sammy slinging passes to ends Wayne Millner and Charlie Malone, or to backs Cliff Battles and Riley Smith, the Redskins romped to the Eastern Division title and defeated the Chicago Bears, 28–21, in the title playoff. A new star and a new team with a loyal

following of devoted fans had been born. Marshall, a born showman, hastened to make capital of both achievements. He brought marching bands and halftime extravaganzas into Griffith Stadium, and soon other owners were following suit. They were all eager to reap the profits of the steadily rising interest in the pro game.

Meanwhile, Sammy Baugh was developing into probably the best and most exciting back pro football has ever known. In 1940 he was magnificent. He completed 111 of 177 attempted passes for a glittering .627 average. He passed for the most touchdowns (12), for the longest gain (81 yards); and in one game against Philadelphia he punted for 85 yards.

Baugh's ability to punt is another reason that he cannot be kept off anyone's all-time team, either collegiate or professional. The majority of his 30 years as a player occurred during the time

when a star had to be equally good at defense and offense. Sammy Baugh was not only a first-class passer and a splendid punter; he could run, too, and he was a superb safetyman. Lanky Sammy was the League's best defender against passes, and he tackled with swift and sure finality. Tackling *him* however, was not so sure. During Baugh's last years as a pro, the poor blocking of his teammates left Sammy exposed to the red-dog rush of enemy linemen. Yet he habitually wrist-snapped the ball away for a successful pass, even when he was only a few inches from the ground.

Moreover, no other back made the transition from the singlewing to the T formation as Baugh did. After two seasons he had mastered it and was leading the Redskins to another Eastern title. Not until 1952 did the indestructible "Beanbag," as he was sometimes called, retire. He completed 11 straight passes in his last game. Behind him he left a hatful of records, most of which have now been surpassed.

Most Seasons: 16
Most Times Led League Passing: 6
Most Passes Completed: 1,709
Most Passes Thrown: 3,016
Most Touchdown Passes: 187
Highest Average: .567
Most Yards Gained: 22,085
Highest Average Gain: 12.5 yards

He was not only great, he was also durable. In his NFL career he wore out more than 60 pairs of shoes, 30 pairs of pants, 100 jerseys, seven helmets and two sets of thigh pads. His shoulder pads were like him: indestructible. From Sid Luckman, superb quarterback of the Bears and another NFL great, came the highest testimony of all.

"I like to just sit and watch him," Luckman said. "Every time he throws, I learn something. But nobody is ever going to equal him. Not anybody."

The Washington Redskin band performs during halftime.

Bowling Along

A Bowl game on New Year's Day is now as typically American as fireworks on the Fourth of July. And it all began because the city of Pasadena in California wanted to publicize its Tournament of Roses.

This was the annual New Year's festival begun at the end of the last century. Throughout the day there were parades with pretty girls tossing roses from gaily decorated floats. There were also speeches, foot races, races between horses and greyhounds, and a concluding event called the Tourney of the Rings. In the latter, mounted horsemen tried to lance a hanging circlet of roses, and from this the Tournament of Roses got its name.

But none of these events impressed the nation's newspaper editors. Crowds grew smaller each year. The tournament seemed to be dying. Then, in 1901, James Wagner, president of the tournament, thought it would be a wonderful thing if two famous colleges played each other in an intersectional football game. In the West the two top teams were California and Stanford. In the East, the likeliest prospects were Michigan, Georgetown and the Carlisle Indians. Two factors swung Wagner toward Michigan.

First, the Wolverines' incredible record of 501 points to 0 against ten opponents. Second, Michigan coach Hurry Up Yost was still smarting from his dismissal by Stanford because he had not gone to school there. Yost thought that the West Coast coaches had adopted the graduate-coaches-only rule because they were jealous of his success. He would be glad to play either California or Stanford for a chance to achieve at least a small revenge. Eventually Stanford was chosen to represent the West. On New Year's Day of 1902 some 8,000 fans saw the revenge-hungry Wolverines devour the Indians by a score of 49–0. Thus was born the granddaddy of all Bowl games.

But, the Wolverine rout had been too crushing. Fourteen years passed before the West Coast hazarded another challenge to the East. And in that 1916 game the West recovered its self-respect when Washington State defeated Brown, 14–0. As a result the tradition of a big Bowl game every New Year's Day became established.

The coming of radio helped to make the annual Rose Bowl games even more attractive, as well as lucrative. Later on, television sent profits skyrocketing, so that the first guarantee of $3,500—to be split between Stanford and Michigan—has increased to a guarantee of more than $200,000 apiece for the competing teams.

Although the Rose Bowl game was a success from 1916 on, the "Bowl" idea did not begin to spread until 1933. That year Miami sponsored a Palm Festival, changing the name to the Orange Bowl two years later. New Orleans came into the picture with the Sugar Bowl in 1935 and Dallas followed with the Cotton Bowl in 1937. These four—Rose, Orange,

Sugar and Cotton—dominated the New Year's Day football festivities until Jacksonville, Florida, added a fifth "prestige" bowl with the 'Gator Bowl in 1946.

There are, of course, other great games taking place at various times during the Christmas season. In 1925 the Shrine East–West Game was begun in San Francisco. Two teams of stars drawn from either side of the Mississippi play each other annually for the benefit of Shrine hospitals for crippled children. A North–South game is also played at this time, and the pros now have their Pro Bowl and the Playoff Bowl. There are also numerous other lesser bowls—so many, in fact, that in one season no less than 47 bowl games were played! After that the National Collegiate Athletic Association stepped in to cut the number of bowl games in half.

But new games such as the Gotham Bowl or the Liberty Bowl spring up each holiday season, while the established fixtures still send their invitation committees out scouting toward the end of each football year. By that time the list of undefeated teams has been narrowed and the potential champions have appeared. The college is then "invited" to this or that bowl. If the faculty is agreeable, then the decision is left to the team. Once, in 1937, a great Pittsburgh team refused to go to the Rose Bowl. The players voted to reject the invitation, 16 to 15. The seniors were tired and wanted their Christmas holidays; the players also wanted more "expense" money.

Another time one of the finest teams ever to come out of the East was completely overlooked in bowl selections.

This was Coach Andy Kerr's Colgate team of 1932. The Red Raiders were one of the few modern elevens to finish a season with their goal line uncrossed. They were eager to go to a bowl, but no one asked them. They went into football annals as the team that was "undefeated, untied, unscored-on—and uninvited."

Some teams such as Notre Dame had a "no bowl" policy. The Irish declined to go "bowling" from 1925 to 1969 when they went to the Cotton Bowl. Navy began to go after World War II, but Army has never gone to a bowl. Although Michigan played in the granddaddy game, the Big Ten followed a no-bowl policy from then until 1946. In that year it was agreed that the Pacific Coast champion and the Big Ten titlist would meet each other annually in the Rose Bowl. Illinois and U.C.L.A. were the first opponents under this agreement and in 1947 Illinois racked up the Bruins, 45–14. The following year Michigan repeated its 49–0 Rose Bowl debut, but this time its victory was at the expense of Southern Cal.

Before the two leagues decided to make the Rose Bowl an annual test of strength, teams from every section of the country appeared in the huge amphitheater at Pasadena. It was the West Coast against all comers, and some of the most thrilling games in football resulted.

At this time, the "Vow Boys" of Stanford were also making history. As freshmen, in 1932, these Stanford boys had vowed that they would never lose to Southern Cal. They never did, and because of their dedicated playing the

Stanford Indians were the only team to appear in the Rose Bowl three times in a row.

In the first of the games, played in 1934, the opponent was Columbia. A howl of derision went up when the Lions were selected to oppose the Indians. Eastern football was "decadent," critics said. Columbia played a "creampuff schedule." Furthermore, the Lions had been beaten by Princeton, 20–0. Could such a weak eleven stand up against such Stanford stars as Bobby Grayson, Horse Reynolds, Monk Moscrip, Keith Topping, Bones Hamilton and Frank Alustiza?

Lou Little, the Columbia coach, thought they could. The big man with the Roman nose and the gravelly voice was one of the game's best coaches, and he believed that his boys might just give the Stanford eleven a real game. Although Columbia's reserves might not have been enough to survive a schedule like mighty Michigan's, Coach Little was confident that on any one day they could play any team in the country on even terms.

Most of the country thought that the idea of pitting Columbia against Stanford was a joke. When the Lions trotted out onto the Rose Bowl's rain-soaked field, the crowd was chanting, "We want Michigan." At first their demand seemed justified. Led by Bobby Grayson, Stanford was pushing Columbia up and down the field. But the Indians could not score. And each time the valiant Lions managed to hold, slender Cliff Montgomery would punt his team out of danger again.

In the second quarter Montgomery

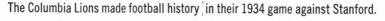

The Columbia Lions made football history in their 1934 game against Stanford.

lofted a high pass to end Tony Matal. Matal made a leaping catch and went skidding and splashing to the Stanford 17-yard line. On the next play Al Barabas fumbled and recovered for a yard loss. In the huddle, Montgomery whispered: "Let's give 'em old KF-79." It was Lou Little's favorite play, one devised for just such a situation. Blockers would switch assignments and Montgomery would have to do some fancy faking. He did. He handed off to Barabas, faked to another back and then pretended to be carrying the ball himself. Meanwhile, the key Stanford defenders were effectively blocked out by this surprise maneuver and Al Barabas went waltzing around end through a team that seemed to be standing still. A successful kick added a point to the touchdown, and that was the end of the scoring.

Next day, a California newspaper quoted from the Bible:

"Now Barabas was a robber."

The following year, 1935, the Vow Boys were pitted against Alabama. The Crimson Tide was coached by Frank Thomas, who had been a substitute quarter behind Harry Stuhldreher of the Four Horsemen. Knute Rockne had always admired Thomas' football brains and had recommended him for a coaching job. Of all the Rock's disciples— Harry Stuhldreher of Wisconsin, Jim Crowley of Fordham, Elmer Layden of Notre Dame, Harry Mehre of Georgia and Mississippi, Buck Shaw of Santa Clara, Clipper Smith of Villanova, Marchie Schwartz of Stanford and Rip Miller of Navy, to name a few—only Frank Leahy of Boston College and Notre Dame would rival Frank Thomas for the title of "the greatest." Thomas came to

Alabama to fill the shoes of the great Wallace Wade, whose last Alabama team had been perhaps his best, whipping Washington State in the Rose Bowl, 24–0.

By 1934 Thomas had fielded an eleven that many thought the equal of the mightiest of Minnesota powerhouses. It was led by Millard "Dixie" Howell and Riley Smith, with Don Hutson and Paul "Bear" Bryant as ends. This team powered its way to the Southern Conference title. So when it went west Stanford braced itself for a running game. But Alabama took to the airways. The band played "Dixie" that day as Dixie Howell passed, ran and caught passes in one of the finest of Rose Bowl individual performances. Smith, Hutson and Bryant backed him up with brilliant plays of their own. The final score was Alabama 29, Stanford 13. The Vow boys had failed again.

But the next year, 1936, they came through with a 7–0 Bowl victory over the Southern Methodist eleven that had topped Texas Christian and Sammy Baugh.

Three years later, two famous teams and two great coaches met in a great Rose Bowl game that football buffs still talk about. Howard Jones with Southern California was meeting Wallace Wade with Duke. Like the Colgate team of 1932, the Duke Blue Devils were that gridiron rarity—an undefeated, untied and *unscored-on* eleven. They had backs such as the peerless punter Eric "The Red" Tipton and powerful George McAfee, and they had a line known as The Seven Iron Dukes. In achieving their spotless record, they had held one of the finest of Pittsburgh teams scoreless.

117

The Blue Devils came into the Rose Bowl determined to keep Howard Jones' conference champions scoreless, too. Red Tipton punted the Trojans into trouble, and in the last quarter he shot out a 24-yard pass that set up what looked to be the game-winning field goal, scored by Ruffa. Duke's 3–0 lead looked good, and the Blue Devils' record was still spotless, when a substitute back named Doyle Nave came into the Southern Cal line-up. He completed seven straight passes, and had the West Coast crowd roaring and gasping as he brought the Trojans downfield. There were only forty-one seconds left to play, and the Seven Iron Dukes were charging madly, when Doyle Nave went back for his eighth pass.

The ball went straight into the arms of Al Krueger over the goal!

Thus the Rose Bowl became a place where reputations are won and lost, where gridiron legends are born and where hearts are likely to burst with joy or break with sorrow on the first day of every New Year.

After starring with the Duke Blue Devils, George McAfee went on to fame with the Bears. Here he makes a run after intercepting a Giant pass.

In the Wake of the Whizzer

In the years between the end of Minnesota's reign and the outbreak of World War II, college football supremacy rotated from section to section.

On the West Coast in 1937 the California Golden Bears won every game except for a tie with Washington, and they defeated undefeated Alabama in the Rose Bowl. The University of North Carolina was right behind in the Southern ratings, while in the East Harvard astounded itself and everyone else by beating Yale and finishing at the top of the Big Three for the first time since 1915. Holy Cross, under Dr. Eddie Anderson, was emerging as an Eastern power. The year before, the Crusaders had gone unbeaten, and they continued to shine in the thirties with such stars as "Bullet Bill" Osmanski.

Villanova and Lafayette were also outstanding, and Earl "Red" Blaik had perhaps his finest Dartmouth team, led by All-America Bob McLeod.

In fact, 1937 turned out to be one of the East's best years since the days when Penn and the Big Three considered football "their game." And the Panthers of Pittsburgh were the top team in the land.

The Pitt eleven was the scourge of the middle thirties. They played and beat the best teams from every section, and played mighty Notre Dame right off their schedule. From 1932 through 1937 Jock Sutherland's powerful Pittsburgh Panthers beat the Irish in five out of six

games and held them to a total of 15 points! "I'm through with Pittsburgh," Coach Elmer Layden told Grantland Rice. "We haven't got a chance. They not only knock our ears back but we are are no good the next week."

And yet, despite their giant line and backs like Biggie Goldberg, John Chickerneo, Curly Stebbins and Frank Patrick, Pittsburgh's mighty team could not defeat Jim Crowley's Fordham Rams.

In one of the most extraordinary football series on record, Fordham and Pitt had played to two successive scoreless ties. The Fordham line, coached by young Frank Leahy, had come to be known as "The Seven Blocks of Granite." (Vince Lombardi, later to become one of the most successful pro coaches, was one of the "Blocks.") But when Pitt and Fordham met in 1937, the experts said that this greatest of Sutherland teams would pulverize the Fordham granite. The final score?

Nothing to nothing.

For the third straight year The Battle of Futility had been waged without a point scored. Pitt finally won in 1938. That was the season when Jock Sutherland had his "Dream Backfield" of Goldberg, Chickerneo, Stebbins and Dick Cassiano. But Carnegie Tech upset this team, and Jock Sutherland quit college coaching. Pittsburgh, like Chicago, had decided there was too much emphasis on "big-time" football. So the "silent doctor" (he was a dentist) stepped down with a lifetime record of 111 victories, 20 defeats and 12 ties. Later he would coach the National Football League's Pittsburgh Steelers.

In the 1938 season the Southwest emerged as the top section. The players were still slinging the ball around down there, and a 150-pound quarterback named "Li'l Davey" O'Brien had taken over for Texas Christian University where Sammy Baugh left off. Little Davey was the leader and spark plug of a giant team that was rated as the best Coach Dutch Meyer ever produced at T.C.U. Some say it was the best in Southwestern Conference history. In the Sugar Bowl, against Carnegie Tech, O'Brien completed 17 of 28 passes and booted a field goal to lead his Horned Frogs to a 15–7 victory.

General Bob Neyland's greatest years at Tennessee began in 1938. During three seasons, the Volunteers won all thirty of their regular season games, beating Oklahoma in the Orange Bowl. But Southern Cal toppled them in the Rose Bowl, and Boston College conquered them in the Sugar Bowl. Neyland's stars were George "Bad News" Cafego and linemen Bowden Wyatt, Bob Suffridge and Ed Molinski.

The thirties also were characterized by the presence of more and more Negro youths starring for college teams. UCLA had a brilliant pair of backs named Kenny Washington and Jackie Robinson. Washington later had a brilliant pro career; Jackie Robinson, of course, was to become a baseball immortal with the Brooklyn Dodgers. Most outstanding of them all was Brud Holland, a two-time All-America end for Cornell. Before

120

Kenny Washington

Jackie Robinson

Holland there had been other Negro players, especially in pro ball, where there had never been a real problem of prejudice. Iowa had had a fine tackle in Duke Slater from 1919 through 1921, and Paul Robeson, later a world-renowned singer, had starred at end for Rutgers. As early as 1915, Fritz Pollard of Brown had been the first member of his race to make the All-America, but Brud Holland's appearance on the glamor team in the thirties was to herald the arrival of a flood of Negro All-Americas.

The Cornell eleven had a large helping of glamor in that decade. The Big Red came out of nowhere in 1939 to go undefeated and to "pull a Notre Dame" against Ohio State by spotting the powerful Buckeyes 14 points and beating them. It was Cornell's first all-victorious season since 1923, and Coach Carl Snavely thought so much of the pluck of his men that he told them, "I have had other good teams. But you—you fellows who have surprised me week after week with your development—you are the greatest. You are my team."

121

The Big Red had a powerhouse again in 1940, until it met Dartmouth in a game that is now celebrated in football lore. With four and a half minutes to play, Dartmouth led, 3–0. Cornell had the ball on its own 48-yard line. Little Pop Scholl, a 159-pound tailback, completed pass after pass, and the Big Red moved to the Dartmouth 5. Here, the Indians braced. Three line smashes got only as far as the one-foot line. With a few seconds left to play, Cornell tried to call a time out and was penalized five yards. On fourth down, Scholl's pass to Russ Murphy was knocked down in the end zone.

Dartmouth, it seemed, had triumphed. But what was this? Referee Red Friesell was signaling that Cornell had another down coming! He put the ball down on the 6-yard line again. Dartmouth protested and the crowd roared. Cornell thought that there had been a double offside nullifying the play, and went into the huddle again. Once more Scholl went back to pass, and once again he threw to Murphy in the end zone. This time Murphy caught it. The point was converted. Cornell had apparently won, 7–3.

But the score never got into the record books. After Coach Snavely saw the films of the game, he realized that there had been no offsides. His team had, in fact, been given a *fifth* down that wasn't due them. So Cornell graciously dashed off a telegram to Dartmouth saying: "Cornell relinquishes claim to victory and extends congratulations to Dartmouth." The Indians had won, 3–0, and the "fifth-down" game was history.

The loss was a big blow to Cornell, but scarcely as big as its disappointment the previous year at having seen the national title elude its splendid 1939 team. The honor that year stayed in the Southwest with Texas A&M and "Jarrin' John" Kimbrough. It was thought that the Aggies had played a harder schedule. They had also played an unusual brand of football for the Southwest—power, power and more power—with big John Kimbrough jarring rival linemen out of their shoes.

Another star in the 1939 season was Nile Kinnick of Iowa, one of the finest triple-threat players the game has ever seen. He was an excellent passer, one of the best kickers in the country and a dangerous runner. Dr. Eddie Anderson had come to the University of Iowa from Holy Cross, and he transformed the Hawkeyes from a Big Ten second-division team to a challenger for first place. Led by the 167-pound Kinnick, the Hawkeyes came within a whisker of the conference title. Kinnick won every individual honor possible: Heisman Trophy, Maxwell, Walter Camp and other trophies; Chicago *Tribune* silver football; All-America and Big Ten's most valuable player. Then Nile Kinnick, like so many other gallant American football stars, went on to give his life for his country during World War II.

Bryon "Whizzer" White was another brilliant All-America who served his country gallantly and well. During World War II he won two Bronze Stars during Pacific naval actions. He also made the years prior to America's entry into the war "the years of the Whizzer" in collegiate and pro football alike.

Whizzer White played for the University of Colorado. He had gone there on an academic rather than a football scholarship, and he had toughened his 190-pound frame by working summers in beet fields, lumber yards and as a railroad section hand. In 1937 the Whizzer put Colorado and the Rocky Mountain area on the football map. He led the country in scoring, rushing and total offense. He was a fast and shifty runner, and too strong to be handled by defensive backs playing him man for man. He could pass. He was a splendid punter. He blocked ferociously, kicked extra points and field goals, kicked off—and specialized in returning kickoffs and punts.

Whizzer was also his team's play-caller and a steady, confident leader. He rarely protested fouls or unfair calls by referees. Once, though, against Colorado College, the Whizzer was off to one of his long, twisting gains. The referee claimed that White's knee had touched the ground, and nullified the run. Everyone on the field knew that White's fingertips, not his knee, had touched turf. Whizzer said: "That was a quick whistle, Ref."

The referee penalized the team 15 yards. Back in the huddle, someone said to Whizzer: "Look, let's have no more of that. If we've got to play against twelve men, we'll do it." Unfortunately, the referee had his head in the huddle, too. He penalized Colorado all the way back to the three. With first down and 40 yards to go, Whizzer's teammates were laughing so hard they could barely huddle. "Do you think you can run it out?" the quarterback asked Whizzer. He nodded. He swept around end to the ten, and in the next three minutes scored three touchdowns.

"Whizzer" White,
the brilliant All-America from Colorado.

In the East, though, there were doubts about Whizzer's real ability. The Rocky Mountain area had never been famous for football. Sports writers were debating about just how good Colorado and Whizzer White really were.

The answer came in the Cotton Bowl. Colorado was matched against a powerful team from Rice Institute, in Texas. Led by Ernie Lain, the Rice eleven were Southwestern Conference champions.

It was obvious almost from the start that Colorado was overmatched. But Byron Whizzer White was also clearly the best man on the field. He ran from short punt formation and threw passes to give the Colorado Grizzlies a score in three minutes. Then he intercepted a pass to run 50 yards for another touchdown. Eventually Rice's power prevailed and the Owls triumphed, 28–14. But Whizzer had displayed his wares, and the nation was now convinced.

Shortly afterward the nation was astounded to learn that this star athlete —he was All-America in basketball as well as football—was also a star scholar. Whizzer White had won a Rhodes Scholarship in competitive examinations. Moreover, he had also refused the $15,000 salary offered him by the Pittsburgh Steelers, who wanted him to play pro ball.

That was a huge salary in those days. Although the pro game was steadily improving and the attendance was growing, the sport was still a poor relation of the collegiate game and far behind professional baseball. Whizzer's reluctance to play rather than continue his law studies was overcome, however, after Pittsburgh pointed out that he could play one season and enter Oxford at mid-year. He agreed and was an immediate sensation.

Pittsburgh won only 2 out of 11 games that year, but Whizzer White still led the league in ground-gaining, with a total of 567 yards. He achieved that record against tacklers eager to make him earn his huge salary. Tuffy Leemans, the Giant star, once slammed into Whizzer with the remark: "I always wondered what it felt like to get my hands on a $15,000 player."

After the season was over, Whizzer went to England. But his stay at Oxford was cut short by the outbreak of war in September, 1939. He returned to the States and entered Yale Law School. The pros came after him again. The Detroit Lions, who had bought up "rights" to Whizzer from the Steelers, suggested that he could play pro football while going to school. He did, and once again he was an outstanding player— the National League's leading rusher— and he was named All-Pro halfback. He also earned the respect of all who played with or against him. His love of the game was always obvious, as was his passion for his studies. When his team was on road trips and the other players were talking or playing cards, Whizzer was at work with his glasses, his pipe and his law books.

When Byron White entered the Navy in World War II, he was an outstanding intelligence officer. It was the Whizzer who interviewed young Lieutenant John F. Kennedy after PT-109 had been cut in two by a Japanese destroyer. The meeting deepened a friendship that had begun when the two young men were students in England together. After John Fitzgerald Kennedy became Presi-

In 1938 White played as a pro for Pittsburgh.
Here he is carrying the ball against the Los Angeles Bulldogs.

dent of the United States in 1960, one of his first appointments to the Supreme Court was Byron R. White.

Justice White, balding and bespectacled, but still a powerful, erect figure of a man in his black judicial robes, was one of the youngest Supreme Court justices ever appointed. But even while serving on the highest court in the land, he has never lost his love for football. When someone raises the old but untrue charge that football is a game for men of great brawn and little brains, the best answer is, "What about Whizzer White?"

125

T for Cinderella

During the 1940 and 1941 seasons, the young men of Europe were marching off to war while the youth of America headed for the football fields.

"Football is the American substitute for war," Frank Leahy said, and many Americans who believed that the United States could "stay out of this one" agreed with him.

Leahy, incidentally, was at Boston College during this period. He had come there in 1939, fielding a team that lost only to Florida during the regular-season games. The next year, the Eagles tore through seven opponents to average 32 points per game against approximately 4 points per game for the opposition. "Chuckin' Charley" O'Rourke, a 147-pound halfback, was the star. He operated behind a huge line, one that was rivaled only by the ponderous forward wall of an undefeated team from Georgetown University.

Under Jack Hagerty the Georgetown Hoyas from the nation's capital had been undefeated in twenty-three successive games. They had a line led by Augie Lio, a great tackler and kicker of field goals who would become a pro star, and a backfield sparked by big Jimmy Castiglia. Lio and Castiglia had been New Jersey high-school stars together, and it seemed that they and their teammates might be able to halt Leahy's high-flying Eagles.

The two teams met in what was called "The Battle of the Brobdingnagians." The players were so huge that they reminded sports writers of Brobdingnag, the mythical land of giants in *Gulliver's Travels*. But it was a Lilliputian, little Charley O'Rourke, who contributed the unforgettable performance. With two minutes left to play, Boston College led, 19–16. But the Hoyas had the Eagles backed up against their own goal. O'Rourke took the ball and retreated into the end zone. For a full half-minute he ran back and forth, twisting and dodging while the crowd roared and Georgetown tacklers frantically tried to corner him. Charley was deliberately "eating the clock" while giving up a two-point safety to protect Boston College's lead. After he had been downed, the Eagles kicked safely downfield from their own 20-yard line and went on to win, 19–18, in one of the most thrilling games in the annals of Eastern College football.

Even though Boston College completed an all-winning season and went on to defeat undefeated Tennessee in the Sugar Bowl, national laurels went elsewhere in the 1940 season. Bernie Bierman had put together another powerhouse at Minnesota. Once again Bierman's formula was maximum power brought to bear on the enemy's weakest point. Bill Daley, a powerful line bucker, and fleet Bruce Smith were the stars. Although this 1940 team of Bierman's was not colorful, it was a fighting one which won all its games, coming from behind six times to do so.

Where they played against Michigan,

the Minnesota Gophers had to stop probably the most exciting player to come out of the Big Ten since Red Grange. He was Tommy Harmon, "Old Ninety-Eight," whose number was retired after he scored three touchdowns against Ohio State in his final game. Harmon's touchdown total was 33, compared with the 31 scored by Grange in four fewer games. He also passed and kicked the extra points and scored 237 points in three seasons. Like Red Grange, Tommy Harmon flashed through enemy backfields with sudden deceptive bursts of speed. He rarely let a tackler get more than his hands on him. Often his jerseys were torn from his back, and it was not a rare thing to see Old Ninety-Eight steaming along without his number. The moment he cut through tackle and got a block, he reversed his field and was off. Generally the man who gave him that block was Forest Evashevski, who was later to compile a fine coaching record at Iowa. Harmon often said that he would never have become famous if "the Ape," as Evashevski was called, had not been blocking for him.

The Ape was blocking when Michigan met Minnesota in 1940 and took a 6–0 lead. It looked as if the Wolverines, under Coach Fritz Crisler, would get another touchdown after a Gopher kick was blocked on the Minnesota 3-yard line. But the big Gopher line held. Harmon was stopped. His pass was intercepted for a touchback, after which Bruce Smith went whirling 80 yards for the score. Minnesota won 7–6.

The following year Minnesota was even better. Bull-like Bill Daley was back, and so were Bruce Smith and running lineman Helge Pukema. Bernie

Bierman thought that this 1941 team was second only to the Gophers of 1934. They, too, played straight-ahead power football. In this respect the Gophers of 1941 were the exact opposite of the Stanford Indians of 1940, the team that many experts had thought was better than Minnesota that year.

Minnesota had been at the top of the Associated Press poll in 1940. But the Helms Foundation pronounced that Stanford was better. That may have been because the Stanford eleven was a "Cinderella team" which fired the public imagination.

Stanford had not won a conference game in 1939. Neither had its new coach, Clark Shaughnessy from Chicago. In fact, the tall, lean, driving Shaughnessy was a man without a job when Stanford hired him. Chicago had dropped football for good at the close of the 1939 season.

Shaughnessy did not impress Palo Alto when he arrived on campus and said, "Stanford will use the T formation."

Protests almost loud enough to echo from coast to coast followed that announcement. The T? The old-fashioned T that had gone out before nose guards and moleskin pants came in? Some wags asked Shaugnessy if he was sure he hadn't meant tackles-back. Shaughnessy shrugged off all the barbs. His was one of the finest of football minds, and he knew what he was talking about. *His* T was to be based upon speed and deception. Moreover, he had quickly seen that he had just the right backfield material to make it work.

There was little Frankie Albert, a so-so tailback in the single wing, but a slick ball handler and left-handed passer who exactly suited Shaughnessy. There was Norm Standlee, a 220-pound bone-crushing fullback who could turn on the speed the moment he broke into the clear. Pete Kmetovic could start like a flash; he was just the shifty runner to burst through a sudden opening and dance through a broken field. Last, there was Hugh Gallarneau, a peerless blocker. Faster than Kmetovic, though not as quick-starting, he had more power and possessed an instinct for picking the right hole.

Like so many other great backfields before them, this foursome fitted together perfectly. But they, too, doubted their new coach's sanity.

"I thought he was crazy," Hugh Gallarneau said. "I was a halfback and when Shaughnessy diagramed a play which sent the halfback into the line without a blocker ahead of him, I laughed."

Laughing had once been a habit with the losing Indians. California sports writers had scorned them as "The Laughing Boys" who would rather crack jokes than crack a line and win games.

Clark Shaughnessy's forbidding expression discouraged laughter. There were no jokes while he drilled them twice a day and held skull sessions at night. Fake, fake, fake, he taught them. Speed and deception were to take the place of blocking. Backs were to scoot through holes which would close as suddenly as Frankie Albert's sleight-of-hand tricks with the ball would open them.

Stanford began to win. The Indians became a Cinderella team. They trampled San Francisco, 27–0, beat Oregon, 13–0, nipped Santa Clara, 7–6, and took

Washington, 26–14. Football fans not only gaped at this record, they were open-mouthed at the Stanford ball-handling. Half the time they didn't even know who had the ball until either Gallerneau, Kmetovic or Standlee appeared in the enemy secondary—or Albert lifted his left hand to throw.

Albert was a magician. The high-spirited little quarterback got better each week, and Shaughnessy winced every time he was tackled. Once, in scrimmage, Albert went down and didn't get up. Shaughnessy moaned. Albert groaned and the coach called wildly for a doctor. Then Albert jumped to his feet with a grin.

"I just wanted to see if you'd miss me, coach," he quipped.

Southern Cal would certainly not have missed him in its annual contest with Stanford. Albert put this big game away with a play that Shaughnessy had outlined between halves. One of the Trojan linebackers had been coming up on Standlee fast on end runs. Albert faked a pitchout to Standlee; Kmetovic faked a block on the eager linebacker—and then slipped past him to take Albert's pass for a touchdown, Stanford University won, 21–7, and finished its season unbeaten.

But in the annual Rose Bowl playoff the miracle comeback of Shaughnessy and Stanford threatened to come to an end. The powerful Cornhuskers of Nebraska seemed to be scoring the upset of the season. Twice Nebraska took the lead, and twice the Wizards of Palo Alto fought back. Behind by a score of 13–7, they turned it into a tie with Frankie Albert's long pass and Hugh Gallarneau's leaping catch. Then Stanford went ahead on Albert's place kick, and drew out of reach after Pete Kmetovic caught a punt on the Nebraska 40 and went drifting like a wraith through a horde of hurtling Cornhuskers to plant the ball across the line.

Stanford won, 21–13. The Cinderella Team had made one of the most sensational comebacks in history—and so had the despised old T formation.

Clark Shaughnessy, the man who brought the T formation and victory to Stanford.

T.N.T.!

The Chicago Bears, with whom Clark Shaughnessy had been associated during his days at Chicago University, had also been using the T formation. They had been using the same idea of a man in motion. Before the ball was snapped, a back would go trailing off to his right or his left. Sometimes an end would line up 15 yards wide.

Rival teams instructed their linebackers to follow the man in motion or to key on the spread end. The Washington Redskins did this and beat the Bears, 7–3. Nevertheless, the Bears won the Western Division title. They were to meet the Redskins for the league championship.

In between the end of his unbeaten season and the Rose Bowl triumph, Clark Shaughnessy helped Halas and assistant coach Ralph Jones of the Bears prepare for the playoff. They studied motion pictures of the last Washington game, and dropped any play that had been stopped consistently. They took the successful plays and devised new variations from them. They also made the Chicago players study the films and analyze their own mistakes until they were red-eyed.

But most important of all, Shaughnessy set up a "counter" play. This meant that the play was to go "against the flow" of the man in motion. If one of the Chicago backs was trotting off to his right and the Redskin secondary was shifting to meet him, then the play would be run to the left.

Sid Luckman, the Bears' splendid quarterback.

By the time of the playoffs the Bears were in a fighting mood. The Redskins' George Preston Marshall had made headlines by claiming that the Bears were "cry-babies" and "front runners."

When the two teams met on the field, Chicago soon got the ball. Sid Luckman, the Bears' splendid quarterback, immediately set about testing the Washington defenses, to discover if they were the same as in the 7–3 defeat. They were. Washington's secondary had keyed on the spread end and had trailed

George McAfee as he went in motion to the right. McAfee carried the ball for eight yards on that play, but the important thing was that Washington was still following "the flow."

Now came the big play. McAfee went trotting to the right and Sid Luckman faked to the other halfback, Ray Nolting, driving straight ahead into the right side of his line. Bullet Bill Osmanski, the fast-starting fullback, also faked right. He twisted his body in that direction, "with the flow," but did not move his feet. And it was then that he took the ball from Luckman and slanted toward his own left tackle. The hole was supposed to open there. But it didn't. Still, the Redskin defense was overshifted with the flow, and Bullet Bill went bellying wide around his left end to break into the clear.

He went racing down the left sideline with only two men, Ed Justice and Jimmy Johnston, in position to head him off. It appeared that they would nail him on their own 35-yard line. But George Wilson of Chicago had come tearing over from his right-end position. He hit Johnston with a blind-side block and knocked him into Justice. Both went sprawling out of bounds, and Osmanski continued on his way for the touchdown.

From then on the game was a rout. The score was 28–0 at the half and 73–0 at the end of the game. The Bears did everything right, and they drove the Redskins mad with their counter plays. By the time the game came to a close, the officials had nearly run out of footballs. So many had been lost by extra-point kicks into the stands that the Bears were asked not to kick for point anymore. They obliged by passing—and completed two!

Thus did the T formation explode on the football world during that memorable year in 1940. Stanford had dazzled the collegians with the T and now the Bears had stunned the pros. From that year on, the T formation was to take over in football.

"Bullet Bill" Osmanski—
first of Holy Cross,
then a star with the Bears.

Touchdown Twins

From the moment that the T formation leaped into prominence, there were coaches at work modifying it.

Don Faurot of Missouri, one of football's finest tacticians, was probably the first innovator. He developed the "split T" after his superb tailback, "Passin' Paul" Christman, was graduated.

In 1941 Faurot stationed his linemen wide apart to open up the defense. His three "setbacks" were also spread wide apart. His quarterback was to slide laterally along either side of the line. From this attack the quarter operated the "option" or "keeper" play. He could dart through holes if enemy linemen kept their eyes on his wide-circling backs. If the linemen went for him, then he pitched out to the backs. Or else, if he had sucked the secondary in close, he dropped back to pass.

With just a good quarterback and a supply of fast, versatile men, Faurot proved that this split T could put greater pressure on the defense and also could spring men into the open more often. With it, the Tigers of Missouri were beaten only by powerful Ohio State in 1941, and they went to the Sugar Bowl, where Fordham upset them, 2–0.

During the following season—the start of the "war years" that ran from 1942 through 1945—the T really caught on. Faurot's variation was ideal for colleges that were short on both good players and coaching staffs. Freshmen were made eligible to play but, even so,

dimout regulations curtailed practice sessions under floodlights.

In 1942 the Rose Bowl was moved to Durham, North Carolina, because it was feared that a West Coast stadium filled with 90,000 people might tempt Japanese naval aircraft. Duke, the host team, was beaten there by Oregon State, 20–16. The Army–Navy game was played at Annapolis for the first time since 1893 because of a ban on running railroad specials. Instead of the usual throng of more than 100,000 people, fewer than 12,000 saw the game. The Yale–Princeton game was played in New York for the first time since the nineties. There was a drastic drop in attendance everywhere, until President Roosevelt decided that the sport should be kept alive during the war. Football's value in keeping home morale high and in conditioning young men was recognized.

Nevertheless, gas rationing and transportation shortages continued to make things difficult for traveling teams during the war years. As early as 1942 travel difficulties wrecked an undefeated season for Ohio State. Twenty-one players became ill as the Buckeyes journeyed to Madison to play Wisconsin, and Ohio State was upended, 17–7.

The uncertain nature of the sport produced a season of upsets. Boston College and Georgia Tech came close to the end of the season with ratings of first and second, respectively. But underdog Holy Cross walloped Boston College

55–12; and a fine Georgia team routed the Ramblin' Wrecks, 34–0. Georgia, incidentally, could boast of having within its ranks the 1942 Heisman Trophy winner—the peerless Frankie Sinkwich, best known for having played the previous season with his broken jaw in a cast. The Georgia eleven, coached by Wally Butts, also won its first Southeastern Conference title in 1942. Nevertheless, good as the Bulldogs were, the national championship went to the Buckeyes of Ohio State.

Their earlier loss to Wisconsin had been a fluke, the AP pollsters decided, and the decision was a personal triumph for Coach Paul Brown. He was in his

Angelo Bertelli

second year at Ohio State, having come there from a sensational career at Severn Academy and Massillon High. He was to go on and make the Cleveland Browns a power among the pros and to become the only man to coach champions on every level: high school, prep school, college and professional. Brown's star at Ohio State was 160-pound Les Horvath, the 1944 Heisman winner. His

offense was 75 percent single wing and 25 percent T.

The next year it was all T, but that season the Fighting Irish were on top.

Frank Leahy had installed the T a year earlier with Angelo Bertelli in charge. Notre Dame won 7 games, lost 2 and tied 2. But in 1943 the Irish had one of the most powerful teams in their history. Bertelli set every kind of passing record for Notre Dame, some of which still stand. In mid-season, however, Bertelli went off to Parris Island to become a Marine—later he fought at Guam and Iwo Jima—and young Johnny Lujack took his place. The Irish still rolled through Army and Northwestern and got past powerful Iowa Pre-Flight by 14–13.

The last game was against Great Lakes Naval Training Station. As in the First World War, Great Lakes had the team of teams. Its roster was crowded with former college stars and studded with All-Americas. For all but 30 seconds Notre Dame held the sailors in check. But then a desperation last-down pass from Steve Lach, formerly of Duke, went 46 yards for a touchdown and Great Lakes won, 19–14.

After that Frank Leahy went into the Navy. Even so, Notre Dame was again winning games in 1944—until the Irish met Army.

In 1944 the Cadets had what was easily the finest team in Army history, and it may very well have been the finest football team in college history. The Cadets were coached by Red Blaik. Three years earlier, Army, humiliated by Penn, 48–0, had lured Blaik away from Dartmouth and home to West Point. Blaik began to build a team. When the "Touchdown Twins" became eligible to play in 1944, he knew he had a winning outfit.

Few running combinations in history have fired the football imagination as did Glenn Davis and Felix "Doc" Blanchard. Davis was known as "Mr. Outside." Swift as the wind, superbly conditioned at 175 pounds, he went wide around the ends, cutting back with a devastating change of pace or faking oncoming tacklers out of their shoes. Blanchard was "Mr. Inside." He was big and bruising at 205 pounds, but he could turn on the speed once he had burst the enemy middle and broken into the clear. Playing with this pair were such other first-class players as huge Barney Poole and Tex Coulter on the line, and the versatile Doug Kenna—and later the matchless Arnold Tucker—at quarterback.

Army, in 1944, rolled to an incredible 504 points. Thirteen years of defeat at the hands of Notre Dame were avenged by an unheard-of 59–0 slaughter, the worst beating in Irish history. Navy, which had not lost to Army in six years, and which boasted many college stars who had transferred to Annapolis, was beaten by a score of 23–7. Penn, the humiliator of 1940, was torn apart, 62–7. The Cadets averaged 56 points a game and stood second only to Hurry Up Yost's point-a-minute team of 1904. They had averaged 58.9.

The team was so good that Red Blaik could say that the best college game he saw all season was the inter-squad scrim-

West Point's fabulous "Touchdown Twins"— Glenn Davis (left) and Felix Blanchard.

mage in which alternate Army teams traded two touchdowns apiece.

The next year, Blaik insisted that Army was even better. The Touchdown Twins were rampaging as before and they had the gifted quarterback, Arnold Tucker, to guide them. They tore through all opponents for a total of 412 points, powdering Penn by a score of 61–0, ripping Navy, 32–13, and swamping Notre Dame, 48–0, thereby handing the Irish their second worst defeat to go with the one administered the previous year. The Cadets were again national champions in the last year of World War II.

In 1946 the Black Knights from West Point were again galloping along. But by 1946 all the stars who had interrupted their schooling to serve their country were back on campus again. So were the coaches. The skeptics sneered that Army wouldn't be playing high-school kids this season. But in the second game,

against a star-studded Oklahoma team coached by Jim Tatum, the Cadets won, 21–7. Then, after beating Cornell, they toppled a fine Michigan eleven, 20–13. The scoffers began to hold their tongues.

By the time Army came to the game with Notre Dame, the Black Knights had won 25 victories in a row. Notre Dame, though, was also undefeated. Frank Leahy had returned to South Bend and put together another splendid machine. The Irish were determined to avenge those two horrendous wartime wallopings. But Earl Blaik was equally eager to gain his first victory over a Leahy-coached team. The game was billed as "The Battle of the Century." There were 74,000 screaming fans in Yankee Stadium as the Touchdown Twins and their cohorts and Johnny Lujack and his mates took the field.

And the contest ended in a scoreless tie.

"Doc" Blanchard (35) weaves away as three Wolverines close in to spill him during a 1945 Army–Michigan game.

Bill Dudley All the Way

In 1940, the year the Chicago Bears went on their 11-touchdown rampage against the Redskins, the National Football League decided that it needed a high commissioner. The position was given to Elmer Layden, then coach of Notre Dame, in 1941.

Layden's job during the next five years was to try to hold the league together in the face of the dwindling crowds that resulted from wartime restrictions. Moreover, the league's annual flow of star players from the ranks of the college seniors had been cut to a trickle. The stars were going into the service, and undoubtedly some of the service elevens like the Great Lakes and Iowa Preflight teams would have been able to play the pros on even terms.

One star, however, did turn pro in those lean years, and he turned out to be one of the greatest of all time.

"Bullet" Bill Dudley had been the nation's leading ground-gainer in his last season with the University of Virginia, and he was named the Maxwell Trophy winner for 1941. The following season he was playing for the Pittsburgh Steelers under Dr. Jock Sutherland. And the NFL fans gasped to see this tiny tailback making monkeys of some of the league's famed 300-pound behemoths.

Bill Dudley had always been outweighed. At high school in Bluefield, Virginia, he was a 136-pound halfback. At the University of Virginia he weighed only 152 pounds. When he entered the pro ranks with the Pittsburgh Steelers, he weighed 170 pounds and stood five feet nine inches tall. How he got his nickname of Bullet Bill remains a mystery. He was not that fast. Once, in a sprint race before an All-Star game, Dudley came in fifteenth in a field of sixteen. But after the game began, he ran back a kickoff for 98 yards and a touchdown.

Dudley's secret was his quick start and his deceptive change of pace. He could cut back or reverse his field at full speed. Moreover, he could kick placements, punt, pass, and he was so good on pass defense that Steve Owen would call him "the best defensive back in the league." Best of all, Bullet Bill Dudley was fearless.

He came to Pittsburgh in 1942 with a bad ankle. But in his first game against the Philadelphia Eagles he still managed to break loose for a 55-yard touchdown run. The following week, against the Redskins, his ankle gave out and he had to be carried from the field. But he returned for the second half with his ankle taped. He took the kickoff and went whirling away for a touchdown.

Bill's fearlessness also carried over onto the practice field. In one of Dudley's first workouts with the Steelers, the dour Dr. Sutherland snapped at him for missing a number of passes.

"It would be a durn sight easier," Bill drawled, "if you'd use different colored jerseys so I could tell the receivers from the defenders."

A hush came over the practice field.

Bill Dudley (left), of the Pittsburgh Steelers, chats with a former Michigan star turned pro—Tom Harmon.

No one ever dared speak to the grim doctor that way.

"Are you coaching this team?" Sutherland asked icily.

"No, sir, I am not," Bill said calmly.

"Then you take orders like everyone else," the doctor snapped.

That was the beginning of Bullet Bill's difficulties with the unbending drillmaster of the Smoky City. They were to multiply after Dudley went into the Army Air Corps and came back to Pittsburgh to star for the 1946 team—Sutherland's best. Even though Dudley led the league in rushing and the Steelers in interceptions, he could not get along with Dr. Jock. Neither could most of the other players, who revolted against Sutherland that year and forced him to soften some of his iron regulations. Dudley merely asked to be traded—and he was, to Detroit.

Bullet Bill had been the NFL's Most Valuable Player in the 1946 season, and while he played with Detroit, and later with Washington, he was the last of the full-time greats. In 1950 the NFL adopted the free-substitution rule which introduced the modern pro game. With the gates steadily increasing, the league teams could afford squads of 35 men. Coaches could train offensive and defensive teams. Specialists appeared. The big man who was hard to move and was fast enough to rush the passer was wanted on the defensive team's forward wall. The fast back who could also tackle and run back intercepted passes for yardage went into the defensive secondary. On the offensive teams were the best passers, runners, blockers and pass receivers. And of course there was the man who came into the game only to kick placements or to punt.

The age of the specialist, with the accent on the forward pass, had actually begun in 1945. In that year Bob Waterfield led the Rams (then in Cleveland) to the league title. Thereafter, no team would win a title without a great quarterback at the helm. In 1946 it was Sid Luckman and the Chicago Bears; in 1947 Passin' Paul Christman and the Chicago Cardinals; in 1948 and 1949 one-eyed Tommy Thompson of Tulsa put the Philadelphia Eagles on top. The following year it was Otto Graham and the Browns; in 1951 it was Waterfield and Norm Van Brocklin with the Los Angeles Rams. Bobby Layne and the Detroit Lions did it in 1952 and 1953; Graham was on top again in 1954 and 1955. In 1956 the elderly gentleman from Mississippi, Chuckin' Charley Conerly, led the Giants home; and Layne was the star again in 1957. Johnny Unitas, the Cinderella slinger, brought the Baltimore Colts out of nowhere to the top in 1958 and 1959. In 1960 it was Van Brocklin again, this time with Philadelphia. For the next two years Bart Starr shone for the Green Bay titlists; and in 1963 Billy Wade put Chicago out in front.

All were stars and all were specialists, and everyone to whom they passed or handed the ball or yelled for a block was a specialist in his own right, too.

But Bill Dudley, like Jim Thorpe and Bronko Nagurski and Ernie Nevers, specialized in everything. And the strange truth is that this small man, who could also pass and lead his league in rushing, would probably—if he played

Bart Starr carries the ball for the Packers.

Johnny Unitas hands off to a Colt teammate.

in today's age of specialists—be put into the defensive secondary to block passes and run back punts. Kickoff and punt returns were his specialty. His average was thirty yards a try. He always fielded every punt that came his way, trying to get even a single extra yard for his team. It was this determination that led to what was perhaps his greatest runback.

Playing for the Redskins against the Steelers, he was back in safety when Joe Geri boomed a diagonal 60-yard punt across the field. It looked as if the ball would surely either sail into the end zone or go out of bounds in the "coffin corner." Bullet Bill Dudley pursued it, but no one in the stadium thought he had a chance to come near it. Twenty-one players stood stock-still watching him. And, with his feet planted firmly in bounds, his hands reaching out of bounds, he caught the ball! Then Dudley looked inquiringly at the referee. Fair? The referee nodded, and Bullet Bill took off.

He faked one oncoming tackler into the turf and went up the sidelines while his teammates suddenly came awake and formed a wall of blockers. Ninety-six yards later he was over the enemy goal.

It was one of the most astonishing runs in pro history, and it capped the career of one of the game's most remarkable players. With it, in 1950, the era of the two-way player came to an end.

Leahy Leads the Irish Back

After Knute Rockne's champions had defeated Army 7–0, in 1929, the Rock's old friend, Bob Zuppke of Illinois, began explaining to the Irish players just how they had won. In concluding, the Dutch Master asked: "Any questions?"

"Yes, sir," said a young tackle, fingering his mouth. "Can you tell me which Cadet knocked out this tooth?"

The remark was typical of Francis William Leahy. Like those Tennessee battlers coached by Fighting Bob Neyland, he would swap a tooth for a touchdown any day. And the one thing which this handsome young man from Winner, South Dakota, wanted to be was a winner.

He was. In eleven years of coaching at Notre Dame, he gave the Irish four national championships and came within a shade of winning two others. His Notre Dame teams won 87 games, lost 11 and tied 9. His record was second only to that of the immortal Knute Rockne, who had a mark of 105–12–5 in 13 years. Because Leahy won more titles in fewer years, and played generally harder schedules, his record may actually have been better than Rockne's. Yet the winner from Winner was as unpopular in the football world as the Rock was beloved.

Although Leahy was a pleasant man and always tried to be courteous to people, he had little of Rockne's warmth. He was typical of the successful coach of the postwar years. Like Earl Blaik of Army, Fritz Crisler of Michigan, Biggie

Frank Leahy of Notre Dame.

Munn of Michigan State and, later, Bud Wilkinson of Oklahoma, he was a perfectionist. His personality seemed to fit that description. Rockne could win a game by five touchdowns and say to his defeated rival, with an impish grin, "You nearly had us, there." And the coach would accept the barb and still like Rock. But Leahy might say, "We were extremely fortunate to have scored at all," and the rival coach would hate him. The Master, as Leahy came to be called, was always predicting disaster

141

for his team. A rival coach picked to lose by three touchdowns would read Saturday morning's sports page and find The Master gloomily forecasting "an Irish debacle." Before each season he would say something like, "Notre Dame will field a representative aggregation this year," and the coaches who knew that the South Bend campus was blooming with 240-pound tackles and rifle-armed quarterbacks would grind their teeth. But the president of Notre Dame may have hit upon the real reason for Leahy's unpopularity when he said, "The trouble with Frank is that he wins too much."

For those Leahy-coached teams of the postwar years really did seem invincible. Throughout four years they were undefeated in 39 straight games, losing to Purdue in the second game of the 1950 season. The parade of Irish stars at that time seemed endless.

On the roster of the 1946 national champions—the team that tied Army and went on to win the rest—there were no less than four All-Americas: linemen George Connor, Johnny Mastrangelo and George Strohmeyer and quarterback Johnny Lujack. On the 1947 championship team, still led by Lujack, was perhaps the finest pair of ends in collegiate history: Jim Martin and huge Leon Hart. Both were to be pro stars and Hart was to be that rarity of modern football: a three-time All-America. The 1947 club also boasted five players who have been elected to the All-Time Notre Dame team: Connor, Hart, Lujack, Martin (as a tackle) and guard Bill Fischer. Connor as a 235-pound tackle, Fischer as a 240-pound guard and Hart as a 265-pound end reflect both the power of that team and the coming of the giant American

athlete, whose diet and workouts with weights and isometrics make him tower over even such "monsters" of the past as Pudge Heffelfinger or Bronko Nagurski.

But that 1947 powerhouse of Leahy's was challenged by eleven lighter speedsters from the north. The team was Michigan, coached by Fritz Crisler, who had shifted from Princeton. The Wolverines didn't have the Irish power, but they had more speed than they could use. They also had "two platoons." In 1945, the canny Crisler realized he didn't have the depth to stop Army. So he trained two elevens, one for defense and the other for offense. In 1947 he was using the same system, and his whirl-away Wolverines, led by a pair of swifties named Bob Chappuis and Bump Elliott, also bowled over all opposition. But after Notre Dame trampled Southern Cal, 38–7, the AP poll decided the Irish were the best.

Then Michigan went to the Rose Bowl to slaughter the very same team of Trojans by a 49–0 score. The AP held a second poll in which Michigan edged out the Irish. But it was decided that the first poll was official, and Notre Dame went into the books as the champion.

In the next season the roles were reversed. Bennie Oosterbaan, the three-time All-America end of the Twenties, was now the Michigan coach. Crisler was the athletic director. With Chuck Ortmann filling the shoes of Bob Chappuis, with Pete Elliott replacing his brother, Bump, and with end Dick Rifenburg catching passes, this team was ranked as the best in the country.

Once again, it was a neck-to-neck race between the Wolverines and the Irish. But in Notre Dame's last game, the Tro-

Johnny Lujack (center) of Notre Dame and Bobby Layne (right) of the University of Texas receive their equipment for the annual 1949 collegiate All-Star game against the NFL champions.

jans of Southern California stunned Leahy's team with a 14–14 tie.

The next season, 1949, Frank Leahy had his fourth and last national champion. Although Kyle "Killer" Rote and Southern Methodist gave the Irish a bad scare, the Notre Dame team, with quarterback Bob Williams and Emil "Six-Yard" Sitko in the backfield, and the great Hart and Martin still at ends, went on to win every game. Hart became the only lineman ever to win the Heisman Trophy.

Leahy's fortune failed for a few years thereafter. But in 1953 he was back with what looked like another champion. Johnny Lattner, a Heisman winner and one of two players to win the Maxwell Trophy twice, became known as "the bread-and-butter player" of that season. But after winning eight games, the Irish were held to a 14–14 upset tie by Iowa— and the number one rating was awarded to unbeaten Maryland.

That was the year Frank Leahy quit coaching. He had collapsed between halves of the Georgia Tech game. His doctors told him that the pressure of being coach at the nation's number one football campus would kill him. Young Terry Brennan, who had played for Leahy's 1946 and 1947 champions and run back a kickoff against Army for a touchdown, was to succeed him as coach of the Irish.

If his two seasons at Boston College are included, Frank Leahy's teams won a total of 107 games, lost 13 and tied 9. During his career as a coach there had been other fine leaders—men such as Blaik, Wilkinson, Crisler, Oosterbaan, Tatum, Munn, Bell of S.M.U., Lynn Waldorf of California, Wally Butts of Georgia and Bob Higgins of Penn State. There had been other stars; for instance, Georgia's Charley Trippi and Johnny Rauch, Harry Gilmer of Alabama and the peerless Otto Graham of Northwestern, Doak Walker of S.M.U., Bobby Layne of Texas, Chuck Bednarik of Penn and Choo-Choo Justice of North Carolina. Yet, it would be hard to say that Frank Leahy was not truly The Master of his era.

143

A New Pro League

On September 3, 1944, Arch Ward, the sportswriter who had originated the annual All-Star Game between the stars and the pro champions, wrote in the Chicago *Tribune:*

"This is an announcement of the organization of the All-America Football Conference, a new major professional league which will begin operation in 1945."

It did, and for the second time in its history the National Football League found itself threatened by a competitor. Actually, the first rival had not been a very serious one. Pyle, the promotor who took Red Grange on tour, had set up an American League with nine teams. Even though "Red Grange's New York Yankees" were the prime attraction, the league lasted only one season.

There had also been minor leagues patterning themselves after organized baseball. These circuits came and went, and the NFL survived them all. Like the Ivy Leaguers of football's infancy, the NFL teams thought that pro football was "our game."

In fact, when the new All-America Conference teams wrote to NFL Commissioner Elmer Layden asking for a meeting, Layden brushed them off with a snort.

"Let them get a football first," he said.

But the new league had more than a football. Even though it did not get started until 1946, it had teams in Los Angeles, Chicago, San Francisco, New York, Buffalo, Baltimore, Cleveland and, for a time, Miami and Brooklyn. They had millionaires backing each franchise, and they were able to sign such stars as Frankie Albert, the great Glenn Dobbs of Tulsa—last of the triple-threat tailbacks—and Bob Steuber of Missouri. They also had Lou Groza, Spec Sanders, George Ratterman, Angelo Bertelli, Y. A. Tittle, Buddy Young and Ben "Automatic" Agajanian, the man who had lost the toes of his right foot in a railway accident and found that it made him kick field goals better. The All-America Football Conference also had coaches such as Red Dawson of Tulane, Clem Crowe, Jimmy Crowley—and Paul Brown.

Brown had been coaching the Great Lakes powerhouse during the war. He was signed to coach the new league's Cleveland team, called the "Browns" as a compliment to him.

Brown's Browns were among the great teams of all time. His quarterback was Otto Graham. Although Sammy Baugh is generally acknowledged as the game's top passer, it is questionable to say that he was a better man than Graham. Otto could run if need be, and he was a master of the sideline pass. He threw to either Mac Speedie or Dante Lavelli, and his passes were seldom intercepted. If these two were not there to catch the ball, it just went out of bounds. When the rival lines were charging, Graham would drop back and slip the ball to Marion Motley on the "draw" play. Motley would then go roaring up the

Otto Graham, star quarterback for the Browns, goes hurtling over a group of Chicago Cardinals for a touchdown.

field shedding tacklers like a runaway express train. Again, it is impossible to compare stars of different eras, but Motley would stand comparison with Bronko Nagurski and his own successor as fullback, Jimmy Brown.

With this Cleveland team, Paul Brown swept to four straight division and league titles. His men were too good. Few other All-America Conference teams could get on the same field with them. The league was suffering from small crowds. San Francisco did well with its Forty-Niners. The Buffalo Bills were a top draw, and so were the

Baltimore Colts. But the Brooklyn Dodgers soon vanished, and the Chicago Rockets discovered, as the Chicago Cardinals would also learn, that in Chicago nobody can compete with the Bears. In New York the Yankees had no chance against the popular Giants.

In Los Angeles it appeared for a time that the Dons could give the Rams a run for their money. The Rams had only recently moved west from Cleveland and had not yet gained a following. But in 1949 the Rams came up with a thrilling team. They had two great passers, Bob Waterfield and Norm Van Brocklin,

The Forty-Niners rush Ram quarterback Norm Van Brocklin (11) as he starts to throw a pass.

throwing to "Crazy Legs" Hirsch and the incomparable Tom Fears. They had Glenn Davis of Army in their backfield along with the blindingly fast Verda "Vitamin" Smith.

The Rams finished off the Dons in the competition for crowds, and their failure destroyed the All-America Conference. The league had failed to draw in any city which also fielded an NFL team. As yet, there were very few television stations in operation. Therefore the television money that would keep the American Football League in business a decade later was not forthcoming.

A "merger" was announced. Actually it was an obituary for all the A-A teams but Cleveland, Baltimore and San Francisco. These three were accepted in an expanded National League, and the All-America Conference and the other teams simply expired.

That happened after the 1949 season. When the 1950 pro season opened, the experts were saying that the A-A had been "a creampuff league." Cleveland would now be "playing with the big boys" of the NFL, and the much-publicized Browns would soon see what real competition was like.

In their first NFL game, Paul Brown's men split the vaunted defense of the league champions, the Philadelphia Eagles, and battered them, 35–10. Then the Browns went on to win the Eastern Division title and beat Los Angeles for the league crown. Brown's Brownies won *seven straight* division titles. Although they won only three of seven playoff games, they still demonstrated that the short-lived All-America Conference had been a top-flight professional league indeed as far as they were concerned.

146

The Mule and the Goat

At the end of every football season there comes a day—usually chilly, often wintry—on which a spotless white goat goes prancing down one side of a football field and a powerful gray mule goes galloping up the other. Great thunderous shouts, coming from the throats of thousands of young men, greet the appearance of the mascots. Frenzied bands play "Anchors Aweigh" or "On, Brave Old Army Team." The blue-coated Brigade of Midshipmen from Annapolis or the long gray line of the Corps of Cadets from West Point go marching and countermarching across the bright green field. They cheer wildly for their helmeted heroes or groan at their failures. They exchange jeers and good-natured taunts and at halftime they present a spectacle unrivaled anywhere in football.

There is, of course, a game. It seldom fails to keep a huge throng enthralled until the very end. It is rarely won or lost much more than a minute before its close. It has produced more upsets than any other rivalry in college football, and it is also the most colorful and thrilling of all the rivalries.

This colorful contest is the annual Army–Navy game, the yearly battle between the Army mule and the Navy goat. There is nothing quite like it in American sports: not the World Series, the Kentucky Derby, a heavyweight championship fight, the NFL playoff contest or even the Olympic Games played on American soil. Within mammoth Kennedy Memorial Stadium in Philadelphia, where the game is now regularly played, gather more than 102,000 persons. Here, even the President of the United States often sits, and there are always ranking government officials, the leading football coaches and the cream of the sports-writing fraternity.

Between halves of the annual Army–Navy game, cadets from West Point mass on the enormous field at Kennedy Memorial Stadium.

For days before the game, there are parties and festive gatherings which have become traditional features of this great sports fixture.

Traditional, too, is the intense and emotional rivalry generated by the Army–Navy game. As early as 1893, in the third game, won by Navy, 6–4, an infuriated general challenged an admiral to a duel. President Grover Cleveland promptly canceled the series for five years to allow tempers to cool. Since then, the rivalry has been more temperate. Generals and admirals now only challenge each other to such bets as a ride on a high-kicking mule against washing down a hard-butting goat.

These mascots, of course, play a central role in the game—and once they were the object of rival raiding parties. In 1953 a group of Cadets kidnaped a goat named Bill XIV. They found Billy grazing in his plot under the stadium and piled him into a car. As soon as they got to Baltimore they telephoned the Navy's duty officer and asked, gloatingly: "Where do you keep the goat?"

There were repercussions. The loudest ones came from Red Blaik, the Army coach, who growled: "Get that goat back."

The officer assigned to take back Bill XIV made a gracious speech to the welcoming crowd at Annapolis.

"In the Army," he explained, "they say that there are four general classes of officers: aides, aviators, adjutants and asses. I am the adjutant at West Point, but today, after playing aide to a goat, I feel like a bit of an ass."

Three years later a group of Midshipmen planned revenge. They intended to kidnap Hannibal, one of many Army

mules, and put him out to graze at an obscure Pennsylvania farm. But the plot was uncovered and the plotters restrained. Now such pranks are banned in both establishments. Even so, Navy now keeps Billy Goat in a building guarded by Marines, and the Cadets are so careful of their mule that they once brought him into Kennedy Stadium behind a tank!

Reciprocal raids are also still in fashion. One year a half-dozen Middies drove to West Point to paint up the town. They scrawled, "Beat Army," on the street at 100-foot intervals. They painted monuments in Navy blue and gold. But they had also brought lady friends with them, and the giggling girls gave them away. Military police caught the culprits and made them scrub off all the paint. But no one caught the villains who climbed the peak of Storm King Range, overlooking West Point, and changed the six-foot letters of Army's electric sign from "Beat Navy" to "Beat Army"!

Another year a Navy corvette steamed up the Hudson to anchor off the Point. During the night a party of Cadets boarded the corvette and painted "Beat Navy" on the starboard side. Fearful that the ship's sailors might erase the insult and pretend that nothing had happened, the Cadets sent two photographers out the next night to record their deed for posterity. The cameramen were caught and forced to remove the paint.

The statue of Tecumseh, the bronze good-luck monument at Annapolis, has always been a favorite object of Army's paint squads. Nowadays, the Middies keep Tecumseh under a round-the-clock guard before an Army–Navy game.

Bill XV romps onto the field with the 1963 first-string Navy backfield (left to right): Dick Earnest, Roger Staubach, Pat Donnelly and John Sai.

Some of the more modern-minded Cadets and Middies have also bombarded the rival academy with propaganda leaflets, dropping thousands of them from hired planes. One of the Navy's leaflets said:

BEAT ARMY

This is a genuine Army sympathy chit. Upon presentation of this chit to any midshipman in Philadelphia following Navy's crushing defeat of Army, bearer is entitled to free and eloquent gestures of sympathy.

On the Thursday nights before a game there are big pep rallies with bonfires, martial music and speeches. At West Point there is the annual Thanksgiving morning football clash between the Goats and the Engineers. The Goats represent the lowest group in the class academically, the Engineers the highest. It is said that if the Goats win, then the Army mule will triumph in the Big Game.

Both teams leave for Philadelphia on the night before the game, and the student bodies depart early Saturday morning. To see them march into cavernous Kennedy Stadium is a stirring sight indeed and, again, there is always horseplay. Once the Middies marched in carrying signs that read, "3,800 Strong." The Army promptly unfurled a banner proclaiming, "3,800 Strong Odors." Mutual mockery is continued during the halftime show. One year the Cadets unveiled a trio of floats. One said, GUNNERY TRAINING, and showed two sailors with slingshots. Another said, SEAMANSHIP, and showed a seasick Middy leaning over the rail. The third was entitled, FIRST COMMAND, and portrayed a naval officer on a garbage scow.

Victory, of course, is the object of the game—and it is celebrated in different ways. At West Point, the Cadets load the

149

team on a victory wagon and pull the players up the steep hill entering the Academy. At Annapolis, the Middies ring the Japanese bell presented to the Academy by Commodore Perry in 1858.

As might be expected in such an intense rivalry, the goddess of victory moves from camp to camp. Of the 64 games played so far, Army has won 31, the Navy 29. Five games have been tied.

The first game, of course, was in 1890. Navy, which had been playing football since 1882, had claimed the "Championship of Dixie" in 1889. Next year the Middies sent a challenge to West Point. The Cadets were eager to accept. But they had little hope that the Academic Board would allow them to. It was well known that in 1850 a Cadet named Philip Sheridan had been disciplined for "kicking football in vicinity of barracks."

Although both General Phil Sheridan and Sheridan's Ride were to become famous in the Civil War, their renown still could not make football popular.

Then there was a cadet named Dennis Mahan Michie, who had played football in prep school. He loved the game, and thought he could persuade the Academic Board to permit it, for he had been born at West Point. Most of the instructors had known Denny when he was a small boy. Denny was also very friendly with "Old Pete," the professor considered most likely to block the game. In fact, Professor Peter S. Michie was Denny's father.

And so the spirited young Cadet for whom Michie Stadium has been named actually did "bring the Board around." The game was played November 29, 1890. Navy appeared in red-and-white stocking-caps and red stockings; Army wore black-and-orange caps, white suits and black stockings. Led by Captain Charley Emrich, the Middies won, 24–0.

An indication of Army's inexperience was the protest raised after the Navy fullback went back for a punt and ran for a touchdown instead. Army wanted the play recalled. "It was clearly a false official statement for an officer and gentleman to announce that he was going to kick a ball and then do something else with it." The following year Captain Denny Michie had the Black Knights roaring back for a 32–16 victory.

From the outset, then, the rivalry has been evenly matched. Of course, there have been prolonged periods of victory for one or the other team. Prior to 1906, the year of the introduction of the forward pass, Army had beaten Navy for five straight games from 1901 to 1904, with a tie in 1905. But the Middies of Coach Paul Dashiell, an Annapolis football hero, upset the Black Knights by 10–0.

In 1924 a crowd of 80,000 people, the largest ever to gather for a game in the East up to that time, saw Army's Ed Garbisch pull off his individual feat of kicking four field goals to defeat the Tars, 12–0.

In 1926 Navy fielded the finest team it had ever had. This was the eleven which many experts thought should have been the national champions rather than Alabama. The Middies had two All-Americas, halfback Tom Hamilton who would later be a fine Navy coach, and Frank Wickhorst at tackle. Army also had two, the great halfback "Lighthorse Harry" Wilson and tackle Bud Sprague, as well as a young halfback named Chris Cagle. Even so, Navy was still favored as the two teams met to dedicate Chicago's new Soldier Field before a record throng of 110,000 persons.

As expected, Navy stormed to a 14–0 lead midway in the second period. It looked like a rout. But before the half was over the score was tied at 14–14. Between them, Wilson and Cagle tore Navy's line apart and Lighthorse Harry plunged over for the score. Then an Army punt struck the Navy safety's shoulder. It bounced off the knee of the covering Army end, Norris Harbold, and went rolling toward Army's goal 25 yards away. Harbold pursued it, caught it and went stumbling over the goal for a touchdown.

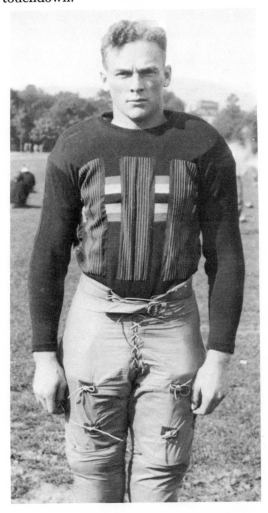

The Cadets' star halfback, Chris Cagle.

As the second half opened, Wilson raced 17 yards. Chris Cagle took the ball next, broke loose, reversed his field and danced 43 yards for a touchdown. Now Army led, 21–14. The Cadets fought furiously to protect that lead. They were still ahead with only four minutes to go when they decided to pass! Alan Shapley intercepted for Navy, and the Tars were back in the game.

But they were tired. Some of them doubted if they could come back, until Wickhorst called time out and pleaded with them to turn the tide. They caught fire. Blocking furiously they drove down to the Army 8-yard line. There, Navy called for a double reverse, with Shapley carrying, and he swept around end for the score.

There was thunder in Soldier Field, but it gradually died down to a hushed silence as Tom Hamilton stood waiting for the pass from center and the kick that meant a tie or a defeat. It came—straight and true—as Hamilton's kick went between the uprights. The greatest cliff-hanger in Army–Navy history ended in a tie.

Nine years later Tom Hamilton was the coach of the team that ended Navy's long victory famine. The Tars had not beaten the Black Knights in thirteen years prior to 1934. But that year the Middies won the game, 3–0.

Another Navy great, Emory "Swede" Larson, became coach at the Naval Academy in 1939. His teams beat Army two years in a row. In 1941, a week before Pearl Harbor, Swede Larson told reporters: "This will be the last football game for me for quite a while. There's a bigger game coming up and I'm going to be in it." The prophetic Swede *was* "in

151

it," as a Marine officer, and that day Barnacle Bill Busik passed and ran Navy to its third straight triumph over Army. It was five straight by 1944, but Red Blaik and his Touchdown Twins put a stop to the Navy's winning streak.

Army continued supreme even through 1947, the year in which Blaik's 32-game winning streak came to a surprise end when Bill Swiacki of Columbia made his sensational diving catch in the end zone. But Blaik had his Black Knights winning again in 1948. By the time they met the Middies, the Cadets had won eight games in a row and Navy had not won any. But the annual contest ended in a 21–21 tie in another one of those memorable upsets.

Two years later, after the incomparable Blaik had put together another string of twenty-six games without defeat, his Cadets met a team of Tars coached by Eddie Erdelatz. The final score was a stunning 14–2 in favor of Navy. Navy went on to dominate the series thereafter, winning 11 of 14 games. In 1958 both Blaik and Erdelatz coached their last Academy teams. The Cadets went undefeated. Led by Pete Dawkins, a Rhodes scholar, Army won 22–6.

Wayne Hardin took over at Navy in 1959 and won five straight games. Joe Bellino, one of the finest of Navy backs, set a record in 1959 by scoring three touchdowns against Army.

Staubach (12) darts through the Army defense to a touchdown in the 1962 Army–Navy contest.

After Bellino came Roger Staubach. "Roger the Dodger," as Staubach was called, was one of the most exciting backs to wear Navy blue. He was a peerless passer who put crowds on their feet while he ducked and dodged among blitzing tacklers, getting the ball away even as he was falling to the turf. Staubach won the Heisman Trophy in 1963, and in 1964 it appeared as though he would lead the Tars to their sixth straight win over Army.

That was the year Memorial Stadium was renamed Kennedy Memorial Stadium. It was also the year the Midshipmen marched in carrying signs that said: EVEN THE SCORE IN '64. Army had a record of 30 wins and Navy had 29, so it was time to bring the series to a tie. Navy was favored to do it, too, but as so often happens, it was the underdog who was inspired. Rollie Stichweh, the Cadet quarter, outshone Roger the Dodger. The final score was Army 11, Navy 8—and Coach Paul Dietzel had his first victory over Navy since coming to West Point from Louisiana State University two years before.

The song that was being played as the great crowd filed from the stadium was "On, Brave Old Army Team," and it was the mule that did the victory prance up the sidelines.

But in any succeeding year, they can be changed to "Anchors Aweigh" and the goat.

Navy coach Wayne Hardin (left) and quarterback Roger Staubach.

Platooners, Sooners and Spartans

In 1950 football fans read the All-America selections and rubbed their eyes. There were *two* teams!

One was made up of stars on offense, the other of stars on defense. That was proof positive that "two-platoon" football had arrived.

Fritz Crisler of Michigan was the man who had begun the platoons in his game against Army in 1945. Red Blaik had noticed and had switched to two platoons while rebuilding West Point's football fortunes in 1948. By 1950 most of the teams in the nation were platooners. Leading them all were the red-shirted Sooners of Oklahoma.

The University of Oklahoma had played good football ever since the memorable year in 1915 when the Sooners gave the Southwest its first "aerial circus" and played an undefeated season. But the team was never the great power that it became in the years following World War II. From 1946 onward the Sooners won no less than *fourteen* straight conference titles. The first two of these were won under Jim Tatum. Then in 1947 Tatum went to Maryland, and his assistant, Bud Wilkinson, took over. Under him Oklahoma's Golden Age began.

With Wilkinson, the Sooners won twelve more conference titles in a row.

They lost the first game of the 1948 season to Santa Clara, after which they won 31 games in a row and met a fine Kentucky team in the 1951 Sugar Bowl. The Wildcats, coached by Paul "Bear" Bryant, and led by the brilliant Babe Parilli, pinned a 13–7 upset defeat on the Sooners. Then, after a loss to Notre Dame in 1952, Oklahoma rolled for 47 more games without defeat until, in 1957, Notre Dame did it again, 7–0, on Dick Lynch's famous end run. That streak of 47 games equalled the string put together by Walter Camp's great teams of yore, and it was achieved during a time when competition was keener and the opposition stronger.

Wilkinson also gave Oklahoma three national championship teams within six years. The Sooners were number one in 1950, and they were on top again in 1955 and 1956. Moreover, the Sooners of 1953 also produced a stunning bowl upset. In the 1954 Orange Bowl game the Oklahoma Sooners of Bud Wilkinson were pitted against the Maryland Terrapins of Wilkinson's old boss, Jim Tatum. This was Tatum's masterpiece at Maryland—the team which had edged out Notre Dame for the number one spot in 1953. But Wilkinson's Sooners shut out Tatum's Terps, 7–0.

In the 1956 Orange Bowl game, Mary-

154

Coach Bud Wilkinson is carried off the field by the victorious Sooners after their 1954 Orange Bowl game against Maryland.

land had a chance to avenge itself on the Oklahoma national champions of 1955. But the Sooners triumphed again, 20–6.

In an eight-year period the Sooners and their handsome, personable, perfectionist coach won 73 regular-season games, lost 5 and tied 2. They also won four bowl games while losing one. The eight-year record, then, was 76-6-2. Few, if any colleges can equal that. Few, if any, played the kind of football that Oklahoma played during that Golden Age. There were thrilling stars such as Darrell Royal, Jim Weatherall, Max Boydston, Billy Vessels, Jerry Tubbs,

Jimmy Harris, Tommy McDonald, Wade Walker, Eddie Crowder, Tom Catlin and Buck McPhail. They played a brand of football that combined the precision Wilkinson had learned while playing for Bernie Bierman at Minnesota with the sudden lightning-like strikes which were the Sooner coach's own trademark.

Football's postwar decade also saw Golden Ages begun or renewed elsewhere. At Princeton, the shining eras associated with the names of Bill Roper or Fritz Crisler were brought back by Charley Caldwell, one of the members of Roper's immortal "Tiger Team of Des-

155

The Tigers' Dick Kazmaier, winner of the Heisman Trophy as the Player of the Year in 1951.

which was voted number one by both AP and UP.

The following year the Spartans were unstoppable; the green-and-white colors of Michigan State were hoisted over the football world. As the national champions, the Spartans ran their victory string up to 28 games until Purdue upset them, 6–0, in the middle of the 1953 season. Even so, they tied Illinois for the Big Ten title. Since this was the first year that the Spartans were eligible for the Rose Bowl (they had to wait five years), they were chosen to go. They beat U.C.L.A., 28–20, and two years later they beat another team of bruising Bruins in a 17–14 thriller that was decided with only seven seconds left to play.

Fans of the Big Ten—probably the toughest football conference in America —were amazed to see how little respect this upstart team had for the league's perennial powers. The Spartans pushed the Gophers and the Wolverines and the Buckeyes around as though it were a long-established habit. Yet before World War II, it had been a rare Michigan State eleven that could begin to stand up to a Big Ten team. As late as 1947 the University of Michigan had trounced the Spartans, 55–0. But four years later the Spartans walloped the Wolverines, 25–0. Before the war, mighty Notre Dame had never deigned to put the lowly Spartans on its schedule. But by 1949 Michigan State was beating Notre Dame, and she kept it up thereafter with astonishing regularity. In twelve games played from 1950 through 1963, the Spartans beat the Irish eleven times. They even won eight in a row. No other team had ever humbled the Irish so.

tiny." Princeton took the Ivy League title in 1950, 1951 and 1955, with stars such as Dick Kazmaier and Royce Flippin.

In 1950, the year that the United Press also began picking a national champion, Michigan State entered a new era. The once-lowly Spartans had been admitted to the Big Ten to replace absent Chicago, and they were a power from the outset. In 1950 they won eight games and lost one, and were number eight in the nation's Top Ten. The next year they took all nine games, whitewashing mighty Notre Dame, 35–0. They were outranked only by Tennessee,

How was it done? Well, there were stars such as Sonny Grandelius and Lynn Chandnois, Billy Wells and Don McAuliffe, Don Coleman, Al Dorow, Dave Kaiser, Earl Morrall and Tom Yewcic. But there were also two fine coaches—Clarence "Biggie" Munn, first, and after him, Hugh Duffy Daugherty. Between them they made the Spartans one of the nation's powers. And, they not only came out of nowhere, they stayed on top after they arrived. That in itself was a rare feat, as many a college which has attempted to "go big-time" has learned, much to its financial hurt.

One of the teams that "made it" during the years 1950 through 1957 was the University of California at Los Angeles, or UCLA. The Bruins, or Uclans, first began to play football in 1919. They rarely had an undefeated season, sometimes they failed to win more games than they lost. UCLA was completely dwarfed by its mighty cross-town neighbor, the University of Southern California. In 1949, a bit weary of its role as a Pacific Coast doormat, UCLA lured Henry "Red" Sanders away from Vanderbilt.

Sanders arrived in Los Angeles with a reputation as a single-wing coach who could do a lot with a little. He was also known as "the clown prince" of football. But Sanders temporarily checked his fondness for practical jokes and got to work with his Bruins. In his second year, he sent them out against the haughty men of Southern California. The result was unbelievable: UCLA 39, Southern Cal 0!

Red Sanders became Mr. Los Angeles. When the Los Angeles *Mirror* ran a popularity contest to name the city's Most Valuable Citizen, he beat such famous celebrities as Bob Hope and Harold Lloyd by a landslide. UCLA's Associated Students presented him a certificate, saying: "We express our humble appreciation to Coach Sanders, the finest, most beloved and respected coach in the nation."

No doubt Red's colleagues respected him, but it was an exaggeration to say that he was "beloved." No coach who compiles a record of 42–12–1 in six seasons can hope to earn the love of his defeated rivals. The record was surpassed in 1954 with an undefeated season and UCLA's first citation as national champion.

Sanders always said that the 1954 team was the best he ever coached. It was the nation's top scorer with 367 points, and it was also number one on defense. Its opponents only scored 40 points combined and were limited to an average of 73.2 yards per game. The United Press's poll of coaches decided that the Uclans were the best in the country, but the AP poll picked Ohio State.

Woody Hayes had already begun his long and successful tenure in Columbus, and his Buckeyes were grounding out the yardage in a split T attack, which almost spurned the forward pass. Why bother to pass, anyway, with an operator like red-haired Howard "Hopalong" Cassady to lug the ball? So Ohio State went undefeated. It was hoped that the Rose Bowl might settle the dispute over who was actually the better, UCLA or Ohio State. But the Uclans had been there the preceding year, and were ineligible. Thus, the record books show a split

Notre Dame's Paul Hornung (5)
carries the ball against Iowa.

championship for that season.

Unlike Ohio State, not all the split-T teams of 1950 through 1956 shunned the pass. In fact, that era could almost be described as the time of the great running quarterbacks. There were, of course, splendid passing tailbacks such as Hank Lauricella of Tennessee and Paul Cameron of UCLA. But it was generally an era of T masters running the deadly option play: keeping, passing or lateraling. Among them were Paul Hornung and Ralph Guglielmi of Notre Dame, George Shaw of Oregon and Jimmy Swink of T.C.U. Navy had George Welsh, who led Eddie Erdelatz's "team named desire" to a 21–0 conquest of Mississippi when the Tars took a trip to New Orleans to appear in their first bowl. There were also Jack Scarbath of Maryland and Eddie Crowder of Oklahoma.

Don Heinrich, a two-time All-America at Washington, led the nation in passing in 1950. And at Georgia Tech, undefeated in 1951 and 1952, Darrell Crawford was passing or feeding the ball to high-stepping Leon Hardeman.

The game had become more exciting than ever before. Much to the delight of the fans, and the despair of the coaches, platoon football had been legislated out of existence. Spectators no longer needed a computer to keep up with the arriving and departing players. Triple-threat tailbacks and split-T quarterbacks added the spice of suspense to the sport. The question always was: will he run or pass?

But in the pro game the attitude was exactly the opposite. Norm Van Brocklin made this clear with his famous quip: "A passer should only run from sheer fright."

The Pro Explosion

In 1946 Elmer Layden resigned as NFL Commissioner and Bert Bell took his place. Bell was the old Penn star who had brought pro football to Philadelphia. Under him, the NFL weathered its battle with the All-America Conference, and pro football began to explode.

By the time of Bell's death in 1959, the twelve-team NFL was playing to more than three million paying customers every year. Under young and energetic Alvin "Pete" Rozelle, who eventually succeeded Bell, the annual "gate" rose to more than four million fans in 1962. It keeps rising every year.

In some cities in the National League it is next to impossible to buy a ticket to a home game. The only way to secure a season's ticket is to inherit one.

In 1963, the franchise of the Los Angeles Rams sold for $7,100,000. In 1941 that same franchise had been worth only $100,000. Twenty years before that, a pro franchise went for $100. Some experts say that the 1963 franchise, worth more than seven million dollars, may be a better risk than the one that went for a mere hundred. That is because the possibility of pay television may open up even more profitable frontiers. And it is also because television has enabled pro football to challenge pro baseball as the national pastime.

Football, with its thrilling combination of brains and brawn, violence and deception, speed and surprise, was always the American *game*. But baseball was the pastime. Stars such as Babe Ruth or Stan Musial played it, and millions went out to watch. They could identify with it. A fan need not have gone to college to root for his favorites. The stars for whom he rooted were back year after year, often for as long as twenty years. They were truly familiar figures. This was not so in college football. Unless he was exceptional, a fine player was on the varsity usually only during his last two years in school. Every year there was a new line-up. Only a loyal alumnus of a particular college would know all the players on that school's team every year.

However, throughout the fifties, and even more so during the early sixties, pro football began to resemble baseball in that it, too, had its *perennial* stars. They came back year after year just like their baseball counterparts. In the age of the specialists, a player lasted longer. As gate receipts rose, he received better medical care. As the size of the squads increased, he was allowed to nurse an injury, to stay out of action for a week or two until he was well again. The pro fans had superstars of their own whom they could discuss in the off-season, just as baseball fans do in the "hot-stove league."

One of the greatest of these stars from 1957 through 1965 was Jimmy Brown of the Cleveland Browns. Perhaps alone among the modern players, Jimmy Brown can stand comparison with either Jim Thorpe or Bronko Nagurski. Certainly in his own time, Jimmy Brown has had no peer as a runner. Six feet two inches tall, weighing 228 pounds, with a beautifully proportioned body tapering to a 32-inch waist, Jim was also known as "Mr. Indestructible." He never got hurt. Nor did he very often get stopped. Most great running backs have 1,000 yards gained from scrimmage as their goal. But in one year—1963—Jim Brown set a record with 1,863 yards. He was running wild again the following year when Cleveland won the Eastern Division and swamped the Baltimore Colts and Johnny Unitas in the playoffs by a score of 27–0. Fans who watched that game saw Jimmy as he usually was: fast, hitting with sledgehammer force, possessed of a savage straight-arm that was more like a powerful backward swipe of the forearm. He was able to turn on a dime while directing his blockers downfield ahead of him like a host of battering tanks.

Perhaps the closest thing to Brown among the pros was Jim Taylor of Green Bay. Powerful as a bull, famous for his "second effort" and his love of bodily contact, Taylor is the only man in the NFL to have gained more than 1,000 yards five years in a row. It was Taylor who teamed up with Paul Hornung to give the Packers their famous "big-man" backfield. Not all the stars, of course, have had to be backs. Giant fans used to shout "Huff-Huff-Huff" whenever Sam Huff shut off the middle with a typical shattering tackle, and in Detroit huge Alex Karras was always a favorite.

Karras and Hornung, unfortunately, figured in the second of two mild scandals connected with the NFL. The first occurred in 1946, when it was discovered that two New York Giant backs—

Merle Hapes and Frank Filchock—had not reported to police that gamblers had offered them a bribe to throw the title game with the Chicago Bears. Later on, both men were exonerated of any wrongdoing.

At the end of the 1962 season it was found that Alex Karras and Paul Hornung, the top point-getter in league history and the most valuable player in 1961, had been betting on games. They were both suspended (for a year, as it turned out). Five Detroit players were also fined $2,000 apiece for having bet on a game that they were watching on television. In neither case, however, was there any evidence that any of the players had bet against themselves or tried to shave points or sell information to gamblers or do anything dishonorable. They had bet on themselves to win, but their contracts expressly forbid gambling of any kind.

Neither scandal did anything to reduce pro football's popularity. In fact, the game was overcoming another former disadvantage. This was the shortness of the season. It had formerly lasted only a few months, with each team playing about ten games each. This was changed to fourteen apiece. There are exhibition games as early as August, and the bowl games continue into January.

Finally, television has been the making of pro football. Millions of persons can now watch this exciting sport at home, and follow the stars just as easily as the lucky spectators with season tickets. Television has kept pro football alive in Canada, where football is played under different rules, and it was responsible for the birth of a second, healthy pro league in America.

The indestructible Jimmy Brown carries the ball
for the Cleveland Browns against the Packers.

The American Football League got started in 1960 with teams in Buffalo, Boston, Houston, Dallas, Los Angeles, Oakland, Denver and New York. The Dallas and Los Angeles franchises were eventually shifted to Kansas City and San Diego, respectively. After four seasons of so-so fortunes during which the older circuit sniffed at the AFL as an upstart and a "minor league," the AFL really arrived. In 1964 the New York Jets played the Buffalo Bills in New York on the same Sunday on which the Giants met the Dallas Cowboys.

The attendance for the Giants at Yankee Stadium was a capacity 63,031 persons. The Jets, in the spanking-new Shea Stadium, drew a capacity 61,929. The total attendance was 124,960. Never before in football, amateur or professional, had so many persons in one city gathered as spectators.

Moreover, the Jets nearly tripled their home attendance in 1964, and capacity crowds were common in Boston and Buffalo. The AFL was not yet, of course, as strong as its older brother, the NFL. But the AFL had also just been given a $36,000,000 five-year telecasting contract by the National Broadcasting System. That meant that for five years the clubs would be guaranteed about $900,000 a year in TV revenue alone. With such backing, the AFL was able to bid for collegiate stars on a more or less equal footing with the NFL. They did that for the first time at the close of the 1964 season, when the entire football world was stunned to hear that the New York Jets had signed Joe Namath, Alabama's star quarterback, to play for three years at an astonishing figure of nearly $400,000. For a rookie to be paid

at the rate of more than $130,000 a year without even putting on his shoes in pro ball was not only unheard-of; it was flabbergasting. And to think that such a salary had been offered by the relatively new AFL was even more preposterous.

The Namath contract was like a starting gun signaling the start of an interleague scramble for the top players. Rival bidding forced the prices higher and higher. After the close of the 1965 season it reached the point where the new Atlanta Falcons of the NFL were reported to have paid $600,000 for the services of Tommy Nobis, the hard-tackling linebacker from Texas. Green Bay was also supposed to have laid out a total of one million dollars for rookie backs Donny Anderson of Texas Tech and Jim Grabowski of Illinois.

Everywhere individual collegiate stars were receiving more money than had been given to entire teams during the twenties and thirties. And in some cases, young men who had signed for as much as $50,000 did not even make the squad! That meant that they had received ten times as much money as a Bronko Nagurski or a Jim Thorpe without ever running out on a major-league field.

Obviously the rival leagues were on the verge of bidding themselves into bankruptcy. In 1966 it appeared that the competition might get even keener, for by then the NFL had agreed to a TV contract with CBS calling for $18.8 million for *only two years*. This meant $1.2 million a year in television revenue alone for each NFL club. The rival circuits, however, finally decided to bury the hatchet.

On June 5, 1966, the NFL and AFL announced that they were going to merge into a single league. Because of existing television contracts, however, the merger would not take place until 1970. Before then each league had the right to add another team. The 15-team NFL quickly expanded to 16 clubs by adding the New Orleans Saints to its roster. The nine-team AFL was expected to follow suit. After 1970, the merged league—to be bossed by NFL chief Pete Rozelle—was to expand to 28 teams.

The two leagues also decided to conduct a common draft of collegiate players. This would put an end to the ruinous competitive bidding. It would also stop the bad practice of secretly approaching college players before their eligibility had expired. Of course players were still receiving salaries much higher than those paid to the old-time stars, but the brief "golden era" introduced by the Namath contract had come to an end.

Finally, the leagues announced that their championship teams would meet in 1967 to decide the world professional football title. Soon this long-awaited game came to be known as the "Super Bowl." Now pro fans rooted not only for their favorite teams to win the league crown but also to become the first world champions.

In the AFL the explosive Kansas City Chiefs were easily the cream of the Western Division. In the East the Buffalo Bills, defending champions, backed into their third straight division title after the New York Jets upset the division-leading Boston Patriots. In the league title game, however, the Bills

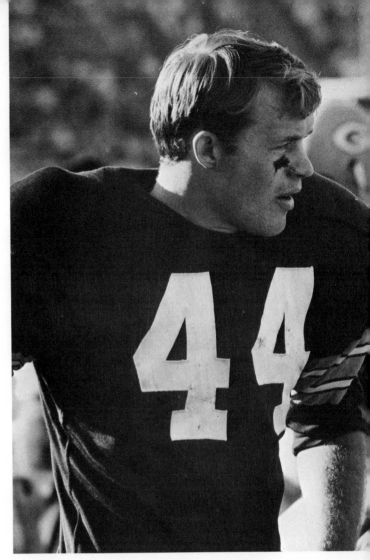

The Green Bay Packers paid dearly for the services of rookie back Donny Anderson.

were outclassed by the Chiefs, 31–7.

In the NFL, the Green Bay Packers played their usual simple, steady game and breezed to the Western Division crown. Eastern supremacy went to the galloping Dallas Cowboys. Came the league championship game and Green Bay again showed that Coach Vince Lombardi's fundamental football was hard to beat. The Packers defeated the Cowboys, 34–27.

Now came the dream game—the much publicized Super Bowl. When Kansas City met Green Bay in the Los Angeles Coliseum, football fans would at last get the answer to that much

163

Quarterback Bart Starr of the Packers lifts a pass over
the Chiefs' Chuck Hurston (85) and E. J. Holub (55).

debated question: can the American
Football League compete on even terms
with the National Football League?

At first, the answer seemed to be
yes. Led by Lenny Dawson, the Chiefs
fought the Packers on nearly even terms,
and when the first half ended they
trailed by only 10–14. In the final 30
minutes, however, the Packers exerted
their superiority. Play by play they

tightened their control of the game. In
the end, the splendid Green Bay quarterback, Bart Starr, and his glue-fingered
receiver, Max McGee, along with a host
of other green-shirted stalwarts smothered the Chiefs by a score of 35–10. As
Coach Lombardi said after the game:
"Kansas City is a good football team.
But their team doesn't compare with
the top NFL teams."

Room at the Top

During the late fifties and early sixties great changes also took place in collegiate football.

In 1956 the very colleges which had begun the sport started to deemphasize it. The Ivy League was officially formed (it had always been an informal group) among Princeton, which had played Rutgers in the first game back in 1869; Yale, football's chief inventor; Harvard, which had introduced running with the ball; Columbia, and such old-time powerhouses as Penn, Cornell and Dartmouth. These teams agreed to play only each other or other Eastern teams. They abolished spring practice. Scholarships were granted only on an academic basis and players were forbidden to play in post-season all-star games.

Even before they took this drastic step away from "big-time" football, many other colleges across the nation dropped the sport entirely. Among them were the former Eastern powers of N.Y.U., Fordham and Georgetown. Oddly enough, these three schools later began a movement which, if it catches on, may take football back to the way it was played when the Ivy Leaguers started it all. In 1964, the student bodies at N.Y.U. and Fordham formed "football clubs." That is, they organized teams which were not supported by college authorities but were allowed to use the school's name. All money for equipment and expenses was raised by the students themselves. The coaches were also students. In the first of the meetings between "football clubs," Fordham defeated N.Y.U. A few weeks later the students at Georgetown formed a club, challenging and beating N.Y.U.

Throughout the East, other colleges which had deemphasized or dropped the sport took note. It appeared that the club movement was gaining momentum.

Generally, though, big-time football with all its paraphernalia of high-priced coaches, trainers, scouts, scholarships and huge crowds remained unaffected by these efforts to deemphasize. In fact, the game had been made even more exciting. In 1958, the Rules Committee made its first change in the scoring system in 46 years. Teams were now permitted an option of trying to kick an extra point after a touchdown or of running or passing for a two-point conversion. This change was made to reduce the number of ties, one of the game's most frustrating aspects. Many of the coaches opposed it, none more strenuously than Darrell Royal, the old Oklahoma star who was coaching Texas. Nevertheless, that very year Royal's Texas Longhorns used the option to defeat his alma mater, under Bud Wilkinson, 15–14.

Bud Wilkinson, incidentally, was the man who had predicted the other great change that was to overtake college football. In 1957, after Notre Dame had ended Oklahoma's 47-game winning streak, Wilkinson said that the era of winning streaks and of perennial powerhouses was at an end. The teams were becoming too evenly matched, he said. Undefeated seasons would become rarer and no one section of the country would dominate the sport.

He was right. That same year, Auburn, led by its brilliant end, Jimmy Phillips, won its first national championship. In 1958, Louisiana State University, coached by the colorful Paul Dietzel and sparked by swivel-hipped Billy Cannon, also gained its first number-one ranking. The following year Ben Schwartzwalder and Syracuse showed the nation that the East was not so weak as had been supposed. A speedy sophomore named Ernie Davis was the star of that first championship Orange team. Fleet-footed Ernie went on to make All-America two years in a row, and then became one of football's tragic figures. When he joined the Cleveland Browns, it appeared that Ernie might team up with that other Syracuse great, Jimmy Brown, to give pro football a stunning running combination. But Ernie was stricken with leukemia. There was no hope, and Ernie Davis went to his death—brave and cheerful to the end.

After Syracuse had won its first championship, those veteran champions, the Golden Gophers of Minnesota, reclaimed the national diadem for the Midwest. Then in 1961 with Paul "Bear" Bryant returned to his alma mater, Alabama came out on top. The next year it was Southern Cal coached by John McKay, and in 1963 Darrell Royal and powerful Ernie Koy gave Texas its first national championship.

Thus, in seven years there had been seven different champions—four of them newcomers—from every section of the country. In the following year it appeared that there would be another different winner, one with the most famous name of all—Notre Dame.

Oklahoma halfback Tommy McDonald races for yardage against Maryland in the 1956 Orange Bowl game.

Two Trojans close in on Notre Dame's John Huarte,
holding him to a 1-yard gain.

Since 1956 the Fighting Irish had been in a disastrous slump. They had lost more than they had won, an incredibly poor performance for Notre Dame. In two seasons they had lost eight and won only two games, and in 1963 they had won only one game! Three famous coaches—young Terry Brennan, Joe Kuharich and Hughie Devore—were unable to pilot the Irish out of the doldrums. Then in 1964 a non-alumnus took over.

He was the handsome and inspirational Ara Parseghian, a graduate of the University of Miami at Oxford, Ohio, where he had played with Paul Dietzel.

Parseghian had coached with great success at Northwestern. Then he came to Notre Dame, and in 1964 the frenzied Irish adherents vowed that "The Era of Ara" had begun.

In one of the greatest comebacks in history, Notre Dame bowled over nine straight opponents and averaged thirty points a game while holding their rivals to an average of six. Week after week the Irish were picked as the nation's top team. In quarterback John Huarte and end Jack Snow they had a fine passing combination. Only one team stood between Ara Parseghian's boys and the national championship.

167

It was Southern California, the same spirited school that had administered that "impossible" upset in 1931 and who had robbed the Irish of the number one spot in 1938. Could they do it again?

It did not seem so. Johnny Huarte, already acclaimed as the Heisman winner for 1964, quickly hooked up with Jack Snow. At the half, the Irish led 17–0. During the intermission, Parseghian spoke hoarsely to his men.

"Thirty minutes stands between us and the greatest sports comeback in history," he said, shaking his fist in emphasis. "Thirty minutes! You've got to go out there and play this second half,

boys—a sixty-minute football team . . . Let's really go out there and give them thirty more minutes of Notre Dame football!"

But the next half-hour belonged to Southern Cal. The red-shirted Trojans were a team obsessed with the idea of springing one of football's greatest upsets. They ripped the huge Irish line apart, and quickly swept to a touchdown with Mike Garrett carrying the ball. Notre Dame struck back in the fourth quarter. Clicking as of old, the Irish marched to the Trojan 1-yard line, from where Joe Kantor bulled over. But the touchdown was called back. A Notre

Southern Cal's Quarterback Craig Fertig uncorks a pass against Notre Dame.

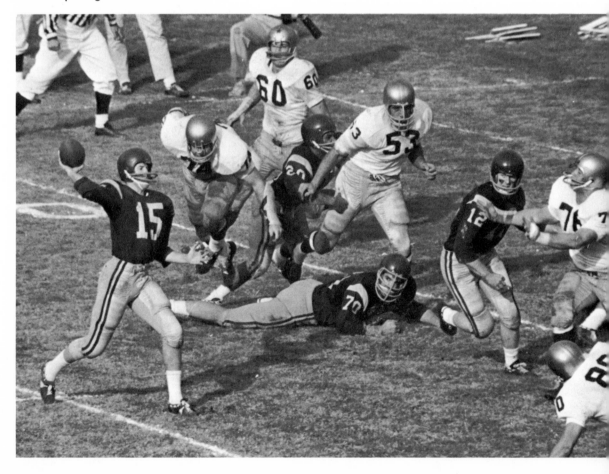

Mike Garrett of USC (with ball) turns the end and attempts to break loose from a determined University of Wyoming defender.

Dame player had been detected holding, and the drive fizzled out.

That was the turning point. From then on Craig Fertig of Southern Cal was in charge. He drove the Trojans 88 yards, passing 23 yards to Fred Hill for a touchdown. The home-town throng of more than 83,000 persons in Los Angeles Colosseum roared with joy. Notre Dame was stunned. Leading 17–13, the Irish seemed powerless to move the ball. They kicked. Jack Snow planted the ball on Southern Cal's 23. But another holding penalty against Notre Dame forced Snow to kick again. This time the Trojans returned the ball to their own 40-yard line, and drove inexorably down-field to the Notre Dame 15.

There, on a last down, with barely two minutes left to play and the huge throng pleading for a touchdown, Craig Fertig dropped back to pass again. He shot a bullet to Rod Sherman on the three, and the Trojan back scampered into the end zone with the roar of a

hysterical crowd in his ears.

The final score was Southern Cal 20, Notre Dame 17. A great comeback had been stopped three points and ninety-five seconds short of its goal.

Alabama, which finished the season undefeated, was named as the number one team. But the Crimson Tide was upended by Texas in the Cotton Bowl a month later, and the National Football Foundation and Hall of Fame still claimed that the Irish were the best, awarding its MacArthur Bowl to Notre Dame.

Only Arkansas, which had beaten Texas by one point, remained undefeated in 1964. This seemed to have proved Bud Wilkinson's contention that the era of the long victory string or the supremacy of a single college was at an end. It also seemed to suggest that something more than a poll or the decision of some unofficial foundation was needed to prove beyond doubt who was really Number One.

A Super Upset

The American Football League began to come of age in 1967. Though critics still scoffed at the younger league, the common draft of players, which had been agreed upon during the merger with the National Football League, bolstered the AFL squads with good young talent. Moreover, the simple fact that the AFL teams had one more year of pro experience under their belts helped. The teams were now developing their own traditions and rivalries. Crowds were up; in some cities, tickets were almost impossible to purchase. With the addition of the Miami Dolphins as the tenth franchise, the AFL looked ahead with a sense of satisfaction.

In 1967, powerful Oakland was probably the most improved team in all pro football. The Raiders also had a new quarterback, Daryle Lamonica. For years the backup signal-caller to Jackie Kemp at Buffalo, Lamonica finally tired of sitting on the bench and asked to be traded. After joining Oakland, he wound up his sturdy right arm and began throwing with a zest that made him the league's top passer and gave his team a sparkling record of 13 wins and one loss. Meeting Houston for the league title, Lamonica and a young Raider team that had speed and strength to spare ran away with the game, and the final score was a lopsided 40–7. Then they sat back to await the NFL outcome.

In the Eastern Conference, the explosive Cowboys of Dallas finally came out on top. In the West, however, there was a three-way donnybrook among the Baltimore Colts, the Los Angeles Rams and the world-champion Green Bay Packers. At first it appeared that the veteran Packers had at last run out of gas and that the peerless Johnny Unitas would lead his Colts back to the top. After all, the injury-ridden Packers had lost four games. But then the Packers steadied, as they had always done, and Unitas and Baltimore ran into the stubborn Los Angeles defense, probably the roughest in pro football. The Rams' front four alone—Deacon Jones, Lamar Lundy, Roger Brown and Merlin Olsen—tipped the scales at a total of 1,100 pounds. After smearing Unitas and leading Los Angeles to a 34–10 victory, the "Fearsome Foursome" appeared to be quite capable of doing the same to the "old men" of the Packers.

Not so. The final score read: Packers 28, Rams 7. Once again, it was done so effortlessly that people who saw the game wondered why anyone thought Los Angeles had a chance. Once again the Packers met the Cowboys for the NFL crown.

This time, the game was in frigid Green Bay, where the temperature was 13 degrees below zero and a 15 m.p.h. wind created a "chilling factor" equivalent to 49 below. It appeared that the hard-charging Cowboys were at last to upend Green Bay. For, with only five minutes left to play, they led by 17–14. But then the "old pro," Packer quarterback Bart Starr, took charge. Coolly mix-

Protected by Gale Gillinghan (68), Travis Williams gains yardage in the 1968 Super Bowl game in Miami.

ing his plays and reading the Dallas defense as though he had written their play book, Starr led the veteran Packers 68 yards downfield to the Dallas goal line. Now, it was fourth down and only 16 seconds left to play. Should the Packers try for the sure-fire field goal that would tie the score and force the game into "sudden death"? Or should they "go for broke"? Like true champions, they risked it all—and Bart Starr went crashing into the end zone with the game-winning score.

After that spine-tingling battle, the second Super Bowl was an anticlimax. Lamonica and his gallant young Raiders fought hard, but they were simply overwhelmed, 33–14. Still, they performed much better than Kansas City had the previous year, actually outgaining the Packers in the air, 186 yards to 162. As they were quick to admit themselves, they just made too many mistakes against a team that turns misplays into touchdowns. Yet Vince Lombardi had kind words for the AFL champion, declaring: "Oakland is a good, well-coached club."

As pro football faced the 1968 season with still another team added to its roster—the AFL Cincinnati Bengals—the same old question remained unanswered: who can beat the Green Bay Packers? Vince Lombardi had become general manager of the club and Phil Bengtson was the new coach.

The answer was not who, but what. As the 1968 season emerged injuries and age began taking their toll of the Packer dynasty. The World Champions were not in shape physically to continue winning. In fact, they stumbled to a 6–7–1 record, finishing third in the NFL's four-team Central Division. The masters of pro football had lost their sure touch. But the new coach couldn't be held at fault. At one point the Packers played without the services of most of their defensive linemen, to say nothing of the games Bart Starr missed.

The 1968 NFL season might well be called "the year of the injury." Again and again the top teams took the field with key players either on the bench or out for the season. Perhaps the most staggering losses were suffered by the Chicago Bears, whose starting quarterback, Jack Concannon, broke his collarbone. Soon after, backup Rudy Bukich went out of action with a shoulder separation. Then the great Gale Sayers, the most feared runner in pro football, was knocked out for the season with a knee injury. This was the most serious loss of all. By the time third-string quarterback Virgil Carter was carried off the field with a broken ankle, Chicago fans had few tears left to shed. Sunday after Sunday, from September to December, NFL coaches watched in misery while their star performers were dragged or carried

from the field. Soon it appeared that the title would be won not by the best first team but by the squad with the best reserves.

Probably the most spectacular casualty of all occurred before the season even started, when Baltimore's matchless Johnny Unitas seriously damaged his right elbow in an exhibition game. At the time Coach Don Shula thought he was staring disaster in the face. The Colt coach had carefully built a great title contender, and he had built it around Unitas. But with the famous quarterback out of action Shula would be forced to rely on Earl Morrall, picked up in an "insurance" trade from the lackluster New York Giants.

Competent but colorless, Morrall had spent 12 indifferent years in the NFL, wearing the uniform of four different clubs—the San Francisco 49ers, the Detroit Lions, the Giants and now the Colts. He certainly didn't seem to be one to replace the inspiring "Johnny U." But events proved otherwise. Morrall became a champion of the underdog, leading his team to the NFL title with a splendid 13–1 record. He won the NFL's Most Valuable Player award.

In the AFL, injuries proved to be only a slightly less serious problem. The limping Buffalo Bills went through six quarterbacks. Nevertheless, the AFL teams surprised the football faithful with the improved quality of their play. They held their own in the inter-league exhibition games with the NFL, and it became obvious that the common draft had provided them with their share of the cream of the college crop. Almost equally startling was the performance of the league's newest expansion club, the Cincinnati Bengals. They won three regular season games under the coaching know-how of Paul Brown, who had won so many titles in the old All-America Football Conference and the NFL. Brown quickly demonstrated that he was back in the game and capable of adding a few more trophies to his showcase.

The AFL Western Division provided the most thrills in 1968. Both the Kansas City Chiefs and the San Diego Chargers came up with fine teams to challenge the defending champion Oakland Raiders. Throughout most of the season, the title race was a three-way struggle. Then the Chargers faded in the waning weeks,

while the Chiefs and Raiders remained neck-and-neck. They finished with identical 12–2 records. In the playoff game for the division title, however, the Raiders were superb. Daryle Lamonica was in top form, throwing four touchdown passes to lead his team to a 41–6 victory.

In the East, Coach Weeb Ewbank's New York Jets simply ran away from the opposition, finishing four full games ahead of the second-place Houston Oilers. In the league playoff game, the Jets squeaked ahead of the Raiders, 27–23, in a contest that wasn't decided until the final seconds. With that, the

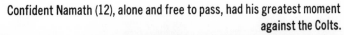

Confident Namath (12), alone and free to pass, had his greatest moment against the Colts.

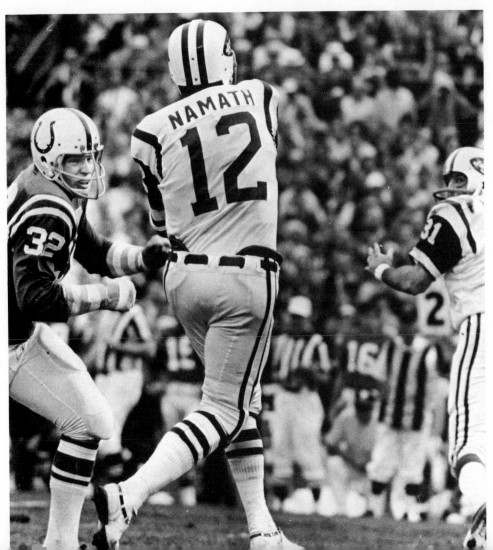

Joe Namath (12) of the Jets hands off to fullback Matt Snell (41) for a gain against the "unbeatable" Baltimore Colts in the 1969 Super Bowl.

Jets won the right to meet the Colts in the third Super Bowl. Immediately football experts began asking: How good is Joe Namath?

Joe—or "Broadway Joe" as he was nicknamed by sportswriters—was such a colorful character that the experts tended to judge him on personality, not performance. Namath was disliked by many for his brash comments and his fondness for bright lights. When news photographs showed him in a full-length fur coat, or when he shaved off his famous mustache for $10,000 in a

in the history of professional sports. Of course, almost everyone agreed that Namath could throw a football. Nevertheless, there remained some doubt about Broadway Joe's ability as a quarterback. He was a good passer, but could he lead a team to victory past a defensive team like the mighty Colts?

Most of the experts did not think he could. Most of them also believed that the AFL's standard of play was still inferior to that of the older league. Thus, as the Super Bowl approached, Joe and his Jets were rated an 18-point underdog. As the game began, it appeared that the experts would be proved correct. The first time the Colts got the ball, they began to tear the Jet defense apart. Then New York stiffened, and Baltimore's deadly place-kicker, Lou Michaels, missed a field goal attempt. Things were never again the same.

A crowd of 75,377 spectators and another 60 million television viewers sat in astonishment while Namath and his high-flying Jets produced the most stunning upset in pro football history. They humbled the mighty Colts, 16–7. Namath passed superbly (17 of 28 for 206 yards). He read the Colt defense with the cool precision of a master field general. When he passed, his interior linemen almost always gave him the time he needed. His fullback, Matt Snell, smashed through the Colt line time after time. On defense, the Jets so hurried Morrall that he threw four interceptions.

And so, much sooner than anyone had expected, the upstart junior league pulled itself up to the level of the senior circuit. As the Jets' Jim Turner, who kicked three field goals, put it after the game: "Welcome to the AFL."

television commercial, his critics said he was not the kind of athlete to serve as an inspiration to American youth. People who liked Joe, however, maintained that the man with the golden arm was actually very frank and witty. Moreover, his fondness for fun was nothing new

175

Who's Number One?

In 1965 that nagging question of "Who's Number One?" arose again in college football. In fact, the major wire services were soon battling each other in the team ratings game. The contest was made more intriguing by football schedules and bowl games that more than once matched the outstanding contenders for the mythical national championship.

At the close of the regular season in 1965, Coach Duffy Daugherty's undefeated, untied Michigan State Spartans were voted the best team in the land. Right behind the Michigan Staters came Alabama, Arkansas and Nebraska. All three were legitimate contenders. That same year another element was added to the annual chase for national rankings. The Associated Press decided, for the first time, to hold its final vote *after* the bowl games. Thus when Michigan State was upset by UCLA in the Rose Bowl, and Alabama defeated Nebraska in the Orange Bowl, the Crimson Tide from the South moved into the top spot.

In 1966, Michigan State and Alabama were back with fine teams—and so was Notre Dame. This time Coach Ara Parseghian unveiled a pair of sophomore stars: quarterback Terry Hanratty and end Jim Seymour. Once again the Notre Dame student body was chanting: "We're Number One." In fact, the high-scoring Irish did displace the Spartans at the top of the polls. But Michigan State was also rolling to impressive victories, and because the two teams were to meet late in the season it seemed that this time a game, not an election, would decide the national championship.

Not since the Army-Notre Dame game of 1946 had any collegiate meeting been as eagerly awaited as this Spartan-Irish clash of 1966. It was called "The Game of the Decade." The Spartans were confident that their tough defense, led by George Webster and the giant Bubba Smith, could stop Notre Dame's Hanratty-to-Seymour combination and contain the running of Nick Eddy and Larry Conjar. And Notre Dame felt that its big line could stop high-stepping Clint Jones and smother the passing of Jimmy Raye. What happened was that each team was able to accomplish about half of what it had predicted. The result was a disappointing 10–10 tie.

Meantime, Alabama claimed the Number One ranking on the strength of its unbeaten *and untied* record. Others declared that, because Alabama does not play so hard a schedule, the Irish and the Spartans should be proclaimed co-champions. Fortunately for the Irish, Notre Dame had another game left: against Southern Cal. And because the Irish rolled to a devastating 51–0 victory over the Pacific Coast champions, the sportswriters and coaches voted them tops for 1966.

Notre Dame was favored to claim the national championship again in 1967. But in the second game of the season the Irish ran into their old nemesis, the Boilermakers of Purdue, and were over-

College football's most exciting player in the 1960's, Southern Cal halfback O. J. Simpson (32), looks for an opening against California.

turned by a 28–21 score. Then the Trojans of Southern Cal came to South Bend vowing to even the score with the Irish for that fearful beating of the previous year. Unveiling a hard-charging, swivel-hipped, fleet-footed halfback named O. J. Simpson, the Trojans got what they wanted and then some: a convincing 24–7 victory.

With that the Trojans were tops, providing of course, they could fight off the challenges of U.C.L.A. and Purdue, the two teams right behind them. Then, just to prove how silly the polls can be, these three top teams in the nation were stopped cold by a comparative unknown: Oregon State.

Among all the major teams in the nation, only Wyoming remained unbeaten and untied. But because Wyoming's schedule was not among the toughest, it was believed that the Cowboys did not rate the top ranking. The arguments went back and forth again, until the Trojans finally met the Uclans in what became, after all, the deciding game.

Pre-game publicity billed it as a contest between Gary Beban, the passer, and O. J. Simpson, the runner. In the end, as is usually the case, the game was decided by superior line play. The powerful Southern Cal forward wall throttled Beban and overpowered the Uclan defense. When one good opening was provided for Simpson, he dashed through for a long touchdown run that gave the Trojans a 21–20 triumph. So, by the narrow margin of a single point, Southern Cal was acclaimed the national champion.

When the 1968 season got rolling, the men of Troy looked like potential national champions again. The pre-season forecasts had selected Purdue to finish Number One, but the Boilermakers faltered early in the year. The Trojans, however, kept galloping along. The chief reason for their success, of course, was O. J. Simpson.

In an age where most of the applause was going to passing quarterbacks and wide receivers, it was something of a welcome relief to have the spotlight focused again on a running back. And as usual, the 210-pound speed demon from Southern Cal lived up to expectations. As a ball carrier, Simpson earned a place alongside Red Grange, Tommy Harmon and Glenn Davis. During the season, he ran for a spectacular total of 1,709 yards against one of the best schedules in the country. He scored 22 touchdowns. Surely, it seemed, O. J. would lead the Trojans to their second straight national crown.

In the Midwest, however, an old football bear was beginning to stir again in Columbus, Ohio. For years the critics had been saying that Coach Woody Hayes had relied too long on old-fashioned football at Ohio State. His system was colorfully described as "three yards and a cloud of dust." Apparently Hayes believed that you can't lose the ball very easily if you are holding onto it. But if you put it into the air, everyone has a chance to get it. And after all, Woody, the dean of Big Ten coaches, had the best win-loss record in the league.

But Woody was wise enough to compromise with modern times. To the roar of fans at Columbus, his sophomore-dominated team dazzled their opponents with a mixture of well-executed passes and rushes. Before the season was half

Coach Woody Hayes, passing on instructions to quarterback Kern, opened up his "cloud of dust" offense in 1968. The result: A national championship.

over, 16 sophomores were listed among Ohio's top 22 players and the Buckeyes were clearly on their way to a Big Ten title. Southern Cal had a tough challenger on its hands.

In the meantime, a brand-new power was emerging in the East. For years Penn State had been among the most outstanding teams in that region, though for decades the East had rarely been on a par with the rest of the country.

Then in 1966 an unusual young coach, Joe Paterno, took charge of the Nittany Lions. Encouraging his players to study, insisting that they call him by his first name, Joe also astounded football ex-

perts by acting as if the game could be fun. Under Paterno, Penn State's fortunes rose steadily, and in 1968 the Nittany Lions climbed rapidly upward through the ranks of the Top Ten.

The East also had another surprise in Harvard. Seldom a strong contender in the lightly rated Ivy League, Harvard had not had an undefeated season since 1931. In 1968, however, the Crimson came up with a strong defensive team. On the other hand, arch-rival Yale had an offensive powerhouse, led by quarterback Brian Dowling and halfback Calvin Hill. Both teams were undefeated and untied when they met in "The Game" at the season's end.

Forty-two seconds from the finish, it looked as if the Yale Bulldogs were going to spoil the Crimson's bid for a perfect season. They led, 29–13. When Harvard got the ball, sportswriters were already beginning to write their accounts of a Yale victory. But Harvard miraculously scored two touchdowns, the second coming on the last play of the game. Then, with time run out, the Crimson passed for the second two-point conversion to tie the score 29–29! Thus, the dogged Crimson remained unbeaten, though tied, and the school's daily newspaper proudly carried the headline: "Harvard *beats* Yale, 29–29."

The following week the spotlight shifted back to the West Coast, where undefeated Southern Cal prepared to nail down its second straight national crown by defeating twice-beaten Notre Dame. But the Irish played the spoiler's role, tying the Trojans, 21–21.

Nevertheless, when Ohio State was selected to represent the Big Ten in the Rose Bowl, the Trojans had a chance to redeem themselves. If they could beat the top-ranked Buckeyes, they could possibly regain their lost laurels. At the outset they quickly spurted to a 10–0 lead on a field goal and a twisting 80-yard touchdown run by the great O. J. But Ohio State's amazingly quick and strong defense gradually smothered the Southern Cal attack. Meanwhile, Ohio's balanced offense began to function smoothly under the expert guidance of sophomore quarterback Rex Kern. Taking complete charge, the Buckeyes won by a final score of 27–16.

That left Ohio State and Penn State (scheduled to play later in the day at the Orange Bowl) as the nation's only major unbeaten teams. Penn State gained a 15–14 victory over Kansas, but with such a narrow victory, they lost all chance of wresting the Number One spot away from Ohio State. For the first time since 1954, the Buckeyes brought the National Championship back to football-mad Columbus.

In 1969—the 100th anniversary of collegiate football—it appeared that Ohio State would breeze to another title. Almost all of the men who had played in the Rose Bowl were back for another season, and Woody Hayes seemed certain to become one of the few coaches to win two straight national championships. In the Big Ten, however, nothing is certain; an eager band of Michigan Wolverines shook the football world by upsetting the mighty Buckeyes.

At Texas, Coach Darrell Royal had introduced football's newest offensive formation. This was the "wishbone-T," three running backs set in an inverted V behind their quarterback in order to provide numerous variations of the "option play." With this attack, Texas simply destroyed the opposition, so much so that the Longhorns supplanted the Buckeyes as Number One. They were so impressive that President Richard Nixon went so far as to give them a plaque symbolic of the national championship after watching them beat Arkansas, 15–14, for the Southwestern Conference Championship.

For 45 years Notre Dame had maintained a "no bowl" policy, but in 1969 the school officials changed their mind. On New Year's Day, 1970, the Irish were in Dallas to meet the lean and hard-charging Texans. The game was a bruis-

180

ing and exciting battle. The lead changed hands twice. With barely a minute left to play, the Irish led, 17–14. Texas had the ball on the Notre Dame two. Stiffening, the Irish stopped the Longhorns cold on three straight plays. It was fourth and two. Texas could still tie the score on an almost certain field goal. But the Longhorns gambled. Substitute halfback Billy Dale drove into the end zone for the touchdown that gave Texas a 21–17 victory and the national championship.

Penn State remained unbeaten, defeating Missouri, 10–3, in the Orange Bowl, but Texas had ripped off a total of 331 yards against an Irish defense that had yielded only 87 yards per game on the ground during the regular season. Most fans were convinced that the Longhorns were tops.

In 1970, it appeared that the band of seniors who had carried the Longhorns to twenty straight victories might finish their collegiate careers undefeated, presenting Texas with a second straight national championship. Similar beautiful visions filled the dreams of another squad of seniors, the veteran Buckeyes of Ohio State, who were burning to recover the title taken from them by Texas.

Interest in the season itself, meantime, had shifted from the race for the Number One spot to the candidates for the Heisman Trophy.

The best of them all, it appeared, was Archie Manning—until the idol of Ole Miss broke his arm halfway through the season. In the end, the award went to big Jim Plunkett. Standing 6' 2½",

Big Jim Plunkett fires the ball over an Ohio State defender in 1971 Rose Bowl.

weighing 212 pounds, he was quick, strong and tough, a born leader and a passer who was accurate at every distance.

It was clear he would be the first pick in the draft for the pro teams. In fact, when the limping Boston Patriots lost their last game, making it certain that they would have first chance at Plunkett, the value of the club's stock increased by $1,500,000 the following Monday.

Plunkett had much to do with Stanford's earning a Rose Bowl invitation for the first time in years. There they would have a shot at unbeaten Ohio State. As expected, the Buckeyes had won all their games, along with Texas.

Another contender for the Number One spot in the country was Nebraska. Since 1915, when they upset Notre Dame, the Cornhuskers had been a major football power. They had come close, but they had never won top honors. In 1962, however, a perfectionist named Bob Devaney took charge in football-happy Lincoln—and the Cornhusker drive for the Big One began. Under Devaney, Nebraska won five Big Eight championships and went to six bowl games. Devaney himself was the winningest coach in collegiate football. In 1970 his Cornhuskers won all their games but one (a 21–21 tie with Southern Cal) only to find themselves ranked Number Three behind Texas and Ohio State. Once again, it seemed, Nebraska had fallen short.

But the bowl games still remained. Stanford would have to upset Ohio State in the Rose Bowl and Notre Dame upend Texas in the Cotton Bowl. Then if Nebraska could defeat L.S.U. in the Sugar Bowl, it would qualify for top honors. This seemed like wishful thinking when New Year's Day of 1971 dawned. And yet, that was exactly what happened. In Pasadena, Jim Plunkett picked the Ohio State defense apart, leading Stanford to its first Rose Bowl victory in thirty years by a score of 27–17. Ara Parseghian of Notre Dame devised a defense that finally contained the wishbone-T of Texas, and Notre Dame ended the Longhorn winning streak at thirty games with a smashing 24–11 victory. Then, with both these upsets on the record books, Nebraska squeezed past L.S.U., 17–12.

Thus, in post-bowl balloting, and despite the protests of Coach Parseghian, who thought that his team's triumph over Texas had established Irish supremacy, the Cornhuskers of Nebraska finally emerged as the national champion.

Victorious at last, both Nebraska and Coach Devaney opened the 1971 season with their sights set on the rarity of a second straight national championship. Nebraska started out strong, but its top competitors, Oklahoma and Alabama, routed opponent after opponent. Both squads had adopted the wishbone-T, which returned the spotlight to running backs like Alabama's Johnny Musso and Oklahoma's Greg Pruitt.

Nebraska, meanwhile, put the emphasis on a balanced power-I attack. The passing of Jerry Tagge, the brutal running of Jeff Kinney and the deadly, methodical blocking of the offensive line combined with the best defense in the nation to make the Cornhuskers nearly unstoppable.

Eventually it became apparent that the Big Eight title game between Ne-

182

Nebraska's great running back, Jeff Kinney, flies past an Oklahoma tackler. Nebraska won the game and the national championship.

braska and Oklahoma on Thanksgiving Day might decide the national championship. The Cornhuskers were rated Number One, the Sooners Number Two. Here, at last, was a *game*, not a vote, that might decide the top college team.

This latest "Game of the Decade" turned out to be all that it was supposed to be. No two teams could have been more evenly matched. They swapped touchdowns back and forth. With five minutes left, Nebraska was trailing, but then it launched a time-consuming 74-yard drive to score a touchdown and win 35–31.

So the Cornhuskers were still Number One. But they still had to meet one more challenge. Nebraska and undefeated Alabama would meet in the Orange Bowl. Could Nebraska stay on top?

This one, however, was no contest. Alabama's wishbone-T and running back Johnny Musso were stopped cold by the Nebraska defense. And Nebraska's Tagge, Kinney and company ran over the 'Bama defense. The result: Nebraska 38, 'Bama 6.

Denied college supremacy for 55 years, Nebraska suddenly had become only the sixth team in history to take two national titles in a row. With that, Bob Devaney set his sights on a third straight crown. He planned to retire at the end of the 1972 season. Already the country's most successful coach, he was looking for one more record.

Although they had lost some stars by graduation, the Cornhuskers were still loaded with such talented players as Johnny Rodgers, the do-everything back, and Rich Glover, probably the nation's best defensive player.

Then Nebraska opened its season against UCLA, looking forward to stretching its unbeaten string to 33 games. UCLA was not expected to be a college power, but it did have sophomore quarterback Mark Harmon, the son of the great Tommy Harmon of Michigan and Heisman Trophy fame. This handsome, articulate youngster, playing in his first varsity game, brought

183

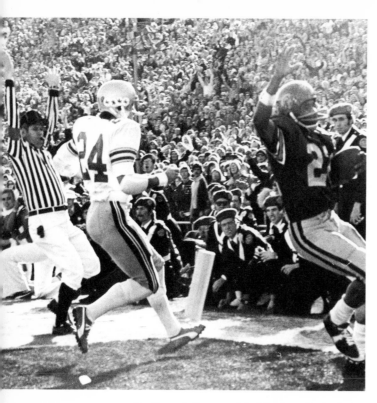

Southern Cal's sensational Anthony Davis scores against Ohio State in the Rose Bowl.

off the impossible: a 20–17 upset of Nebraska.

The Cornhuskers never recovered from that opening-day shock. Iowa State tied them, Oklahoma beat them and they sank far down in the rankings.

Meanwhile, interest in the 1972 season had focused on two other surprises. The first was the appearance of freshman football stars. Since 1951, first-year men had not been eligible for varsity play. But in January 1972, the NCAA made them eligible again and 1972 became known as the Year of the Freshman.

No less than 84 frosh won starting berths on major college teams and 303 made the traveling squads. A few of them became standout performers. Ohio State running back Archie Griffin

had much to do with the Buckeyes' winning the Big Ten Crown. Against North Carolina he ran for 239 yards, a new school record. Notre Dame's defensive goliath, Steve Niehaus, made the Irish almost immovable until he was hurt in a freak practice accident. And receiver Tinker Owens of Oklahoma, the brother of Heisman Trophy winner Steve, was another offensive ace.

Among sophomores, the most celebrated was little Anthony Davis of Southern California. Not even Mike Garrett or O.J. Simpson had gained national fame so spectacularly. Against Notre Dame in front of a nationwide TV audience, Davis returned two kickoffs for touchdowns and scored a total of six as the Trojans trounced the Irish.

Anthony Davis was part of the season's second surprise—the powerful but underrated U.S.C. squad. Preseason polls ranked the Trojans no better than eighth, but they turned out to be one of the finest teams in the annals of collegiate football. Big and fast, quick and steady, almost like professionals in their ability to make rapid adjustments, the Trojans were so good that no team got closer to them than nine points.

Yet, their No. 1 position was disputed right up until New Year's Day. Then in the Rose Bowl, where they met once-beaten Ohio State, Coach John McKay's fired-up Trojans blew the Buckeyes off the field, 42–17.

That silenced all critics. As silver-haired Coach McKay quipped: "Is there anyone else they want us to play now to prove that we're really Number One?"

Ohio State coach Woody Hayes gave a solemn answer: "This is the best college team I've ever seen."

Exits and Entrances

With the approach of the 1969 season, it appeared that the World Champion Jets might have to take the field without Broadway Joe. Rather than obey Commissioner Pete Rozelle's order to sell his interest in a New York bar allegedly frequented by gamblers, Namath went into retirement. Then, just a month before opening day, Joe finally sold out, and his familiar number 12 once again began to draw fans into AFL stadiums.

As expected, the Jets won the Eastern Division championship. As was *not* expected, they were upset in the playoffs, 13–6, by the rejuvenated Kansas City Chiefs. Then the Chiefs, who had lost twice to the Oakland Raiders during the regular season, went on to upend the Raiders, 17–7, and win the AFL title.

Meanwhile, in the NFL a new power had emerged: the Minnesota Vikings. They were led by Joe Kapp, a bruising quarterback who horrified football purists by his awkward lunges and wobbly passes, while he kept the home folks happy with his fondness for running with the ball and his habit of winning games. The Vikings were victorious in the league's tough Central Division, though they barely got past a rugged band of Los Angeles Rams, 23–20, in the Western Division playoff. However, they routed a very good Cleveland Browns team, 27–7, to win the NFL championship.

Going into the fourth Super Bowl, played this time in New Orleans, the Vikings were 13-point favorites to give the NFL a 3–1 edge in victories. Sportswriters insisted that the awesome Minnesota front four—Jim Marshall, Alan Page, Gary Larsen and Carl Eller—who had simply devoured the Cleveland offense, would be too much for the Chiefs. The Chiefs' veteran quarterback, 34-year-old Lenny Dawson, the goat of the first Super Bowl, missed six games in 1969 because of a torn ligament in his left knee. He was therefore considered to be outclassed by the aggressive Kapp.

But once again the experts were wrong. The underdog from the AFL pinned a stunning defeat on the favored NFL champion. The final score was 23–7. Both the Chiefs and Dawson had their revenge for their humiliating loss to the Packers four seasons earlier.

The Viking–Chief contest was the last meeting between the AFL and the NFL. In 1970 the two circuits merged to form the 26-team National Football League, divided into a National and an American Conference. So it was particularly fitting that the once-despised American Football League had evened the Superbowl count at 2–2 in the last year of its existence. The bitterness which had once divided pro football had ended in a happy marriage.

But then, just before the merged new league's first season began, joy gave way to sorrow at the death of the great

Coach Vince Lombardi signals a Packer victory in the 1967 Super Bowl game against Kansas City.

Vince Lombardi. Lombardi had left the Packers and become part-owner and coach of the listless Washington Redskins. To the surprise of practically no one, he turned the losing 'Skins into a winning team, posting a 7–5–2 record in 1969. He served notice that in 1970 Washington would be in the thick of the title fight. Unfortunately, he had no chance to add new laurels to the most illustrious coaching career in pro football history. In September of 1970, at the age of 57, Vince Lombardi died of cancer.

Lombardi left a lasting mark on the game. He had been to pro football what Knute Rockne had been to the collegiate sport. A fierce, proud, lonely and emotional man, he had been dedicated to one purpose: winning. To win, Lombardi relied upon simple execution of the basics. Intricate defenses and multiple offenses were not for him. "Football," he often said, "is blocking and tackling. If you block and tackle better than the team you're playing, you'll win."

He won wherever he went—as a star

fullback for St. Francis Prep in New York, as one of Fordham's celebrated Seven Blocks of Granite, as a coach at St. Cecilia High School of Englewood, N. J. Later he contributed to winning teams as assistant coach at Army and for the New York Giants. But it was with the Green Bay Packers that he reached his peak. At the close of the 1958 season Green Bay had stumbled to a dismal 1–10–1 record. Exactly one decade later, coached by the hard-driving, perfectionist Lombardi, the green-and-gold "Pack" had won five NFL championships (1961, 1962, 1965, 1966, 1967) and the first two Super Bowls. They had compiled an astonishing record of 99 wins, 31 losses and four ties. Such was the incomparable career of Vince Lombardi.

During 1970 the football world watched with amazement as two men who shouldn't have been in the game turned in amazing performances. The 43-year-old George Blanda, back-up quarterback of the Oakland Raiders was years past the usual retirement age. Yet on five consecutive Sunday afternoons, the ageless Blanda came off the bench to lead the Raiders to four victories and a tie. Against Cleveland, for instance, he relieved Daryle Lamonica with the Raiders trailing, 20–13. He threw a touchdown pass and kicked an extra point. Then in the last seconds he booted a 52-yard field goal to give his team a 23–20 triumph.

On that same afternoon, more NFL history was being made in New Orleans. The Saints' Tom Dempsey kicked the longest field goal in NFL history—63 yards—against Detroit, winning for New Orleans on the last play of the game.

Dempsey's feat emphasized the growing importance of the last-ditch field goal in pro football. Game after game was decided in the final moments by a clutch kick. This was again demonstrated by "Miracle Man" Blanda two weeks later when he booted a 16-yarder in the last seven seconds to beat San Diego, 20–17. This victory kept Oakland in the running for the AFC title.

The Raiders finally met Baltimore in the AFC championship game. This time, however, even Blanda could not overcome the magic of Johnny Unitas. Blanda kicked a 48-yard field goal and connected on two touchdown passes, but Unitas threw one touchdown pass and set up two other scores. The final score was: Baltimore 27, Oakland 17. In the NFC, meanwhile, the alert Dallas Cowboys scored a 17-10 upset victory over San Francisco.

So the Cowboys met the Colts in the Super Bowl in a match that was expected to display all that was finest in pro ball. In fact, the game became a contest of mistakes. For three and a half periods, the Colts fumbled and stumbled. At the same time the Cowboys missed chance after chance to take a commanding lead. Midway in the fourth period, the score was Dallas 13, Baltimore 6.

Then the Cowboys began to err in earnest. The Colts scored after intercepting a pass to tie the game. Then Mike Curtis of the Colts intercepted another Cowboy pass and returned the ball to the Dallas 26.

With five seconds remaining, rookie placekicker Jim O'Brien came on the field for Baltimore. In a fitting climax

With five seconds left, Baltimore's Jim O'Brien kicks the field goal that gave the Colts a 16-13 victory over Dallas.

to what could be called the Last-Seconds Season, O'Brien booted the ball squarely between the posts, winning the game 16–13. The Colts, who had been humiliated in the third Super Bowl, had at last vindicated themselves in the fifth big game.

Coach Tom Landry and the Cowboys had failed again. Three times in five years they had lost a championship game. Fans and writers insisted that they were "choke artists." They won every game but the big one, it was said.

When the 1971 season opened, Dallas was again the best team on paper. No other team was so loaded with talent. They were awesome on defense with such stalwarts as Jethro Pugh and Bob Lilly and they seemed nearly unstoppable on offense with runners Calvin Hill and Duane Thomas, receivers Bob Hayes and Lance Alworth and two big-time quarterbacks, Craig Morton and Roger Staubach.

Landry's problem was to choose a quarterback. Craig Morton was the veteran, an orthodox pocket passer whose performance was unpredictable. On some days he was great and on others he was ineffective. Roger Staubach, starting his third year as a pro, liked to scramble with the ball — and call his own plays instead of the ones Landry sent in from the sidelines.

Halfway through the season Landry finally chose Staubach as *the* starter. Roger came through. Conquering his urge to scramble, he learned to drop straight back into the pocket and to "eat" the ball when his receivers were covered rather than risk an interception. Thus, passing and occasionally running, Staubach made the Cowboys winners again.

The Cowboys' leadership of the Eastern Division was challenged by the surprising Washington Redskins. Coach George Allen had taken Lombardi's place and built his team around quarterback Billy Kilmer, slick-running Larry Brown and a collection of veterans. Known as the "Over-the-Hill Gang," the revamped Redskins gave Dallas quite a scare, but the Cowboys finally won the Division crown.

The Cowboys sailed through their playoff games, defeating Minnesota on the strength of their defense, 20–12, and turning back San Francisco 14–3, to earn their second straight shot at the Super Bowl.

In the American Conference a new star had risen. Two years before, veteran coach Don Shula had come to the lackluster Miami Dolphins from Baltimore. Now his new team was challenging his old team for the division championship.

The Dolphins had a potent offense based on the passing of Bob Griese, the power running of Larry Csonka and Jim Kiick and the speed and sure hands of receiver Paul Warfield.

But Baltimore was not about to surrender. Young running back Norm Bulaich had given them an unexpected burst of running power to go along with the signal-calling of veteran Johnny Unitas. When Miami met the Colts in the game that decided the division championship, they were unable to stop Bulaich and Unitas and they lost 14–3.

Yet the Dolphins did get into the playoffs as the AFC's best runner-up. They met the Kansas City Chiefs in the first round in a contest that made football history. It became the longest play-off game in history, going 22 minutes and 40 seconds into sudden-death overtime—and it was decided by the performance of a foreign-born field-goal kicker.

Miami's left-footed Garo Yepremian, born in Cyprus, kicked one Dolphin field goal in regulation time. But he got his big chance with more than 22 minutes gone in the overtime. He booted a perfect 37-yarder to win the game.

The Colts methodically tore up the Cleveland Browns in the other AFC playoff, winning 20–3. So once again Miami met Baltimore, this time for the conference title and a place in the Super Bowl.

In this one it was the Colts who made all the mistakes and the Dolphins who made all the points. Without Norm Bulaich, who had been injured, Johnny Unitas could do little. The astonishing Dolphins won 21–0.

The Cowboys, grim and determined, were out to prove that for once they could win the big one. The young and high-hearted Dolphins were confident that if they could play in their usual relaxed style they would win. But experience and determination told. In Super Bowl VI the Dolphins made the kind of mistakes they had not made all season. And the Cowboys, playing at their best, not only sank the Dolphins, but almost drowned them, winning 24–3.

In 1972 the actors in the pro football drama changed. In the place of the contenders of recent years—Kansas City, Oakland, New York, Baltimore and Dallas—there were new and reconditioned teams on every hand.

First among these was Miami. The Dolphins had nearly reached the top in Super Bowl VI, but many fans thought their season had been a fluke. The Dolphins were out to prove otherwise.

Other "new faces" included the Pittsburgh Steelers, who had never won an

Three top running backs: Pittsburgh's Franco Harris, Washington's Larry Brown and Miami's Larry Csonka.

NFL title and had seldom been in contention; Washington's "Over-the-Hill" gang; and the Green Bay Packers, contenders for the first time since Vince Lombardi's departure after the 1966 season.

One thing all of these teams had in common was great running backs. After many seasons in which passers and receivers had been in the spotlight, 1972 was the Year of the Runner.

Pittsburgh's rookie Franco Harris tied Jimmy Brown's record by rushing for 100 yards or more in six straight games. Teamed with Terry Bradshaw and a fine defensive line, Harris helped bring the Steelers their first conference championship in history.

At Washington, the runner was Larry Brown. Time after time he gave the Redskins the yards they needed in crucial situations. He would have been far ahead of all other rushers in yards

gained if he had not been injured and out of action in the last two games. Buffalo's O.J. Simpson won the rushing title with 1,251 yards, compared to Brown's 1,216.

In Green Bay, it almost seemed that the days of Jim Taylor and Paul Hornung had returned. John Brockington, who had gained 1,000-plus yards as a rookie in 1971, went over the mark again, and the Packers made the play-offs.

But again it was the mighty Dolphins who led the way. At one point it appeared that three of their running backs might gain 1,000 yards—Larry Csonka, Jim Kiick and the new sensation, Mercury Morris. Only Csonka and Morris made it, but the three rushers gained a total of 2,951 yards, a record.

With their three runners, a tough defense and quarterback Bob Griese, the Dolphins began the season in top

190

form. Then early in the season Griese was injured and put out of the line-up for most of the season. The Dolphins called on a familiar old man to call the signals: Earl Morrall, who had come off the bench in 1968 to lead Baltimore to the Super Bowl. Morrall repeated his performance and was named Most Valuable Player in the league.

The question halfway through the season was whether Miami would even lose a game. Each week they rolled over another opponent, and soon sportswriters were looking in the record book to compare other winning streaks. Some complained that Miami had an easy schedule (only two of the teams they beat ended up with winning records). But when the season was over, no one could deny that the Dolphins had won 14 straight. They rolled over Cleveland and Pittsburgh in the play-offs, leaving only the Super Bowl to win for a perfect season.

Meanwhile in the NFC, the Redskins beat out Dallas for the Eastern Division title with an 11–3 record. Two of their losses came at the end of the season when the title had been clinched and coach George Allen was resting his aging troops. The Redskins beat the Packers and the Cowboys in the play-offs, so it was the young Dolphins against the old Redskins in Super Bowl VII.

Washington was actually favored to win. Although it had a poorer record than Miami, it had played tougher competition. And many observers were confident that emotional, perfectionist George Allen could inspire his team to win the big one.

But when the teams took the field, Miami took charge. The Dolphin defense stymied Larry Brown, and with Bob Griese back at quarterback, the offense rolled up a 14–0 lead with two minutes left.

At this point, field-goal kicker Garo Yepremian almost gave away the Dolphins' 17th straight win. When his field goal attempt was blocked, little Garo picked up the ball and tried to throw it. It rolled off his fingers and into the hands of Washington's Mike Bass, who ran all the way for a touchdown, making the score 14–7.

The Redskins seemed to have a chance when they got the ball again with seconds left. But the Miami defense rose up to hold the 'Skins until time ran out.

Finishing the most successful season in NFL history, the Dolphins were truly champs.

Index

Library of Congress Cataloging in Publication Data

Leckie, Robert. The story of football. (Landmark giant, 9) SUMMARY: Traces the history of football in the United States from the first intercollegiate game in 1869 to the most current Super Bowl game. 1. Football—History—Juvenile literature. [1. Football—History] I. Title.

GV950.7.L35 1973   796.33′2′09   73-3321

ISBN 0-394-81679-X

ISBN 0-394-91679-4 (lib. bdg.)

Photograph Credits: Bettmann Archive, viii, 3, 5, 11, 18; Vernon J. Biever, i, ii, iii, vi, vii, 139, 140, 161, 164, 171, 173; Brown Brothers, 34, 52 (bottom), 56, 64 (bottom); Cornell University, 33, 52 (top); Culver Pictures, 9, 16, 35, 42, 43, 62, 64 (top), 67, 73, 104, 151; Malcolm Emmons, 191; Eric S. Monberg, 7; University of Notre Dame, 69, 78, 133, 141; Princeton University, 27, 156; Ken Regan—Camera Five: 174–175; Fred Roe from Roy Cummings, Inc., 163; Herb Stein, 137; United Press International, iv, v, 8, 22, 29, 30, 36, 39, 49, 50, 51, 55, 61, 71, 75, 84, 89, 96–100, 102, 105, 108, 112–113, 116, 118, 121, 125, 129, 130, 131, 145, 146, 152, 153, 155, 158, 166, 167, 177, 179, 181, 183, 184, 186, 188, 190 (both); Wide World, 15, 23, 25, 44, 59, 76, 81, 82, 87, 90, 92, 106, 107, 110, 111, 120, 123, 134, 135, 143, 147, 149, 168, 169.